WORLD RELIGIONS

With contributions by Li Deman,
Birgit Falkenberg, Kora Perle, Brigitte Selbig

The texts and illustrations in this book have been written and selected with the
utmost consideration for the sensibilities and beliefs of the faiths concerned.
Nevertheless, it is possible that individual depictions are coloured by the
understanding imposed by the western culture of the authors and as such
may not always concur with the understanding of some readers.
No offence is intended by this.

© Könemann Verlagsgesellschaft mbH
Bonner Str. 126, D-50968 Köln

Editor: Peter Delius
Layout: Brigitte Selbig
Index: Julia Niehaus
English translation: Chris Charlesworth for Hart McLeod
Typesetting: Goodfellow & Egan, Cambridge
Design: Peter Feierabend
Production manager: Detlev Schaper
Reproductions: Imago Publishing Ltd., Thame
Printed and bound: Leefung Asco Printers, Hong Kong/China

ISBN 3-89508-854-4

Markus Hattstein

WORLD RELIGIONS

KÖNEMANN

Contents

HINDUISM OR BRAHMANISM

BUDDHISM

THE RELIGIONS OF CHINA

THE RELIGIONS OF JAPAN

JUDAISM

CHRISTIANITY

ISLAM

APPENDIX

HINDUISM OR BRAHMANISM

Hinduism is the most diverse of all the major religions and comprises almost all religious forms of expression known to humankind – from the worship of nature gods, to polytheism, to a philosophically sophisticated monotheism and the belief in a universal law (dharma). It is closely interconnected with the social order (caste system) and requires distinctive ritual sacrifices. It does not prescribe any universally binding metaphysical or religious views, but emphasizes the working of the universal law, which is also understood in a moral sense. The theory of retribution inherent in the teaching on karma, with its cycle of re-births and world eras (yugas), is characteristic of Hinduism.

BASIC CONCEPT AND DISTINCTIVE FEATURES

The "Eternal Religion"

The indigenous religion of India is known as Brahmanism or Hinduism. The two terms are often used synonymously although they have different origins. "Brahmanism" is the name the religion gives itself; the word is derived from the Indian priest or Brahman caste (Sanskrit: brahmana) and refers generally to those Indians who recognise the Brahmans and their teaching as their religion. The word "Hinduism" was originally a foreign term coined by the Muslims who were advancing into India. Derived from the River Indus, it was used to designate all Indians who were not Muslims. The term "Brahmanism" has been in use since around 1000 B.C. when the Brahman priest caste first attained their prime status, while Hinduism can be traced back further to the ancient Indian autochthonous religion, which was essentially nature worship, and was later systematised and reformed by the Brahman caste.

What is striking about Hinduism is the rich diversity of both its religious practices and its social life: it is extremely creative and adaptable. The bond holding it together is neither a founder nor a sacred book, but the continuity of development from ancient times to the present day. For this reason the Hindus themselves call their faith the "Eternal Religion" (sanatana dharma) and a central feature of it is the fact that at different times wise men and religious teachers appear and proclaim their teachings in different forms.

Helmuth von Glasenapp talks of three distinctive features of Hinduism. It is a religion that has "developed" not one which has been founded, it has no fixed dogma, and it is a specifically Indian phenomenon. The Hindus believe in the eternity of a world that is constantly renewing itself; they therefore do not think of the world as having an absolute beginning, nor of there being a unique process in history for salvation. There is no particular person as a saviour at the centre of Hinduism, which is why different systems of thoughts and different cults have essentially equal rights and are considered equally true.

The believer can have a personal creator God or can instead adhere to the idea of a non-personal law governing the world. The paths to salvation are similarly many and varied. The faith is nevertheless not completely arbitrary, but revolves around a number of specific philosophies: the idea of the cosmos as an ordered whole ruled by a universal law (dharma), the earthly representation of this order by a strictly hierarchical caste system and its purity laws, the belief in cosmic periods and world eras (calpas) with the world constantly ending and beginning again, and the belief that this natural world order also acts as a moral order.

The Wheel of Life

On the Black Pagoda in Konarak The wheel is the central symbol in Hinduism, and represents the course of the cosmos with its cycles of birth and death, coming into being, maturing, decay, dissolution and re-emergence that characterize all living things. It is also a symbol for the cycle of the four Hindu world eras (yugas), which every world goes through until it sinks into darkness and comes into being again. The turning of the wheel stands for the continuity and unalterability of cosmic events. Wisdom in Hinduism means insight into this cyclical change of the universe that never ends and is thought of as a biological event. The sun temple at Konarak was in the shape of a sun chariot, a form dating back to the worship of the Vedic sun god Surya, who was thought to be the driver of the sun chariot and thus one of the architects of the cosmic cycles.

Hinduism is a specifically Indian religion which undertakes no obvious spiritual mission beyond that culture. Although it has engaged in missionary work in southeast Asia and in Indonesia, it is not interested in winning "individual souls," but if anything in incorporating entire tribes as "new castes." Nevertheless some Brahmanist thinkers or holy men have quite consciously influenced the thoughts of non-Indians who turn to Hinduism - as was the case, for example, during the "India Craze" of the 1960s and 1970s in Europe and the U.S.A.

THE RELIGIOUS HISTORY OF HINDUISM

The Pre-Aryan Culture

Hinduism is a fusion of two different religious developments which gradually merged into a single entity: the ancient Indian autochthonous religion and the religion of the Aryans who invaded India from the North.

The era of pre-Aryan culture lies back in the murky depths of history. The original population was probably negroid people who were pushed further and further south by other peoples advancing from the north. It was a matriarchal, agricultural culture which introduced into Hinduism certain elements which play no role in the Vedic writings – such as the cult of the phallus and the worship of fertile earth-goddesses. This Indus culture was already developed socially and had a well-formed cult of images based around phallus stones (lingams) and certain religious symbols, such as the swastika as a symbol of the sun. The worship of sacred animals also dates back to this specific culture.

The Aryan or Vedic Period

The Aryans advanced over the mountains of the northwest into India in the second millennium B.C. They were warriors, rural people with no urban culture, who overthrew the native population. They brought with them to India a developed religious system which had a pantheon with many different branches. Their faith was written down in the "Veda" (= Holy Knowledge), whose oldest hymn, the Rig Veda, mainly describes the gods as personified forces of nature. In the course of time, as they became clothed in myths, many of the gods

Worship of the Lingam
Indian miniature, page from a Ragamala series, 18th century, Rajasthan, Savar

The cult of the phallus, counterpart to the cult of the mother, goes back to the time of pre-Vedic deities, and was only later transposed onto Shiva. Shiva is the god of fertility and destruction, and the lingam, the stone phallus, before which sacrificial offerings for fertility are laid, is the main symbol of his creative power and the central focus of Shiva's cult. Initially, only naturally formed stones were worshipped, but later they were also made of clay for worship in the home. The shaping of the lingam is accompanied by religious litanies and followed by ritual washing. After this puja ceremony the clay lingam is thrown into water and destroyed again.

underwent radical transformation. The principal gods were initially the sun god Mitra and the god of the sky Varuna. Both of them are seen as the guardians of the "eternal world order" (Rita) which is seen in nature, morals and rituals as the ordering force of the cosmos.

The Aryan faith is henotheistic (one God at a time), i.e. different gods are each worshipped with the title of Supreme Lord of the World. The views varied between the belief in a transpersonal universal law that stood above all the gods, and the belief in a Supreme God who directed the universal law, a split which still runs through the whole of Hinduism.

Around 1000 B.C. the Aryans advanced east and south from the Punjab to the fertile Ganges Plain and conquered the local population by introducing the caste system. The Aryans themselves made up the top three castes, while the indigenous people and their descendants became the "Sudras" (fourth caste). As a result of the complicated system of rituals and sacrifices, the Brahmin caste gained an influence hitherto unknown in any religion through their claim that even the gods themselves had to bow to their knowledge and could be influenced by them, the priests. This claim of the priest caste to have a monopoly on knowledge and the sole ability to carry out all acts of worship has been retained right through to contemporary Hinduism.

The Classical Period

The period beginning around 500 B.C. in India is referred to as the Classical Period, in which

Ganga, the River Goddess
Terracotta tile, 5th century, Northern India

The Ganges is the archetype and most revered of all Indian rivers. It is personified as the river goddess Ganga who rides the lake monster Makara and holds an overflowing pitcher symbolizing life force as flowing water. According to tradition, she originally lived with the gods – as the second wife of Vishnu and later of Shiva – and could only be persuaded to come down to earth after prolonged human pleading. She flows as seven rivers out of Shiva's hair, one of which is the Ganges.

Episode from the Ramayana Epic
Indian miniature, 1st quarter of the
19th century, Pahari style, Kangra

The Ramayana epic tells in 24,000
double verses of the heroic deeds of
Rama, the accomplished warrior and
prince. As the 7th incarnation of
Vishnu, at the instigation of his step-
mother, Rama had to live 14 years in
exile in the jungle with his wife Sita,
the epitome of purity, and his loyal
half-brother Lakshmana. In permanent
conflict with furious armies of
demons, Rama kills 14,000 such
demons in the first battle alone.
When the 10-headed prince of the
demons, Ravana, uses trickery to
abduct Sita, the brothers turn to the
monkey king, Hanuman, who with
his gigantic army of monkeys and
bears, goes into a final battle
(illustrated) against Ravana's cavalry
of demons. In the course of the
battle all the demons are killed and
Rama kills Ravana in one-to-one
combat. Rama then rules Ayodhya
as the rightful king, and in gratitude
for his loyalty the gods grant
immortality to Hanuman. The epic
ends with a description of the
extraordinary circumstances of the
death of Sita, Lakshmana and Rama,
who are assumed into the "Glory of
Vishnu."

Hinduism took on the form it has essentially
retained. This period was Hinduism's heyday
and the time when it spread most rapidly. This
was particularly thanks to the language of classical Sanskrit, which is an artificial language of
poets and scholars and was used almost
exclusively for religious purposes. The word
"sanskrita" also means "artistically prepared"
and is clearly distinct from the everyday Indian
language, Prakrita.

The influence of the Aryans now extended
across the entire sub-continent of India and
spread to all earlier cults and religions. The
new gods Brahma, Vishnu and Shiva took
centre stage. Worship of these new gods was
very different from the former kind of worship:
the gods were no longer commemorated
at open sacrifice sites with grass scattered
around them; instead, temples were built containing statues of the gods in front of which
offerings were placed in the form of food,
drinks or flowers. Even today, 16 sacraments
(sanskaras) are distinguished in Hinduism, and
these are carried out by the male members
of the three highest castes. The cult of the
dead and the afterlife took on a distinct form
through the practice of making offerings to the
dead (shraddha) in annual commemoration
ceremonies.

From the 4th century B.C. onwards, Hinduism in
India was in a decidedly defensive position and
lost large numbers of its followers to Buddhism,
which was beginning to flourish. As Buddhism
turned more and more to the east, Hinduism
underwent a noticeable recovery in India, but it
was not until the 4th century under the dynasty

of the Gupta Emperors (320–647 A.D.), the
only significant native dynasty of India, that it
was officially recognised.

The Period of Islamic Supremacy

After the gradual elimination of Buddhism and
the decline of Jainism, Hinduism regained spiritual dominance in India, but it was soon
threatened by the advance of Islam. Since the
8th century Islam had been steadily conquering the north of India and had also converted
many Indians. A number of people founded
sects devoted to Vishnu and Shiva and tried to
impose a monotheistic faith on Hinduism. In
this context the religious community of the
Sikhs (Hindi for "learners") grew up in what is
now the Punjab. They see themselves as a
completely separate religion. With their strict
monotheism and devotion to ten religious
masters (gurus), their faith is a curious mixture
of Hindu and Islamic elements. The members
of the religion can be recognised by their distinctive clothing and hairstyles and by the addition of the word "Singh" (= lion) to their names.

The Period of British Supremacy

From the early 16th century, India moved
increasingly into the field of vision of the
European colonial powers, beginning with the
Portuguese. Gradually, however, the British East
India Company cleared the field of all competition and set up trading posts to guarantee their
export monopolies. The British intervened more
and more directly in Indian politics, enlisted the
support of the majority of local Indian rulers,
and in 1857 overthrew the by then almost far-
cical rule of the Moghuls. In 1877, Queen
Victoria of England accepted the title of
Empress of India. In the 19th century many
attempts were made by educated Indians to
reform Hinduism. Through their engagement
with the technical achievements and modern
philosophies of Europe, the reformers tried to
declare that modern orthodox Hinduism could
be reconciled with other religions. They did not
want Hinduism to continue to be an exclusive
religion, but wanted to allow space for the worship of other prophets and religious teachers.

The New India

India was finally granted her independence by
the British on 15 August 1947, for which many
Hindus and Muslims had fought long and

hard. The flag of the Indian National Congress combined the colours saffron-red (Hindus), green (Muslims) and white (Christians, Jews, Parsees and others).

The time of independence was, however, also a time of great re-settlement and reciprocal persecution between Hindus and Muslims. The direct consequence of this was that as early as 1947 the State of Pakistan (= "Land of the Pure") split off as a purely Muslim state. A symbol of the religious conflicts and riots was the murder of Mahatma Gandhi in January 1948 by a fanatic Hindu who saw Gandhi's tolerance as a betrayal of the religion.

In the ensuing years, Jawaharlal Pandit Nehru, alongside Gandhi one of the driving forces of the struggle for independence, steered India through a moderate socialist course into the non-aligned movement. The huge social problems of the country led to repeated outbreaks of religious conflict. Both politically and from a religious viewpoint, India is still quite unstable today and those in positions of responsibility must exercise great caution.

THE HOLY SCRIPTURES

The Foundations of all Orthodox Systems

The Hindu scriptures are a rather diverse assemblage, but are considered to be the authoritative source of knowledge about the moral world order, the law of cause and effect of deeds, the rights and duties of all living beings, and natural, spiritual and social hierarchies.

The most important texts are the four Vedas (Holy Hymns) with the associated Brahmanas (Holy Treatises) and the Uphanishads (Secret Teachings). These scriptures are believed by orthodox Hindus to be of supernatural origin and constitute the "Basic Dogmas" of all Hindu systems. The texts are the source of a broad common ground in Hinduism: the belief in certain gods, initiation rites and the necessity of sacrifices, the strict social rules of the caste system, the belief in an eternal law (dharma) and the system of retribution through a hierarchy of rebirths.

The works are all written in the scholarly language of Sanskrit and are divided into two groups: those which are considered to be superhuman revelation (sruti) and those that were created by human hand and are handed down from memory (smriti).

The Four Vedas

The Vedas are thought to be the epitome of holy revelation and comprise an immense collection of texts written between 1500 B.C. and 1500 A.D., in other words over a period of 3000 years. They consist of four collections of sayings and songs (sanhitas).

1) The Rig Veda: This is the oldest collection and consists of 1028 hymns, probably written between 1500 and 1200 B.C. which were used to evoke the gods during rites of sacrifice. It contains different creation myths in which sacrifice is in the foreground. For example, it tells of the origin of mankind and the world through the sacrifice of the giant cosmic man Purusha from whom all creatures are descended. The tone of the songs is full of the joy of living and contains no hint of world-weariness. Rita, as the dynamic order of the cosmos, ensures that the forces are balanced.

2) The Sama Veda: A collection of chants which accompanied the preparation and offering of sacrifices. The subject matter is to a large degree similar to that of the Rig Veda.

3) The Yajur Veda: This is a collection of prayers that were murmured during the completion of sacrifices. It represents the transition to the Brahmana sacrificial texts which began around 1000 B.C. and which were introduced with the advance of the Aryans.

4) The Atharva Veda: A collection of magical songs which are probably only a little younger than the Rig Veda [my reference says these were added after 600 B.C. - ed. The verse form prayers and hymns are magical or are concerned with the creation of the world.

Ritual Ablutions in the Ganges (Benares)

Orthodox Hindus are convinced of the divine purity of the water of the Ganges. Benares, as the "City of Light" (its religious name) is the centre of Shiva and Ganges worship and the goal of major pilgrimages. Strict Hindus carry out extensive ablutions here each morning, accompanied by prayers; many people also fill cans and buckets so that they can take the holy water home with them. Submersion in the water of the Ganges, drinking it and performing ablutions are accompanied by the hope that purity will enable them to depart the cycle of re-births and attain salvation directly. A special ritual bathing feast "Kumbh-Mela" is celebrated every three years at the holy rivers, particularly at Allahabad, where the Yamuna flows into the Ganges. As many Hindus make pilgrimages to Benares in order to die on the banks of the Ganges, the city is the centre of Hindu cremations. The corpses are burnt on the bank on a Ghat, and the ashes scattered in the Ganges.

Krishna and Arjuna go into battle
Indian miniature, page from the series on the Mahabharata Epic, 18th century, Pahari style, Kangra

As a powerful killer of demons, Krishna (literally: "The Black One") is one of the most popular and celebrated heroes of Hinduism. Brought into safety from the cruel usurper Kansa, whom he later conquers and kills, Krishna grows up with herdsmen, plays countless pranks in his youth and, as the shepherdesses' favourite, is the hero of countless amorous adventures. For Krishnaism, Krishna, actually the 8th incarnation of Vishnu, has become the Supreme God. In the heroic epic, the Mahabharata, Krishna is king of the charioteers of his allies Arjuna and the the Pandava clan. Before the battle against the hostile Kauravas, Krishna, in an attempt to strengthen the vacillating Arjuna's fighting power, announced to him the didactic poem, the Bhagavadgita, which for many Hindus is the fundamental religious and philosophical text of Hinduism. The Bhagavadgita promulgates a warrior and ascetic ethos that elevates the fight between good and evil to a cosmic principle, but also develops a formulated teaching of serenity through yoga and insight. The path of faithful devotion (bhakti) is also outlined by Krishna.

The name means "Veda of the Atharvans" – those who know magic spells. They were probably intended for the warrior caste, expressed most notably in the hymns to the war drums.

Each of these four sanhitas has as "appendixes," two types of writings of a different character: the Brahmanas, sacrificial texts that describe and explain the sacred rituals, and the Uphanishads, philosophical texts that are concerned particularly with the universal spirit in which all beings participate.

The Brahmanas (actually "Brahmana of the 100 ways") are written in prose and contain formulae for sacrificial rituals (mantras) and mythological plots. They probably originated after 1000 B.C. and have a leaning towards philosophical speculation. They also attempt to record, list and catalogue the individual forces of existence, gods and powers, and contain the oldest theories on the Brahma or principle of the Absolute. The Veda hymns had already to some extent told of how the Many proceeded from the original cosmic One; these speculations are systematically taken further in the Brahmanas with the intention of advancing to the ultimate unity of all existence.

The Uphanishads are appendixed to or incorporated into the Brahmana texts. They are tracts with a ritual and cosmological view and form the conclusion of the Vedic literature. They represent the beginning of systematic speculative thought in India.

Brahma, the Absolute, is seen as identical with Atman, the "Self," the innermost core of each individual being, because each individual being (the Many) proceeded from the original cosmic being (the One). The Uphanishads

also contain the first pronouncement of the theory of retribution for good and evil deeds (karma) in a subsequent life (rebirth) which particularly determines the Hindu world view (Brihadaranyaka Uphanishad 3,2, verse 13). It is not clear whether this theory was brought into Hinduism by the Aryans or whether it originates from the pre-Aryan era. The belief that the processes of the world have neither beginning nor end, the hope for salvation from the fetters of the changing world through renunciation (asceticism) and the idea that all living beings, even humans and animals, are different not in essence but only in degree, is also formulated in the Uphanishads.

The Sacred Tradition (Smriti)

The sacred tradition comprises scriptures (sutras) and "teaching books" (sastras), covering the most varied areas of knowledge and philosophical questions connected with religious and social problems. Works are also counted as part of this tradition even if they are only partially didactic in character and are on the whole more narrative. The principal works in this category are the two great popular epics, the Mahabharata and the Ramayana.

The Mahabharata is an epic of over 90,000 double verses in which entertainment and religious instruction are juxtaposed. Of all its components, the most important is the Bhagavadgita ("Song of the Exalted"), in which Krishna, as the highest being, leads mankind. The god Krishna explains to the hero Arjuna the nature of God, the world and the human soul. This "Bible of Krishnaism" has become one of the texts best known outside the Hindu culture. The much shorter epic Ramayana, probably the most popular in the Indian language, tells of the fate of the hero Rama and of his battles against Ravana, the king of the demons, who abducts the hero's wife. Rama survives these battles with the help of Hanuman, the clever monkey king, and his army.

The 18 puranas ("the old writings") originated after the great epics and form the basic of popular Hinduism. They are concerned with the creation of the world, destruction and recreation, the world periods and the deeds of heroes and genealogies of individual gods and kings.

A variety of newer writings were added to these (mostly dating from between 500 and

1000 A.D.): the samhitas (collections) concerned with Vishnu, the agamas (traditions) concerned with Shiva and above all the tantras (literally: weaving), which are texts about the regulations of religion, with a decidedly esoteric character. However, the core message of Hinduism is found in the middle part of the Uphanishads, the Bhagavadgita and the Bhagavata Purana.

THE TEACHING

The Cosmos as an Ordered Whole: the Caste System as a Social Order

For Hinduism the cosmos is an ordered whole, on both macro and micro levels. It is ruled by the law of the world (dharma) which at the same time acts as a natural and moral order. The principle of this order is that all living things are strictly different from one another from the moment of birth, and as a consequence of this have different tasks, obligations, rights and abilities. In human beings there are different classes (castes) that are strictly separated from one another. The dharma is the one, eternal law of the world for all living things, but it is expressed differently for the different castes and stages of life (ashramas), which means that special religious and ritual rules are needed for the individual castes. The orthodox caste rules affect all areas of daily life and are expressed in commandments prescribing clear separation, affecting, for example, meals and marriages. The caste system is peculiar to Hinduism and is very difficult for other religions and philosophies to understand and accept.

At the top of the caste hierarchy is the priesthood, the caste of the Brahmans, who particularly emphasise the purity law, concern themselves almost exclusively with spiritual things and, through performing rituals and sacrifices, are "closest" to the gods. The second class is the warrior caste (kshatriya), who are charged with protecting the social order. Rulers and kings are normally from this class. As the "military class," they originally lived on the taxes and levies they gathered from the lower classes. The third class is made up of farmers and herdsmen, business people and traders (vaisyas); they are the actual "nourishing class." These three top castes, formed after the Aryan expansion, by virtue of belonging to the higher castes, have experienced in a certain sense

a social rebirth and are therefore called the "twice-born." For orthodox Hinduism these upper castes are the only ones with the right to study the sacred Vedas.

The lower castes are forever separate from these higher castes. The fourth class, the "sudras," are workers and artisans of the "lower" occupations whose duty is to serve the upper classes. There are further strict gradations according to purity. Thus, for example, weavers and potters are higher than laundry people, butchers, fishermen or leather tanners. The lowest group, the fifth class, is known as "pancamas," "parias" or "untouchables" (asprishyas). In traditional Indian society they often live a miserable existence and do "unclean" or "dishonest" work such as sweeping streets, cleaning toilets or are members of the various begging and thieving castes. The two lower classes were created largely by the Aryans from the original Indian population they overthrew.

Each of the five castes is broken down into numerous internal sub-divisions, so that

Temple of Minakshi in Madurai

India's temples display very rich ornamentation, particularly on their facades and roofs. All available surfaces are covered with relief work depicting the gods and goddesses, demons and heroes, animals, plants and fantastic creatures. Each temple constitutes its own cosmos of highly turbulent, lively scenes, bursting with activity. The two huge gate-towers (gopuras) of the Temple of Minakshi in Madurai are also covered with thousands of stucco figures in magnificent colours. The temple complex in Madurai, with its numerous halls and courtyards, was completed in the 17th century. The temple is one of Hinduism's most important centres of pilgrimage and is visited by around 10,000 believers each day. Tradition has it that Shiva married Parvati here. The temple complex, which are mainly covered, extend over six hectares. The interiors are full of festively decorated images of gods and altars at which people constantly pray and offer sacrifices.

**Krishna and Radha sitting on a
lotus blossom**
Miniature of the Parkari school,
Basohli, 1715

The lotus is the cosmic plant of
Hinduism. When the divine
substance of life is in the process of
bringing forth the universe, a
thousand-leafed lotus grows out of
the cosmic waters and is the
opening, gateway and mouth for the
development of the universe. The
cosmic lotus is the organ of
procreation of the Absolute that
gives birth to the universe and
symbolizes the never-ending
succession of existences. In pre-
Vedic times, the lotus was the
symbol of the Great Mother Goddess
or "Earth Goddess," Shri or Lakshmi.
In the post-Vedic period the image
of the one born of the lotus was
transferred to Brahma, and shortly
after a number of gods were
depicted sitting on the lotus.

Hinduism has a total of some 2000 or 3000
castes, each of which has a fixed definition and
fixed tasks. For Hindus all other possible cate-
gorisations – for example by place, language,
nation or culture – are considered to be secondary and "artificial." The lack of a caste system
is seen as a break with the natural order.

Modern India, which since Pandit Nehru
regards itself in the social realm as a secular
state, is attempting in many areas to mitigate
the harshness of the caste system, but for
pious Hindus this is regarded as the valid
social order that has existed for thousands of
years. Right back in the earliest Hindu text,
the Rig Veda (10,90, verse 12), the caste
system is seen as a divine institution and the
different castes are described as having been
made from the different limbs of the original
cosmic being, Purusha. The different castes
are therefore meant to work together like one
body.

Karmic Retribution: the Cosmos as Moral Order

The hierarchy of the caste system is strongly
linked to the idea that the natural order is at the
same time a moral world order. Since the
Uphanishads a particular expression of this has
been the teaching on karma. This says that the
existence and fate of the individual are the necessary consequence of actions performed in a
former life, by which the good deeds will be
rewarded with a "good rebirth," i.e. birth into a
higher caste, and bad deeds will be punished
with a lower rebirth.

The diversity of living things is seen as an
expression of the diversity of deeds that need
to be rewarded or punished. The similarities
and differences between living things are
measured according to the similarities and differences of deeds carried out in former lives.
Since the world is without end and the world
systems eternally die and are re-born, Hindus
do not see the process of retribution as having
a beginning. The ends of world systems and
cosmic periods of rest do not interrupt the
cycle of reward and punishment, which will be
continued when the next world is formed. The
moral order of the world includes not only retribution for deeds but also the possibility of
living things gradually perfecting themselves
and ultimately experiencing salvation.

It is a moot point whether Hinduism really
assumes that all living things will one day be
saved and released from repeated reincarnation into the changing world (samsara). Specific
to Hinduism is that all life, plants and animals
too, are part of these two hierarchies, since
every living thing is different from everything
else by degree only and not in essence.

THE DIFFERENT IDEAS OF GOD

The Diversity of the Systems

Hinduism, like no other religion, gives its
believers freedom in metaphysical and philosophical questions. It is up to the individual
whether he sees himself as a theist, pantheist
or atheist, whether he sees Vishnu or Shiva as
the highest personal guiding force in the
world, or prefers to think of this concept in
apersonal terms.

The theories about the formation of worlds
and the interplay between their material and
non-material components, as well as the relationship between body and soul, are similarly
not universally binding. The Indian mind does
not have a need to systematise this wide
range of religious views and practices.
Nowhere is this diversity better expressed than
in the metaphysical and philosophical declara-
tions. The philosophical views are fixed in the
"sutras" (scriptures) and certain systems of
thought known in Sanskrit as "darshana" (literally: way of seeing from "drishti = to see, see
the truth), and are often intended merely as
guidelines.

The Six Orthodox Darshanas

Tradition distinguishes six darshanas, which are all considered to be orthodox because they all recognise the Vedas as revelation, although they otherwise interpret the world in completely different ways.

The six systems are usually ordered in pairs; samkhya or sankhya (based on intellectual knowledge) and yoga (control of the senses and inner forces) belong together; vaisheshika (which is experimental and based on sensory perception) and nyaya (which proceeds logically and is based on dialectics) are paired and vedanta (metaphysical speculation) and karma mimansa (which is deistic and ritualistic and based on sacred scriptures) belong together. In each of the three pairs the first system is the more metaphysical and philosophical while the second is dedicated more to methodology.

1) Samkhya or sankhya (literally: enumerating) represents dualistic realism. It is a very old system and recognises two final eternal realities: the mind (purusa) and nature (prakriti). Prakriti is an all-pervasive force, a kind of substance which consists of three main components or elements (gunas). These three gunas contradict each other in a certain sense and thus keep each other in balance. Purusa is non-matter or pure spirit. Yoga can be used to influence the play of forces. Our material (earthly) existence is arduous and full of sorrow because we do not know the difference between self and not-self. Freedom can be found only in meditation.

2) Yoga (literally, "harnessing, training") can be traced back to the teaching book of the Patanjali in the first half of the 1st century A.D., but parts of it are considerably older. It is a theistic system based on the modified ("classical") samkhya as a practical teaching of meditation to reach an attachment-free state which leads to salvation. There are eight stages of yoga, ranging from overcoming the self to complete contemplation.

3) Vaisesika is originally an atheistic system. It sets out an atomistic interpretation of the world according to which everything (apart from the spirit) is composed of atoms that do not become visible until they connect as matter. In the night of dissolution (end of the world) the atoms separate again and form new combinations in new worlds. The natural philosophy of vaisesika analyses the real differences (vishesda) between everything that exists by classifying all that is into categories. Nine substances account for the interconnection of events in the world: four elements consisting of atoms (earth, water, fire, air), three identical all-pervasive entities (ether, space, time), the countless individual souls (the 8th substance) and the atomically small thought substances that belong to them (the 9th substance).

4) Nyaya (literally, "logic") supports a theory of logical realism. It is a system of logic and dialectics which corresponds to vaisheshika in its basic view of the world and was later fused with it. It distinguishes real from false know-

Yogi in front of the Temple of Warwari in Madras

The meditating yogi has the clearly visible signs of the followers of Vishnu: white make-up on his forehead with a vertical red line between the eyebrows.

Pilgrim fakir in Malaysia

On pilgrimages Hindu ascetics demonstrate their insensitivity to physical pain and indifference to the difficulties of daily life, attained principally through concentration, meditation and trance. A popular practice is to pierce the cheeks and tongue with silver rods or spikes to which small chains are often attached. Other fakirs hang on pilgrims' wagons on hooks through the skin of their backs. These wagons are often pushed for weeks by their fellow pilgrims to the goal of their pilgrimage. The ascetics particularly worship the nagas (from "naga" = serpent, serpent demon), who are seen as the guardians of the faith. They are well-versed in the martial arts and often live naked and in complete poverty, usually wearing only a spike and pilgrim's chain that is used as prayer beads.

Stele of the God Brahma
Chlorite slate, 12th century, North Bengal

Brahma, the personification of the Vedic neutral "Brahman" (= universal soul, universe) always wears the Sacred Thread of the top three castes and rides on a goose (hansa) which is regarded as an intelligent animal. Brahma is not the creator, but the designer or architect of the universe and guardian of the world. Many myths tell how Brahma was deprived of power and became clearly subordinate to the supreme gods Vishnu and Shiva.

The God Brahma at a Sacrificial Fire
Indian miniature, page from a Ragamala series, around 1660, Central India, Malva style

Brahman is the supreme god of the Brahmin priest caste. As such he is depicted as having four heads and four hands, each head standing for one of the four holy Vedas and holding in his hands the requisites of a priest: Veda manuscript, vessel containing holy water, sacrificial spoon and sling.

ledge by means of five members (statements) and claims that the existence of ideas is dependent on a mind that thinks them. It sees liberation as being brought about by experiencing the independence of the self, which is thought of as separate from the body and pure mind. A god was originally not named in nyaya and only came into the system later when it was unified with vaisesika.

5) Vedanta (literally, "culmination of the Vedas") attempts to convey the final statement of the Uphanishads. Its great teaching text is the "Brahmasutra." It is the culmination of Vedic speculation. The short aphorisms are difficult to interpret because of their riddle-like character, and there are countless commentaries on the Vedanta.

6) Karma-Mimamsa (literally: scriptural exegesis or "critical explanation") was originally a theological or religious text. The work was not philosophical, but an interpretation of the sacred texts on sacrificial rituals which are important for the preservation of the world and human life. In the 7th to 8th century A.D. it was developed into a philosophical system teaching the real existence of a multitude of souls and substances.

All six darshanas make different statements about the divine. The karma-mimansa and classical sanskhya deny the existence of an eternal ruler of the world and see the cosmos as being ruled by natural and moral law (dharma). Yoga recognises an eternal, omniscient God, but gives him no influence over what happens in the world (a stance known in European philosophy as deism). Vaisesika and nyaya believe in a personal and interventionalist God who is, however, in origin identical with the eternal soul and eternal matter. Older vedanta teaches a pantheism in which God is the original substance of the world and yet at the same time a being who is higher than this world. This idea is understood by some as a non-personal principle and by others as a personal supreme God. This system was later transposed onto the gods Vishnu and Shiva. The central concept of these schools or sects is "bhakti." Bhakti means a pious state of being in passionate relationship with the Lord of the World as a means of achieving personal salvation, in the face of which philosophy and science recede sharply.

Shankara

The Brahmin Shankara (788–820 A.D.) made a great attempt to unify religious views and practices by re-interpreting the Vedanta texts, and this had an enormous effect on Hindu thought. Influenced by Buddhist systems, Shankara upheld a two-stage theory of the truth, according to which all forms of belief in this world have a right to exist, but that all can only inadequately grasp the highest truth.

The holy and ultimate is for him beyond the appearance of diversity, beyond the "veil of maya" (= worldly illusion) and may only be experienced by wise people in meditative contemplation. Shankara combines the "knowledge" of a supreme all-uniting universal spirit with the belief in a personal Lord of the World who has validity for the realm of "maya," in other words for our illusionary" changing world." All earthly religions are for him merely preliminary stages on the way to insight into the absolute truth, which is beyond words and thoughts. Shankara's teaching has been largely adopted into orthodox Hinduism.

The Yoga Teachings

The word yoga literally means "to harness," and originally referred to the actual comparison with guiding horses through the use of a harness. The techniques of yoga, whose teaching refers to both the samkhya and yoga darshanas, are methods of spiritual and physical discipline and a way of concentrating on intuitive knowledge and the unity behind the world of diverse phenomena.

There are nine systems of yoga, sub-divided into four main paths and five complementary methods. The aim of yoga is the achievement of true insight through the liberation of the soul. The means to achieve this are renunciation, abstinence and asceticism, rejection of all comforts and possessions, the killing of desires and through this the attainment of spiritual serenity and inner gentleness, expressed as inner retreat in contemplative meditation.

Tantrism

From around 500 A.D. the sacred practices of Hinduism were significantly revalued. The ritual movement that emerged, in which magical elements play a major role, is called Tantrism after its texts, the tantras.

In this cult, the spirit of the non-Aryan peoples of India gains greater influence. It culminates in the belief in "shaktis," the feminine consorts and companions of the gods and in the theory that the male god can only be effective through the energy given to him by his wife. The tantric cult is often connected with secret rituals, has a complicated mystical system of numbers and letters, and a sophisticated cult of images. The support of a guru is considered to be absolutely essential. So-called "left-handed Tantrism" is, exactly like in Buddhism, a cult of sexuality with partially orgiastic character; there are extreme esoteric and magical forms of Tantrism.

Vishnuites and Shivaites

The Vishnuite and Shivaite systems are later philosophical systems of Hinduism which originated to some extent in competition with the strict monotheism of the advancing Islam (from the 8th century A.D.) but which were primarily a reaction to Shankara's philosophy and Tantrism. The followers have the objective of ensuring that the god they believe to be Lord of the World – Vishnu or Shiva – is considered to be the only true God.

Both movements also adopted a number of local cults and characteristics of the gods. The basic form of Vishnuite piety is the "way of loving devotion to God" (bhakti-marga), while Shiva is mainly worshipped in the form of the phallus (lingam) but also as a (destructive) feminine force. Both belief systems have large communities of adherents, following different rites.

Worship and Ritual

After the Vedic epoch, ritual steadily lost significance while external religious practices – particularly under the influence of Tantrism – became increasingly important. This was reflected in the spread of figurative representations of the gods and monumental holy sculptures.

"Puja" (adoration) became the central focus of religious life: god is greeted as a guest of honour and welcomed with incense and flowers. Sometimes the god image is seen as being identical with the god; it is also possible for the god to be present through a symbol, such as in the lingam as a symbol of Shiva. Ritual purity is a key concept in serving the gods. During prayer, particular formulae are recited (man-

tras), and temple dancers and house priests also play a part in the adoration of the gods, with particular movements and body postures prescribed for these religious dances. Tantrism also has its own religious emblems, the often artistically crafted yantras or mandalas, mystical diagrams in the form of a circle or square, which are thought to evoke the presence of the corresponding god for ritual or meditation.

It is particularly difficult for non-Hindus to understand the religious symbolism in Hinduism. With, or rather in, the symbols of the gods, the gods themselves are worshipped. For example, the image of a god carried in a procession "is" the god himself, although educated Hindus, of course, do not deny the difference between the symbol and that which it symbolises. What is happening is that abstract principles are being depicted in images that affirm them.

The temples of India that have been preserved were for the most part built in the 7th century A.D. or later when the temples and images of the gods replaced the older open-air sacrificial sites. Walking around temples and shrines is an element of most religious pilgrimages. The temples in the north of the country are pyramid-shaped towers, while those in the south are usually more truncated and rectangular.

THE HINDU PANTHEON

Inexhaustible Diversity

The word for God in Hinduism is "Deva" (from "div" = to shine or radiate). The Vedic pantheon

Worship of Ganesha
Indian miniature, illustration at the beginning of the text of the Bhagavadgita, 18th century, Moghul style, Kashmir

The good-humoured and warm-hearted Ganesha, thought to be the son or creation of Shiva, is one of Hinduism's most popular gods. As his father gave him the power to grant anything that mankind asked him for, he is called upon for help before every difficult undertaking or journey. He has the head of an elephant with only one tusk and there are a number of legends about his form. All the versions, however, relate that the god originally had a human head which he either lost or had chopped off, and was then given the head of an elephant by Shiva or Brahma. He has a fat belly because he is partial to the sacrificial offerings people make, particularly fruit and candy, which is why he is often depicted with servant girls handing fruit to him. As the god of wisdom and custodian of science he is thought to have written down the sacred epic Mahabharata as dictated to him by the sage Vyasa. In the fight against the demons he is the leader of Shiva's army (Ganadevatas), and as this "Great Lord of the Hordes" (Mahaganapati) he has become the Supreme Deity for one of the sects of tantric Hinduism.

Stele of the God Vishnu
Late Pallara, 9th century

Vishnu, whose rise did not begin until the late-Vedic period, is now, along with Shiva, the main god of Hinduism. By contrast to Shiva, Vishnu personifies the kind and helpful supreme god to whose strength coupled with gentleness the believer surrenders in faithful devotion (bhakti). He is always seen as the moderate preserver and conserver of the world.

Vishnu in his Incarnation as a Boar (varaha) at the Hoysala Temple in Belur

In his 3rd incarnation, as a boar (varaha), Vishnu hauled the earth that had been pushed into the ocean by a demon up from the bottom of the sea with his tusks, killed the demon and emerged from the waters with the rescued earth goddess Prithivi in his arms. Prithivi, the Earth, then became his wife.

underwent a complete transformation at the time of the Uphanishads: the Vedic gods Mitra and Varuna, Indra and Agni were still worshipped, but receded more and more into the background.

Instead, three new gods became the all-powerful figures of the Indian pantheon: Brahma, Vishnu and Shiva. They sometimes appear as a triad (trimurti) and are connected with the theory that the three gods are only three different aspects or forms of the one original being in its activity as creator, preserver and destroyer of the universe. Most modern Hindu theologians belong either to the Vishnuites or the Shivaites and see one of the two as the supreme God to whom the other gods are subordinate subjects or manifestations (incarnations).

Brahma, the Creator

As creator god, Brahma played a substantial part in the creation of the world. He did not, however, create the world according to his own free will, nor did he create it out of nothing, which is why he can only with some reservation be called a "creator god." Nevertheless, he did pronounce the sacred Vedas. He is a personification of the originally neuter Brahman, mentioned in the Uphanishads as meaning the Absolute (universal spirit) which is identical with the Atman, the innermost eternal self of each individual. Brahma is also a merging of other cosmogonic figures such as Prajapati, the "Lord of Creatures," who is often mentioned in the Brahmana texts.

However, Brahma – maybe because he is still tinged by his origins in a neutral or rather impersonal principle – has not become a supreme God towering above the other gods. Contemporary Hinduism sees him as the demiurge, the architect of the worlds, who constantly re-orders the existing components of the world and gives the souls caught in the cycle of the worlds new bodies each time they are reborn. The Brahman of the Uphanishads was an Absolute without colour or form. In the Vedic period, the creator or demiurge was not yet identified as the god Brahma; he was called Prajapati and was a creative energy. The Vishnuites and Shivaites, who were beginning to hold sway, took decisive action against Brahma, deprived him of any claim to absoluteness and caricatured him as a creator god – for instance

through the story that he took his daughter Savritri as his wife and lived with her in an incestuous relationship. The legend of his birth is a particular example of his claim to absoluteness being undermined: Brahma is said to have emerged from a lotus blossom growing out of Vishnu's navel. As he is a purely theistic and not originally a natural god, Brahma is not connected with the opposing tendencies of destruction and re-creation (like Shiva).

Vishnu, the Preserver

Vishnu had a more successful career than Brahma. Although little attention is paid to him in the Vedas, he later became one of India's most powerful gods, particularly through his identification with various deities and his incarnation in the various heroes of the great Indian epics. He embodies the principle of the preservation of the world through ethical or heroic deeds. Whenever the world or humanity is in danger of falling into decay due to evil forces or moral decline, Vishnu comes to the rescue as a hero in the form of an animal or a human being. Vishnu appears in ten incarnations divided between the four world ages. In the complicated time structure of the aeons of the gods each world age ends with moral decline, at the end of which Vishnu appears and fights the demons of evil so that a new world can be formed.

Vishnu's ten incarnations are as: 1) fish (Matsyavatara); 2) turtle (Kurmavatara); 3) boar (Varhavatara); 4) man-lion (Narasimhavatara); 5) dwarf (Vamanavatara); 6) Rama with the axe (Parashu-Ramavatara); 7) Rama the hero (Ramavatara); 8) Krishna; 9) Buddha; 10) horse (Kalki). Of these incarnations (avataras, literally: descents) of Vishnu, the 7th incarnation as Rama the hero and the 8th incarnation as Krishna enjoy particular popularity. In the Ramayana epic Rama is a prince and later King of Ayodha who lives with his virtuous wife Sita, the epitome of fidelity, ruling as an ideal king. Rama is revered as a statesman, commander, legislator and artist.

Krishna is thought to be the only complete incarnation of Vishnu and is therefore worshipped as a separate deity. Krishna is also a prince. It was prophesied to his uncle, the cruel King Kamsa of Mathura, that Krishna would kill him, so Kamsa had all newborn baby boys in his kingdom killed. However, Krishna grew up unrecognised amongst herdsmen in

Brindaban, where even as a boy he performed wondrous deeds and as a youth was the favourite of all the shepherdesses (Gopi). Later he killed Kamsa and became ruler of Mathura, conducted victorious campaigns, and moved to Gujarat where in Dvaraka he fathered 180,000 sons with 16,000 women, which is why he is also the fertility patron. His heroic deeds, amorous adventures and words of wisdom are among the most popular themes in Indian literature. Vishnu's 10th incarnation will be as Kalki, the god of the future who overcomes evil, restores righteousness and ushers in a new and happy world age.

In Vedic times Vishnu was merely one of twelve sun gods and symbolised the course of the sun, and his role as preserver of the world was ascribed to him relatively late. Vishnuism also grew up later than Shivaitism. As preserver of the world he is also seen as the embodiment of goodness and mercy. He has called the world and all the living things in it into existence through emanation and preserves life until the dissolution of the universe. At the end of each world Vishnu returns to his original form and after a rest lets everything form anew. His depiction as Narayana, the god at the beginning of a new age, is particularly popular: Vishnu rests in contemplative sleep on the five-headed world serpent and dreams the new order into existence. Out of his navel grows the lotus which brings forth the creator god, Brahma.

Shiva, the Destroyer

Today Shiva, whose name means "The Merciful One," along with Vishnu, is the most popular god in Hinduism. He is prefigured in the Vedic Rudra, the terrible archer who sends diseases and drives them away again. But with him is merged the pre-Aryan god of virility, who is worshipped in the symbol of the phallus (lingam). Shiva is the "double-headed" god par excellence, who embodies both the creative and destructive forces of the cosmos – depending on his different forms and incarnations. Looked at in spiritual terms he is also the archetype of the great ascetic who overcomes the world through self-castigation, thus creating new existence, and the redeeming saviour.

Like Vishnu, Shiva is also seen by his followers as the highest Lord of the World. He is the deity with the greatest number of different forms and facets in Hinduism, and is one of the oldest gods. As an originally natural character through and through he was the god of storms, of illnesses and of the great death, but he was also the helper and saviour of mankind. He has a total of 1,008 different names. As Rudra the god of storms he lived in cemeteries and forests, a god of the wilderness and boundary areas, depicted wearing a necklace of skulls.

The Aryans saw him in his manifestation as Rudra as being equal with Vishnu, and his uncultivated and wild natural powers were in a manner of speaking "civilised." In contemporary Hinduism Shiva is sometimes mascu-

Battle of the Gods against the Demons
Indian miniature, page from a Sanskrit manuscript of the Devimahatmya, 2nd half of the 18th century, Pahari region, Guler style

In the battle of the gods against the demons, Shiva's wife Durga, "she who is difficult to approach," plays an important part. She is an aspect of the great goddess Devi. She was born from flames flowing from the mouth of a great god, and was from the start a magnificent woman with the task of killing the demons of evil. The gods immediately put her into battle against the mighty buffalo demon Mahisha who was a threat even to the gods (the illustration shows Durga in battle against Mahisha). She fought him with ten arms, in each hand a weapon given to her by a different god. After a long struggle, Durga finally killed the demon with a spear.

Shiva Nataraja
Bronze, Southern India, 19th century

As "Lord of the Dance" (Nataraja), Shiva performs his dance on the body of the dwarf demon Apasmara, who stands for evil and ignorance. Shiva's dance has cosmic significance as it heralds the new creation and re-establishment of divine order in a new age. The halo of flames surrounding him symbolizes the cycle of creation, decay and re-birth.

Sacred Cows

Since the Vedic period the cow has enjoyed extraordinary religious adoration in India, and the point of the Vedic sacrifice to the gods was to ask for wealth in cows. Some of the holy cows in India belong to temples, but most of them roam around freely in the cities, relying upon the faithful to feed them. They are also often given garlands of flowers and saffron as a sign of adoration. For the faithful Hindu, the eating of beef is taboo and killing a cow is one of the gravest of sins.

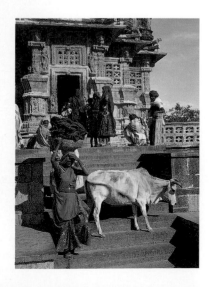

line, sometimes feminine and sometimes androgynous. The androgynous aspect of the god is constitutive. The androgynous Shiva (Ardhanarishvara) is represented by a figure with a body that is half male and half female. The male Shiva is also depicted with his Shakti (feminine deity) from whom he derives his energy. In this form the masculine principle symbolises the passive element of space and the feminine principle symbolises the active element of time. A particular form of representation is Shiva as the Lord of the Dance (Nataraja). The cosmic dance is considered to be the creative act par excellence, in which the dancer symbolises the impersonal, constantly changing life force which is shown in different poses and postures. At the same time, the cosmic dancer releases the world from ignorance, as symbolised by the evil dwarf Apasmara on whom the dancer Nataraja stands.

Shiva as Feminine Deity

As he is the only one of the trimurti gods who still has natural features, Shiva is also considered to be an incarnation or incarnations of the feminine deities, particularly the goddesses of natural forces (such as sunrise, night-time and fertility). The feminine forces of nature were revalued in the Vedas by the concept of the "shakti" which means "power" and refers to the feminine deities as giving energy to the masculine deities to whom they correspond. The highest collective term for the gods, "devi," originally meant mother goddess and mother of the world, and then the earth goddess Prithivi. All of these diverse shaktis are connected with the forces of Shiva. Shiva is well known and feared as a goddess in her terrifying aspects, particularly as "Black Kali," the goddess of time, portrayed Medusa-like with teeth bared, blazing hair and outstretched tongue, holding a skull, sword and noose.

Miscellaneous Gods – the Vedic Gods

There are countless deities in Hinduism particularly those gods in animal form which are often spoken of as the children or servants of the three great trimurti gods. Ganesha, the pot-bellied god with the head of an elephant, deserves particular mention as the god of wisdom who clears away all obstacles. He is seen as intelligent, good-humoured and full of character, and is invoked before examinations or difficult undertakings.

Of the Vedic gods, the main one to mention is the sun god Surya as the giver of life, depicted in a horse-drawn chariot. He was initially thought to be the origin of all things and creator of the universe, and his friendly overall image was greatly adored. Temples were dedicated to him until into the 12th century.

Four gods act in the Vedas as the "guardians of the cardinal points" (dikpala): the god of storms, Indra (East); the god of water, Varuna (West); the god of death, Yama (South); and the god of wealth, Kubera (North). Additionally there are the guardians of the secondary cardinal points: the god of fire, Agni (Southeast); the god of wind, Vayu (Northwest); the god of misfortune, Nirrti (Southwest); and the moon god Candra (Northeast).

The god of thunder and war, Indra, was also called "King of the gods" and is depicted with all the insignia of royal power, including the diamond thunderbolt Vajra. The Vajrayana, the "diamond vehicle," was introduced later as the third way of Tantric Buddhism. The myths tell of how Indra's power became weaker and weaker as a result of intoxicating drinks (soma) until he was finally "dethroned" by Vishnu and Shiva, a story which illustrates the shifting significance of the Indian pantheon.

The fire god Agni, with Indra and the sun god Surya, formed a kind of trinity in early Vedic time. He was also responsible for ritual sacrificial fire and was seen as the god of warmth and light. The god of death, Yama, was thought to be the son of Surya, the sun god, and was regarded as the first person on earth and thus the first mortal. He is also imagined as the lord of hell and judge of death, recording the deeds of human beings. Varuna is the god of water, who was also regarded as the omnipotent guardian of the cosmic order who made the sun, moon and stars shine, and as the eternal witness to human deeds. The fact that water is so highly worshipped in Hinduism is probably connected with him.

Hinduism also has countless gods of planets and stars, the ancestors of the gods (rishis) who are imagined as aimlessly wandering spirits, as well as all manner of demons who are mostly regarded as the enemies of both gods and humans. Yakshas and yakshis are eerie beings, magical masculine and feminine creatures who have a great influence on human life and who can be both friendly and hostile. The bhutas are regarded as ominous spirits of the night who are connected with death and misfortune.

The majority of the supernatural beings act as guardians or are heavenly musicians or protective deities with local functions. The gods are nearly all depicted as riding a particular animal and have a number of dwarf-like servants or companions.

The Feminine Deities

As already mentioned in connection with the feminine aspects of Shiva, feminine deities have been worshipped in India from time immemorial, but there is little mention of them in the Vedas. Increasing attention was paid to them in the classical period as a result of the rising influence of non-Aryan thought.

Today the most important feminine deities are the wives of the three main gods: Lakshmi, the wife of Vishnu as the goddess of fortune; Sarasvati, the wife of Brahma as the patron of learning; and Durga ("she who is difficult to approach"), the wife of Shiva as a symbol of the eternal primeval force, who gives birth and destroys again.

Durga is regarded by some Hindus as the highest ruler of the world and the primeval force (shakti) par excellence. Since almost all the Vedic goddesses embody the perpetual forces of nature, they almost all bear the "double face" of creative and destructive aspects, familiar in Shiva in his incarnations as feminine deities. One of the very early symbols of Indian religion was the "Great Mother" who is equated with the cosmic cow; the special worship of "sacred cows" in India can no doubt be traced back to this.

THE WORLD VIEW OF HINDUISM

Hindu Cosmography and Humans

Hindu cosmography consists of the earth's disc with Mount Meru in the centre, surrounded by continents and seas. Beneath the earth are the nether worlds, populated by demons, and the hells as places of punishment for evil-doers. Above the earth are the upper worlds, like separate stories stacked one on top of the other, where the spirits and gods live. The whole world is surrounded by a shell and is seen as the "world egg;" an infinite number of world eggs rest in empty space.

These ideas have existed since the time of the Uphanishads and were adopted virtually wholesale from Buddhism. An infinite number of living things inhabit the world; each of these beings consists of a soul made of pure spirit (jiva) and a material body. The souls have always existed, since time has no beginning, and depending on their karma (deeds performed) they repeatedly take on new bodies. There are a number of discussions in Hinduism about the nature of souls; some systems see them as being surrounded by an invisible body of fine matter during the transmigration stage or even when they are in the physical body.

There are different ideas about the relationship of the soul to matter or to the body, particularly in the case of human beings. The main belief, however, is that it is only out of ignorance that people believe thier immortal souls really form one unity with their mortal bodies, which in fact are made of completely different matter.

The Emergence from the Primal Matter and the World Eras (calpas)

Most schools of Hinduism today accept the sankhya teaching on the emergence, or rather emanation, of all matter from the primal matter (prakriti). During the period of rest that follows the end of a world, the primal matter is in a very fine, undeveloped stage. It consists of three substances (gunas): 1) sattva = light, bright, causing joy; 2) rajas = nimble, stimulating, causing pain; and 3) tamas = heavy, dark, inhibiting.

In the state of rest between worlds these three gunas are in equilibrium, but when the world is

Worshippers
Temple in Calcutta

Hinduism's numerous religious festivals are a particular attraction for believers of every caste. The five-day autumn festival of Lakshmi the goddess of fortune (Diwali), and the spring festival, Holi, which is celebrated with carnival-like processions and bonfires, are particularly popular. In Bengal, the festival "Durga Puja" is celebrated in October in honour of the goddess Durga. It involves grand processions, with each village or neighbourhood making its own image of Durga out of clay and papier machè, painting it in bright colours, and carrying it through the streets. At the end of the festival week the image is cast into the waters of the holy rivers, where it sinks. All of Hinduism's religious rites and events are colourful and appeal to the senses. The photograph shows the interior of a temple in Calcutta dedicated to Kali, the patron god of the city. Fresh flowers and Ganges water are offered by the faithful in front of black and white lingam stones.

Young Woman and Ascetic

The great religious variety and the direct juxtaposition of completely different forms of piety and worship in Hinduism are striking and fascinating. Even the strictest asceticism and the different rituals are openly practised in public and characterize the image of this religion and of India. Even demonstrations of renunciation and of overcoming the world take place amidst everyday life.

being formed they are thrown out of balance through divine intervention. They work against each other and are mixed together. In this way the matter becomes slightly dense and then progressively denser. After the souls have begun to have insight and thought (slightly more dense state) and the five elements have been formed (increased density), the "world egg" is finally formed as a combination of all these powers (high density). Into this world egg, God (the universal spirit) now penetrates and as a demiurge brings forth the god Brahma who establishes the world according to the eternal laws (dharma). Brahma helps the souls who are sleeping between worlds to enter new bodies according to their karma.

Brahma has alternating periods of activity and rest, just as humans have times of sleep and wakefulness. When Brahma's day comes to a close, the end of the world follows, and when he awakens a new world is created. Each great world era (mahayuga) consists of four world eras (yuga), which decrease in duration and quality.

Calculating the duration of the individual world eras is very complicated. While in the first world era (kritayuga) justice, truth and virtue always reign, these decrease further and further throughout the next three world eras until there is complete moral and natural decay, so that a new first world era can begin again. Our world thus has a long bad period ahead of it, at the end of which Vishnu in his 10th incarnation as Kalki will appear – like a Messiah – on a white horse to punish the wicked and usher in a new age of happiness. At the end of

Brahma's life, i.e. after 100 Brahma years, the world egg sinks back into undifferentiated primal matter and after a long period of rest a new world egg emerges again.

The Highest World Principle (Dharma)

The eternal law which rules all things and all beings is both a natural and a moral world order. For most philosophical systems of Hinduism, dharma is the highest and ultimate principle that is at work in everything, and which rules everything. The gods are also subject to it and therefore, like human beings, are regarded as "impermanent" and subject to karmic rebirth. It is therefore possible to regard this system, with its non-personal world order, as in some sense ultimately "atheistic."

The natural philosophies of yoga and vaisheshika-nyaya on the other hand teach the existence of an eternal personal God who stands alongside the eternal souls and eternal matter and does not create them but simply orders them as a demiurge. Even this God, however, is only the executor of the dharma that is above everything. There are, however, systems in Hinduism which see the world as emerging from an eternal God and see dharma as the will and law of this one God.

Transmigration of Souls and Redemption

The doctrine of karma and the transmigration of souls that goes with it is central to all Hindu systems, regardless of how they view God. The aim of each human life is to ensure a good reincarnation through good deeds.

However, as all existences end when a world ends, each existence, including that of the gods, is "limited" in time. Thus any wise person who has recognised the frailty and impermanence of all earthly existence will strive for eternal salvation.

Vishnuites and Shivaites teach that one cannot achieve redemption from the changing world by virtue of his own strength, but needs the grace of God, which can be gained through faithful and loving devotion (bhakti) and trusting surrender (prapatti).

Certain systems teach that it is necessary for human beings to participate in this work of God, saying that man should cling to God like a young monkey to his mother. For this reason they are called the "Monkey Schools" (theologically: synergists). Other systems claim man will be brought to safety without having to do anything, just as a cat takes its helpless young into its mouth and carries it out of the danger zone. They are called "Cat Schools" and rely entirely on the grace of God without any human merit (theologically: monergists).

Still other schools, by contrast, claim that one can attain redemption alone, and in this are comparable to Buddhism. According to them, true knowledge and true insight into the world make it possible to rein in all passion, which will have a positive influence both on the current karma and on the karma of former existences which is potentially still present and can be "paid off" in this way. Some schools believe that redemption is not possible until death, while others see a possibility of redemption in this earthly existence through intensive meditation and asceticism. Various schools offer different answers to the question of the redemption or eternal condemnation of the soul. While the solution of this problem is met with considerable difficulty, most theories do not believe in eternal condemnation because of the constant changes of a state of being.

Reformers of Hinduism

There have always been important thinkers and interpreters in this religion, but it is only since the beginning of the 19th century that attempts have been made to integrate Indian traditions with European thought and with new ideologies and world views.

The highly educated Bengali Brahmin Ram Mohan Roy (1772–1833), who founded the reform movement of Brahma-Samaj in 1828, undertook the first systematic analysis in the context of European culture which earned him the honourary title "Father of Modern India." He sought to purify Hinduism by reflecting on its original elements and aspired ultimately to a unity of all world religions. In his analysis of Christianity, from which he adopted certain philosophies (monotheism, ethics), it emerged that Hinduism was not inferior to Christianity. This movement gave rise to numerous Hindu reformers in the 19th century.

The Brahmin Ramakrishna (1836–1886, born Gadadhar Chatterjee) was the most important and effective Indian thinker of the 19th century. He had a strong mystical bent and described paths of inner enlightenment. His aim was the simple pious life, respect for each living creature and the synthesis of all religions through a visionary idea of God and inner experience.

His dynamic pupil, Vivekananda (1863–1902, born Narendranath Datta), was a missionary philanthropist and campaigned for Hinduism on his travels in Europe and the U.S.A. In 1897 he founded the Ramakrishna Mission with its centre in Bellur, near Calcutta. Mohandas Karamchand Gandhi (1869–1948), known as "Mahatma" (= "great soul") was an orthodox Hindu but was also influenced by European thought (e.g. liberalism, Tolstoy). He led the Indian struggle for independence from Britain under the banner of non-violence and emphasised the truth of all religions in the belief in one and the same God. He advocated a just social order and equal rights for women. After a spell in jail for participation in the fight for liberation, Sri Aurobindo Ghose (1872– 1950) had mystical experiences and developed his philosophy of "Integral Yoga." He set up an ashram at Pondicherry and published semi-religious, semi-philosophical works and interpretations of the Vedas and Uphanishads. His revival of Indian spirituality had a strong influence on people in Europe, who began to turn toward the inner life. Sarvepalli Radhakrishnan (1888–1975) was an important philosopher of Indian religion and culture, who was also the president of India between 1962 and 1967. He worked for a spiritual exchange between Hinduism and western ideas and in particular strove for political and religious reconciliation.

Mahatma Gandhi (1869–1948)

Mahatma Gandhi is one of modern Hinduism's most important thinkers. He propagated a deeply pious religious universalism and respect for the truth of all religions, and also undertook a strong politicization of Hindu religious thought. An early follower of the ascetic ideal, he also used religious fasting as a means of political pressure. From 1919 on he emerged as the most famous leader of the Indian independence movement and organized the strategic defiance toward the British colonial power, the "Non-Cooperation Movement," a mass movement with a policy of non-violence. In his writings he advocated an all-inclusive concept of peace and the ideal of a moderate way of life characterized by esteem for every living thing.

BUDDHISM

The term Buddhism comes from the Sanskrit word "buddh" (to awaken) and means the awakening out of the darkness of ignorance into the light of the teaching. Original Buddhism played down the figure of the Buddha Gautama, who did not move into center-stage until later, but emphasized instead the importance of gaining knowledge by virtue of one's own strength, independent of divine revelation. This came about principally through meditation on the "Four Noble Truths," which bring about inner serenity and extinguish belief in one's own individuality. Buddhism dissolves all persistent substances into non-fixed aggregates of existence and thus stresses the impermanence of all earthly things. Later teachings made great compromises to popular faith and magical healing practices, and in this way a belief in gods, Buddhas and helpful beings like Bodhisattvas, who help others to attain salvation, gained great significance.

Buddha with the Wheel of Teaching
Relief, Black Pagoda, 936/941, Fuzhou, China

The wheel is the symbol most frequently used in Buddhist imagery and iconography. It symbolizes the never-ending cycle of the flow of consciousness of each human being through the six realms of existence (rebirth, wheel of life) and the teachings of the historical Buddha Gautama. After Gautama, through meditation, had recognized the Eightfold Path that leads to deliverance from the cycle of life (Wheel of the Law) he set the "Wheel of Teaching" in motion by passing on his message. Depictions of the Buddha meditating in the lotus position refer to the buddha power nature, manifested in history in the person of Gautama.

THE ORIGINAL TEACHINGS

Human Knowledge and Eternal Truth

The human being, the individual, is thought of in Buddhism as a not-self (anatta), that is as something without a soul and without essence. The ego, therefore, is seen as a mere "accumulation" of elements of existence (dharmas). These dharmas determining the individual are categorized into five groups or factors (khandhas): a) body, senses, physical form (rupa); b) feeling (vedana); c) perceptions and ideas (samjna); d) driving forces (sankhara); e) consciousness (vijnana). These khandhas together constitute individuality.

Buddhism seeks to eliminate the false belief in individuality expressed typically in phrases such as "I am," "I have," "mine" (possession) or any talk of a "self." Buddhist teaching therefore breaks down the acts of perceiving or feeling, which in common parlance are assumed to have a soul or person as subject, into a series of impersonal processes. For example, "I perceive" would be replaced by: "a process of perception in the five groups is taking place."

Buddhism recognizes different ways and methods of de-individualisation, based ultimately on the insight that life means suffering and is painful, since it is subject to illness, ageing and death. Characteristics both of the individual and of the world are impermanence, suffering and non-selfhood. Neither humans, nor the world as we experience it, is a coherent whole, but are a combination of individual components that are constantly coming together, dis-

solving and coming together again. The individual therefore does not possess an immortal soul (self) that continues to exist unchanged when the body decays.

The individual and his worlds are subject to a constant process of becoming and dying. The individual constituents of this process (dharmas) are, however, subject to a strict set of laws, since there is a moral law of the world (also known as dharma) and all the individual constituents are merely different forms of expression of this one law of the world. That is why the individual aggregates are also called dharmas; there are many of these, and they are thought of as forces, even though they have a material nature. The process by which they combine and co-operate gives an appearance of coherence; for instance in humans the illusion of a "self" is created. The constant flow of these aggregates is not interrupted, even by death. They endure beyond the death of the specific "individual" and form new combinations to create the basis for the existence of a new "individual." In Buddhism (more clearly than in Hinduism) this process must be called rebirth, rather than the migration of souls, because Buddhism does not assume the existence of a soul in the classical sense.

Buddha explains this position in his teaching on "Dependent Origination" which, transposed to Western thought, is also known as "Conditioned Arising" or the "Formula of Causal Connection." In brief, it says that the aggregates are mutually dependent on and determine one another. The teaching names 12 links in the chain of aggregates (dharmas), in which links 1 and 2 are the dharmas which, in a past form of existence, constitute the prerequisite for a new "individual" to come into being in the present time (= past), links 3 to 10 explain the new "individual's" process of becoming (links 3 to 5) and the forces that are created in him (links 6 to 10 = present), while links 11 and 12 determine the aggregates of a future existence (= future).

The idea of the 12 conditioning links may be represented as follows:

Out of the precondition of ignorance (1) the driving forces (2) arise, out of the driving forces a consciousness (3) arises, out of consciousness a spiritual and physical individuality (4) arises, through this individuality the six senses (5) come into being, through the senses touch

(6), through touch feeling (7), through feeling "thirst" or craving (8), through craving the inclination toward life (9), through the inclination toward life karmic becoming (10), through karmic becoming rebirth (11), and through rebirth ageing, dying, worry, lamentation, suffering, sorrow and despair (12).

The 8th stage, "thirst" or craving, means the sensory desires, in particular the sex drive; the 9th link, the inclination towards life, means "grasping at" the realm of the senses, "like the flame grasps fuel."

Knowledge of these connections can prevent the karmic drives from repeatedly setting in motion new rebirths, and can thus usher in deliverance. Knowledge is essential, since in the Buddhist view the entire cycle of unhappiness begins with ignorance (link 1).

The Cycle of Rebirth

The death of a person who is ignorant and thus who has not attained salvation is inevitably followed by their rebirth. There is no fear of death in Buddhism, since final death means entrance to nirvana, but only a fear of being reborn. But this horror must also be encountered with calm. The Buddhist theory of rebirth is closely based on the Indian, or rather Hindu, theory of karma: a better rebirth can be brought about by good deeds, a worse one is risked by evil deeds.

However, in Buddhism (more strongly than in Hinduism), it is not so much the deeds that are decisive but the motives behind them or the spiritual attitude of the person doing the deeds. Whatever we do without desire, hatred or blindness will have a positive effect; acting without desiring success, without the desire to harm anyone and quite generally any action guided by reason, will promote salvation.

The driving force behind the rebirths is craving or thirst (the 8th dharma) that bind beings to existence through the ideas "mine" and "I." Thus the state of salvation, the extinguishing entrance into nirvana, is also seen as a state of absolute lack of craving and thirst. The unredeemed person, by contrast, is chained to the world through ignorance and lack of knowledge of the causality connected with suffering. Craving and ignorance rank alongside one another as causes of suffering and set in motion the formula of the 12 links (or stages) of causal or conditioned interconnection.

Buddhism as Psychology and Philosophy

The philosophy of Buddhism was described by Edward Conze as "dialectic pragmatism." Its objective is a theory of salvation which accounts for its psychological and practical stance. All speculations that do not directly serve the purpose of achieving salvation are considered in the original teaching to be futile and useless. In its advice, descriptions and attitudes, it represents a pragmatic philosophy of life which strives for inner independence, contentment and a rejection of worldly gain. It was not until later that silence was added as a particular value.

The "Four Noble (or Holy) Truths" are considered to be a means to reach salvation and a way of promoting contemplation and self-discipline. Buddhism likes to use dialectics, in other words, to demonstrate wisdom through a love of contradictions and paradoxes (similar to Chinese thinking) in order to show the limitations of thought and logic. The self (individual) is considered the main cause of all suffering, which is why liberation from suffering is linked to attaining the state of not-self (anatta).

The theory of the not-self is difficult to grasp, and even in sections of Buddhism is thought to be unfathomable. As the world and the self and their daily life are rejected as being impermanent, unsatisfactory and full of suffering, it is possible to speak of the radical pessimism of Buddhism. And yet there is no sense of pessimistic sorrow or misanthropy; what Buddhism calls for is a good-natured calmness in self-denial.

In Buddhism "Immortality," or rather the state of salvation, does not mean the continuation of individual existence. From the moment of birth, individual life is linked to death; it seems to be "designed" for death and is dominated by suffering since it constantly clings to the transitory in the misguided belief that it can possess it. Immortality in Buddhism, therefore, means the overcoming or elimination of individuality. Life is suffering, therefore the way to salvation in Buddhism is concerned mainly with self-denial and the casting off of worldly ties.

Buddhist Cosmology and the Deities

Buddhism inherited Hindu cosmology, which it largely adopted. Time is seen as cosmic time,

Golden Buddha
Shwedagon Stupa, 15th century or later, Rangoon, Burma

The link to the historical Buddha Gautama and the school of the "Small Vehicle" has been preserved in a marked form in southeast Asian Buddhism, and has led to a rich tradition of legends. Buddha Gautama appears here as the completion and redeemer of a mythical, chaotic era, not simply as the historical manifestation of the Buddha power. The veneration of relics, said to be connected with Buddha Gautama, is therefore given particular significance. The value placed on them has led to impressive magnificence in the design of the relic shrines (stupas), their interiors and their figurative sculptures and ornamentation.

Head of the Great Buddha
713-803, Leshan, China

Unnaturally large ear lobes as a sign of extensive knowledge, along with half-closed eyes and slightly parted lips, are the physiognomical characteristics of all depictions of the Buddha. They symbolise the unity of knowledge of the visible and invisible, the revealed teaching, and silent, meditative contemplation through extinction of the self, of earthliness and nirvana. The distinctiveness of each of the countless manifestations of the Buddha nature and their iconography can be recognized primarily through hand gestures (mudras) and assigned attributes. The Buddha statue at Leshan, which at 71 metres high is the largest to be carved out of a cliff wall, is an exception in the canon of Buddha figures. Most of them depict him either in a seated meditation posture or standing, whereas here he is sitting up straight with his hands on his knees. The head alone of this colossal statue measures 15 metres.

calculated not in years but in eons (calpas) – a calpa being the period between the birth and death of a world system and usually said to be several million human years. Each world system goes through a certain development, from its creation to its final incineration. There are countless world systems and therefore countless, even parallel, worlds, with our own being neither unique nor special. The series of worlds ending and beginning is infinite and each world system is constructed in layers that range from regions of coarse matter to fine matter with the "region of no form" (no physical form) above them. Each world consists of an endless host of aggregates of existence (dharmas), some of which are unconditional and indestructible (such as nirvana and empty space), while the others are all reciprocally dependent and therefore impermanent and inconstant.

Later, or organized, Buddhism does assume the existence of heavens and hells, and divides each world system into realms of life which are further divided into 3 upper and 3 lower regions. The 3 upper realms constitute first and foremost the region of the gods (devas), who stand above humankind and are materially refined. They are thought to live longer, but are equally subject to suffering and mortality. The second region is that of the asuras, also heavenly beings, but envisaged as angry spirits who do battle with the gods. The third region is the human world.

These 3 upper worlds are separated from the 3 "dark fates" or "miserable states." They are divided into the world of the spirits (preta), which originally meant the spirits of the dead but which today also includes all manner of demons; then the world of animals; and finally the lowest region of hells of which there are many, divided into hot and cold hells.

Suffering is the fate of all life and all regions. There is a certain "state of holy privilege" for mankind since for Buddhism being reborn as a human being is necessary for the attainment of knowledge and insight into dharma (law of the world). Man alone, when he has gained true knowledge, reaches a point at which he no longer has to be reborn into the states of the world in which suffering is inherent. Due to its lack of statements about the gods, original Buddhism has often been said to be an atheistic doctrine. It has never disputed the existence of a personal God, but has simply never accor-

ded this question any significance, and views speculation about the nature and characteristics of the gods as a waste of time. At the same time it claimed that Nirvana is eternal and named it bliss, truth or the highest reality. Later, when Buddha had become increasingly transfigured, he began to be seen as the embodiment of nirvana and himself became the object of religious veneration.

The Four Noble or Holy Truths

The Four Noble Truths of Buddhism consist of the answers to four decisive questions: 1) What is suffering? 2) What is the origin of suffering? 3) How can suffering be eliminated? 4) What is the path to eliminate suffering?

Birth, ageing, illness and death, but also separation from a loved one and the futility of striving are all seen as suffering (dukkha). The thirst that leads from rebirth to rebirth and which is accompanied by joy and passion is thought to be responsible for the origination of suffering; it is the craving of pleasure, the attachment to the very ideas of existence or non-existence. The elimination of suffering consists in suppressing or, better yet, eliminating this thirst or craving. The way of eliminating it is embodied in the "Eightfold Path" – the way to salvation.

In order to understand life as suffering it is necessary to see the five khandhas of man as five ways of clinging to earthly things and avoid relinquishing the suffering aspect of life. Anyone who clings to their body and to the "self" with their consciousness and feelings will of necessity fall prey to suffering. Suffering is universal.

The Eightfold Path to overcoming thirst or craving (desire) consists of the following factors: right view or understanding, right directed thought or intention, right speech, right action, right livelihood, right effort, right mindfulness, and right concentration. The Path is divided into three sections that are understood as wisdom (factors 1 and 2), discipline or moral virtue (factors 3 to 5) and concentration or meditative cultivation of the heart/mind (factors 6 to 8).

The individual factors are explained in more detail in various writings. Right concentration (factor 8), for example, is divided into five meditation techniques: guarding of the gateways to the senses, mindfulness in all actions, contemplation or trance, analytical techniques (introspective and extrospective) and synthetic technique.

The Synthetic Technique is also known as "The Four Sublime States," or "Four Divine Dwelling Places." These are friendliness, compassion, sympathy and equanimity. The mind loses its boundaries when through meditation it has generated the four sublime states consecutively. Added to that is an ethical catalogue to be adopted by the person meditating. The goal of salvation, nirvana, is understood not as nothingness but is described as something positive, particularly as the absence of the elements of suffering that characterize life. Nirvana means the elimination or rather the dissolution of the individual person.

THE LIFE OF THE BUDDHA

About the concept of Buddha

The Buddha can be seen in three different ways: as a human being, as a spiritual principle and as a being somewhere between the two.

The historical Gautama Buddha was of little interest to original Buddhism. The Buddha is an enlightened one, an archetype of the wise teacher who manifests at different times in different individuals. Seen as a spiritual principle, a Buddha nature, namely the dharma body (tathagata), was hidden in the "individual" Gautama. The historical Buddha is thus no isolated or historically unique teacher, but one of an endless series of tathagatas who preach the same teaching in all ages on the earth.

Finally, the Buddha can be observed in his "transformed body," also called the "unfalsified body" or "body of the true nature." This transformed body was practically hidden by the mortal human body of the historical Buddha, but can be recognized by the 32 distinguishing characteristics of the "super-human" which are a favourite motif in Buddhist art.

The Historical Buddha

The historical Buddha was actually called Siddharta, but was known as Gautama (after a Vedic teacher from whom his family was descended) or Shakyamuni (= sage from the clan of the Shakyas). He came from a noble North Indian family and is often referred to as a prince, although his father, Suddhodana, as a Raja, was more like the "doge" of an aristocratic republic. His dates are disputed, but are generally given as 560-480 B.C.

The Buddha legends reveal a great deal about Gautama's previous existences, but they also mention that his mother, Mahamaya, dreamt at the time he was conceived that she was transported to the Himalayas where a being in the form of a white elephant entered her right side. This event was taken to indicate an important birth. She died seven days after Gautama's birth.

Numerous miracles from his childhood are recounted. He was raised by Mahapajapati, his mother's sister, who was also one of his father's wives. He married young and his wife Yasodhara bore him a son, Rahula, when he was 29.

At the age of 29, Gautama underwent a radical change in his nature. The legend says that in pondering the states that are free of the suffering of illness, old age and death he met on four consecutive outings an old man, a sick man, a corpse (funeral procession) and finally an ascetic. In this process the ideas about impermanence and overcoming the world came to him. This account, however, denies the strong influence of Hinduism on his thinking.

After the fourth outing, Gautama was given the news of the birth of his son but decided in the same night to go away, and wandered around in what is today the province of Bihar. He joined with different masters (gurus) but found them all unsatisfactory. He then led the life of an ascetic, through fasting and castigation, until he was completely weakened and realized that this was not the right path.

Finally, he sat beneath a pipal or bo-tree (Ficus religiosa) and meditated (in four stages),

Buddha's Death Amidst his Pupils

The depiction of Buddha Gautama passing away is one of the most impressive motifs in Buddhist art. Paintings tend to emphasize the narrative aspects of this historical and legendary character, relating the different reactions of the disciples and the gracious and demonic spirits of all the different worlds. Sculptures generally portray the uniqueness represented by Gautama's death, namely the historical manifestation of this act of extinguishing consciousness and feeling, and the entry into complete nirvana. The coming together of the world that can be experienced and that which cannot be experienced in the depiction of the "sleeping Buddha" gives the motif of Gautama's death a special character, contrasting with the many and varied representations of Buddha's power.

remaining nearby for three or four weeks. Here he achieved enlightenment (bodhi), becoming a Tathagata (one who has attained truth). He wrestled with himself about whether he should keep his wisdom to himself or announce it to other people. Finally, he made five ascetics his first disciples and thus set in motion the "Wheel of Teaching" (or dharma-wheel).

He chose the Middle Way of renunciation of the world without extreme asceticism, understood life as being inextricably connected with suffering, and dedicated his teaching to overcoming suffering. The small community travelled around as itinerant monks, and with the Five Moral Precepts Gautama established the first Rules of the Order which varied in strictness depending on whether they were applied to monks or lay people.

Buddha's followers increased rapidly and came from different classes, and Gautama was promoted by different local rulers whom he also counselled. He paid no attention to the Hindu caste system in choosing his followers, although he did not strive to fundamentally overthrow it. Gautama led the community through the persuasive power of his harmonious personality, and placed high intellectual demands on his monks, who were not allowed any possessions other than their personal utensils. His family also adhered to his teaching.

At the age of 80, after a brief illness, Gautama took his leave of everyone and passed peacefully into nirvana. His body was cremated and the ashes divided among different groups of followers, forming the basis of the later cult of relics in Buddhism.

Gautama the Buddha was a thoroughly aristocratic personage, but was open and compassionate. He was completely familiar with the philosophical speculation of his time and understood the Hindu systems. He outlined an extensive, diverse and sophisticated world view and strove to achieve harmony between his teaching and his life, a high level of morality and the attainment of a peaceable and kind attitude toward life. He possessed a spiritual equanimity that resisted many temptations and his supernatural serenity formed the basis for the later transfiguration of his being.

The Buddhist Scriptures

Gautama left nothing in writing and his teachings were originally deliberately handed down in oral form only. Any attempt to separate the original teachings from later additions is therefore fraught with difficulties. The continual development of his teachings in the early days is therefore also a part of Buddhism, which in this sense has no fundamental canon of dogma.

The earliest teachings were probably the Four Noble or Holy Truths, the Eightfold Path, the teachings on Dependent Origination and on the non-existence of a constant self, and the statements about nirvana as the ultimate goal. The first records dealing with Buddhism date from around 200 years after Gautama's death, in the time of the Emperor Ashoka (272-232 B.C.).

Early on, the writings were divided into "dharma" = teaching, and "vinaya" = monastic disciplines. The most important texts are the "sutras," or discourses, alleged to originate with Gautama himself. The later sutras are treated differently by the different schools of Buddhism. Hinayana (small vehicle) Buddhism sees them as poetry and disputes their authenticity; Mahayana (great vehicle) Buddhism assumes that certain of Gautama's texts were not meant for his contemporaries and were kept in the underworld, to be retrieved later by other great teachers.

A further part of the canon are the "shastras," texts by authoritative authors whose names are not known (in other words a kind of "church teachers"). In many cases only fragments of the texts have been preserved and it is difficult to date them with any certainty. Many texts were also subsequently ascribed to famous

Buddhist teachers. All the writings considered authentic are divided into 3 great collections or canons: 1) the Pali Tripitaka; 2) the Chinese Tripitaka and 3) the Tibetan Kanjur and Tanjur. The division refers roughly to the region in which the collection originated and the language of origin. Some writings in Indian Sanskrit also exist but they do not form a separate canon.

THE TEACHINGS OF EARLY MONASTIC BUDDHISM

Monastic Buddhism (Sangha)

The most important distinction in the Buddhist community is between monks and lay people. The monks form the core of the Buddhist movement and live either in society or as hermits. The community of monks and hermits is called "sangha." Its strength has varied throughout the course of the history of Buddhism and from one region to another. For example, the number of monks and nuns in China grew from 77,258 in 450 A.D. to 2 million in 525 A.D. In Tibet there have been times when every third male inhabitant lived in a Buddhist monastery.

The monks see themselves as the "true Buddhists." Their original teaching, the Hinayana, prescribes through the monastic rules a strict self-monitoring, purity laws and a warning against the life of the senses and its temptations. The monastic rules are called "vinaya" (from "vi-nayati = leading away, i.e. from suffering to discipline). The rules were codified early on, and before they were recorded in writing, used to be recited at the assemblies.

The vinaya has three ideals: poverty, celibacy and peaceableness. The monk has no possessions apart from his begging bowl, sewing needle, prayer beads, razor and drinking water filter. The monks were originally itinerant, committed to the ideal of being without house or home, but this was later relaxed, and monasteries were built. As possession of money was also prohibited, food was meant to be procured by begging alone. In doing so the rule was that the monks should beg from rich and poor alike, favouring no one. Hinayana saw begging as a school of self-discipline, while Mahayana later emphasized altruism, love and compassion. Today only certain sections of the

Zen Buddhist monastic community of Japan beg, although not for themselves but for charitable causes.

The rules of celibacy established how the monks were to treat women. Both desire and sex as a way of relaxation had to be suppressed since the only path to inner peace open to the monk was to practice the techniques of meditation. Later, however, there were some married monks.

In its ideal of peaceableness, Buddhism has much in common with Jainism which originated in India at the same time. In this respect Jains and Buddhists follow two basic principles: 1) the belief in the interrelatedness of all living things and the teaching that each living thing could be a reincarnation of a human being (a radicalisation of Hindu beliefs); and 2) the deduction from the saying of Buddha "Everything I encounter is myself" that one should not harm anyone else because each person wants to preserve himself, in other words compassion for all other living things "as if they were me." Both teachings had a strong humanising influence in Asia. Due to its peaceableness, Buddhism was politically encouraged and thought of benevolently, particularly in its early days, and yet the history of Buddhism has also seen involvement in worldly and political power right up to the present day.

The Main Currents and Schools in Early Buddhism

After Gautama's death, three councils tried to set down the master's teachings. There were

Veneration of Bodhisattva Guanyin
on Mount Putuo Shan, consecrated to the Bodhisattva, near Ningpo, China

The monastic Buddhist community does not have regular services. Communal recitation of sutras (several times a day) and the worship of statues characterize the temple activities of the monasteries. In contrast to popular devotional practice, figurative depictions of the Buddhas, the world eras, Bodhisattvas, Medicine Buddhas, Sin-forgiving Buddhas, and others are not meant to represent transcendent divine beings, but are symbols of spiritual and cosmic forces and principles and are seen as aids to meditation, helping to direct concentration to the object of the contemplation. However, in popular devotion in its different national and cultural forms, numerous emanations of the Buddha power have arisen and a Buddhist pantheon has been created which has influenced the monastic community's rituals. An example of this is the transformation of the Bodhisattva Avalokiteshvara into the gracious and helpful goddess Guanyin in China between the 6th and 10th century. She is still the most popular deity in popular Chinese Buddhism.

early splits between the followers of the Theravada tradition (sanskrit: sthaviravadin), the followers of the "Doctrine of the Elders," who essentially formulated the stricter Hinayana Buddhism, and the Mahasanghikas, the followers of the "Great Assembly," who had a far more liberal attitude and prepared the way for the later Mahayana Buddhism.

To the "Ancient Doctrine of Wisdom" of Hinayana was added the "New Doctrine of Wisdom" of Mahayana with its belief in Buddhas and Bodhisattvas as higher beings and the schools of yoga (Yogacarins). Then in 500 A.D., Vajrayana or "Diamond Vehicle," a specific form of magic Buddhism influenced by the Hindu Tantric school, became particularly widespread in Nepal, Tibet, China, Java and Sumatra. In Tibet, Buddhism in the form of Lamaism entered a special relationship with the old shamanist Bon religion. The lines of the Theravada and Mahayana followers splintered in the course of time into a number of sub-schools. The schools of Buddhism are considered to have been fully formed from the 11th century A.D. onwards (after 1500 years of Buddhism).

The Position and Influence of Lay People

The monks and ascetics always had to rely on the goodwill of the Buddhist lay people. Furthermore, the Buddhist ethos is fundamentally concerned with the spiritual well-being of all people. It is therefore necessary to share the teaching (dharma) with others, and (unlike in Hinduism) to undertake missionary work. Buddhism also had to cover the need for

mythology and faith and did this through its theory of "acquiring merit." It was said that by leading a good life merits could be acquired for a richer existence in a better rebirth, culminating in future enlightenment. The yearning of the faithful for another world was also absorbed by the worship of the Buddha and of relics in so-called "caityas" or shrines. The central focus of this veneration is the Holy Place in Bodhgaya, the bo-tree under which Gautama gained enlightenment.

In this way a rich cult of sacrifice grew up, as well as veneration of holy images of patron saints and a well-developed symbolism centered around the tree, the wheel as a symbol of dharma, and the throne and the stupa (stylized burial mound for holy relics; often pagoda-like). Emperor Ashoka's (272–232 B.C.) patronage of Buddhism had great influence on the relationship between monks and lay people. As a reformer he introduced far-reaching changes and persuaded the monks to popularize their teachings.

Originally, the monks had been in favour of the lay people having little influence, and of a strict separation of the two classes. The monks laid down five precepts and 3 "treasures" or "jewels," so-called refuge phrases which, if repeated three times by the lay person (upasaka), would grant admission to the Buddhist community. The threefold formula is: "I go the Buddha for refuge; I go to the teachings (dharma) for refuge; I go to the holy order (sangha) for refuge." The five precepts also applied to the lay person: (1) do not kill, (2) do not steal, (3) do not commit adultery, (4) do not lie and (5) do not take intoxicating drink.

Under the direction of Ashoka, the orders moderated their strict rules, thus making Buddhism more universal, which was the emperor's intention. Worship and veneration of the Buddha was simplified by his depiction in human form, and promoted the growth of popular literature recounting the Buddha legends. The teachings on karma and rebirth, with which the faithful were familiar from Hinduism, were emphasized. Overall, the increased influence of the lay people prepared the way for Mahayana Buddhism.

Buddhism and Worldly Power

Emperor Ashoka was the first person to make Buddhism into a world religion. He sent mis-

The Hanging Monastery
7th/8th century, Hengshan, southern Datong, China

Remoteness from the world as a prerequisite for undisturbed meditation and the ascetic ideal of the Buddhist monastic orders have led to remote mountain tops, islands, wilderness and other places that are difficult to reach being chosen as sites for hermitages or monasteries. They have frequently become lively places of pilgrimages, and with time developed into major temple complexes. The hanging monastery in Hengshan is one of the most impressive examples of how a hermitage hewn into a steep cliff has become a monastery temple with a total of 40 buildings. As the monastery is also a hostel for pilgrims of all kinds, it also contains other places of remembrance for Lao-tzu and Confucius.

sionaries into neighbouring countries, had the texts made more precise, and ensured that the "good teaching" was spread through the whole of India and Sri Lanka. He issued edicts on leading a moral life, and prohibited disputes among the monks. It was also important for the development of Mahayana Buddhism that the Ashoka edicts rejected the excessive value placed on external rules and rituals in Hinayana Buddhism and called instead for virtuous actions and useful deeds. Emperor Ashoka is considered by all schools to be the epitome of a just Buddhist ruler.

From then on, particularly in North India and Bengal, Buddhism came under the protection of the ruler, since it called for peacableness, good humour and conciliation. Many rulers gave themselves Buddhist titles of honour and in some countries under the influence of Buddhism, such as Indochina, Java and Tibet, theocracies grew up. This was facilitated by the fact that Buddhism has no notion of hostility to science or culture, does not emphasize caste barriers or class taboos, and is compatible both with the thinking of modern industrial countries and with high technological achievements and the increased mobility of modern men and women.

HINAYANA: THE ANCIENT SCHOOL OF WISDOM

The Ideal of the Arhat

Buddha's passing into nirvana in the year 480 B.C. confronted his followers with a difficult situation, since the tradition had been handed down only orally. At the first council, 500 monks gathered and immediately split up into different sects and schools. In Buddhism, as in early Christianity, the teaching was not codified by the founder himself but by his early disciples and followers.

The monk Sariputra drew up the methodical system of contemplation according to the rules of abhidharma, and developed the doctrine of the Ancient School of Wisdom. His interpretations influenced the Buddhism of the first 15 to 20 generations. The Hinayana or "lesser vehicle" is the canon of rules of the Ancient School of Wisdom. This canon is divided into three compendia, each of which is called a "basket" (pitaka) after the places in which they were kept. The three compendia are the vinaya-

Schwedagon Stupa
15th century or later, Rangoon, Burma

The Schwedagon Stupa, the golden hallmark of Buddhism in Burma, is both a religious and a national monument. Its splendour is due to donations by enthusiastic Buddhists and the self-glorification wishes of Buddhist rulers who linked Buddha's fame to their own. Stone stupas (pagodas) were built as memorials and mausoleums for important Buddhist teachers. Particularly elaborate ones, like the Schwedagon Stupa, were built over the relics of Buddha Gautama, in which eight hairs from his head have been preserved. The more sacred a relic is considered, the stronger the positive influence on the individual's future fate.

pitaka (monastic discipline; the rules of the order), the sutta-pitaka (discourses; the sermons of the master and his monks, in five texts) and the abhidharma-pitaka (the seven texts comprising the "basket of further teachings").

Arhat means a holy or wise person of the highest level, and represents the ideal of completion in Hinayana Buddhism. The word means "destroyer of enemies," referring to worldly pleasures and passions and the belief in an ego or a self. The arhat sees in human beings a conglomeration of the five khandhas or aggregates, and has renounced his ties to the "threefold world" – the world of sensory desires, the world of form and the world without form. He has achieved a kind of "super-insight" and is entirely focused on the supernatural world of unchanging reality (nirvana), which he approaches in meditation.

This meditation happens in three stages: moral discipline; lucid trance; wisdom. By moral discipline, Hinayana means a disciplined attitude to one's own body, refraining from sensory pleasures and craving, and liberation from the illusion of individuality. Various exercises show the human body as being repulsive and inadequate. "Monitoring the sensory organs" trains concentration of awareness, while "monitoring the gateways to the senses" is tantamount to a conscious interruption of the stimulus-response chain. The idea is to keep the stimuli in check and to see the mind as being purely for itself without external affections, so that our desires do not cling so much to worldly things.

Three kinds of concentration exercise come under the category of "lucid trance": 1) the four jhanas, 2) the four states of the formless realm

Bodhisattva Avalokiteshvara
Gilded bronze, 18th century, temple monastery of Tanzhesi, near Beijing, China

Bodhisattvas are those who reach complete Buddhahood but decide not to enter nirvana in order to help people who are caught in the cycle of rebirths. With this concept, the Mahayana school made a significant contribution to transforming Buddhism from a school of monastic teaching into a popular religion. Avalokiteshvara, the Bodhisattva of boundless mercy, has always enjoyed particular popularity amongst his followers. His eleven faces and thousand arms symbolize the omnipresent power of the Buddha to recognize the suffering of those in need of help and to offer aid and comfort.

and 3) the occult powers. The jhanas are the stages of interrupting our responses to external sensory stimuli. At first the concentration is focused on a particular object and all personal inclinations towards it are suppressed (1st stage). From paying attention to the external object, the meditator progresses into the areas of belief and non-discursive thought, through which he experiences inner peace and delight (2nd stage). There is a progressive development of deeper calm and "one-pointedness" (3rd stage) and then the loss of any feeling for the comfort or discomfort of his own person (4th stage).

Above these stages are the four states of the formless realm, in which all object relationship is overcome, and unbounded space or rather emptiness (nirvana) becomes "visible." The person meditating finally reaches a state beyond perception and non-perception in which all consciousness is extinguished and he or she experiences the union of nothingness with nothingness or of the One with the One. This state is also called the "divine abyss" or the "desert of the godhead." It is a path of progressive extinguishing of the self.

The four formless states (apramana) are methods of controlling the feelings: a) loving-kindness b) compassion, c) empathetic joy and d) equanimity. For these exercises it is important to eliminate the boundaries between one's own self and the self of the other, without paying attention to one's own likes and dislikes. Kindness promotes the concern for the well-being of all living things and liberation from any malice towards others; compassion means concentration on the suffering of other living

creatures and the will to alleviate it; when this has been achieved, a cheerful sharing in the joy of others can take place; when equanimity has been reached this attitude becomes universal and boundless.

From the fourth jhana, progression to the "higher knowledges" may be developed. These include psychic powers and clairvoyance, culminating in the conscious attainment of nirvana. However, in the strictly rationalist school of early Buddhism the occult powers play only a very subordinate role; yet an enhanced spiritual life has always made parapsychological powers more acute.

Wisdom

Wisdom is considered the highest virtue in Buddhism and means methodical contemplation of the dharma (law). It is above all laid down in the 7 texts of the abhidharma. As the abhidharma is systematically concerned with overcoming individuality it may be regarded as the oldest formulated system of psychology.

The abhidharma undertakes the systematic transformation of personal expressions into impersonal ones according to the dharma (law). To illustrate, consider the personally worded sentence: "I have toothache." Division into the five khandhas would render this as: 1) this is a form (the tooth as matter); 2) this is a painful feeling; 3) this is the perception of the tooth by the face, by touch and pain; 4) this is a reaction of the will: dislike of pain, fear of the consequences for future well-being, craving for well-being; 5) this is consciousness – consciousness of the points realized under 1 to 4. Contrary to normal, everyday understanding, the abhidharma breaks down reality into 79 to 174 basic processes which serve to transform the usual, cohesive view into a play of impersonal forces. And yet this way of looking at things is by no means purely theoretical, but serves solely the "therapeutic" purpose of dealing with the burdens and suffering of the world. The possessive thinking of individualism alienates us from our true self and causes suffering through identification with conditioned and changing things. Meditation serves to extinguish the self and thus to dissociate with everything that is conditioned.

In these definitions, some contradictions about the "Absolute," nirvana in Buddhism remain unresolved. For example, the Absolute has by definition no relationship to the "other;" yet the very idea of deliverance from the fetters of the changing world into the Absolute assumes attachment to the conditioned as one in need of deliverance. Furthermore, no statement can be made about the Absolute, because all statements are conditioned and at best have only temporary validity; so nothing positive can be said about the Absolute with respect to its being in the world (immanent) or outside of the world (transcendental). Nevertheless, the Absolute (nirvana) is defined by contrast to the world, as not being the world. The world is considered to be impermanent, decaying and causing suffering; the Absolute by contrast is unconditioned, unchanging and is even called "undisturbed, blissful peace." Buddhism has always been aware of these difficulties and therefore often uses paradoxes to describe these kinds of teachings.

MAHAYANA: THE NEW SCHOOL OF WISDOM

Mahayana: the "Great Vehicle"

The time of Emperor Ashoka saw the first significant split in the Buddhist monastic order into the conservative Sthaviravadins and the more "democratic" Mahasanghikas. The latter accorded greater influence to lay people and prepared the ground for Mahayana Buddhism, which expanded Buddhism beyond the exclusive community of monks. It was not until the decline of Buddhism in India around 800 A.D. that the number of followers of the Mahayana movement exceeded the Hinayana followers, and Mahayana Buddhism was developed particularly in different schools in China, Japan and Tibet; whilst Sri Lanka, Burma, Cambodia and Thailand remained the strongholds of Hinayana. Generally speaking, Mahayana Buddhism teaches the existence of an Absolute and projects the characteristics of the Absolute onto the figure of the Buddha. In contrast to Hinayana which seeks to overcome the world, Mahayana wants to help the world attain salvation and therefore believes it possible to transfer karmic merits from one person to another, thus creating a completely new ethic of compassion.

Between 100 B.C. and 200 A.D., Mahayana produced a great wealth of sutras, particularly the "Lotus of the Good Law" and the comprehensive "Perfection of Wisdom" (Sanskrit: prajnaparamita, literally "wisdom passed over to the other side," in other words transcendental wisdom). The philosophically sophisticated writings of the prajnaparamita came from Dekkan (southeast India) around 150 A.D. and were for the most part formulated by the monks Nagarjuna and Aryadeva.

Nagarjuna was one of the most important dialecticians of all time, and claimed that all affirmative statements, particularly about the Absolute, were untenable, which is why he worked with logic and paradox. He made "essentialness" the criterion for distinguishing between the authentic and inauthentic, and drew up the theory of emptiness as the basis for the changing world and impermanence. Recognising these truths can break the cycle of rebirths and makes it possible to die into the Absolute in an "attitude of emptiness."

Under the direction of Nagarjuna, Mahayana Buddhism, influenced by Hindu thought patterns, broke with the strict dualism of the Hinayana, which interpreted the relationship between nirvana and the changing world as unbridgable opposites. Nagarjuna taught a monist theory, according to which everything changeable is merely appearance, and in truth only "the void" (shunya) as a kind of "relative nothingness" (similar to nirvana) or universal spirit exists, in which every difference between being and non-being and between the One and the Many is eliminated. Thus ultimately the difference between nirvana and the changing world exists only in the region of the illusory, in other words in the changing world, but not in truth. The activist and altruistic ethos of

Buddha Maitreya
5th century, Yungang caves near Datong, China

Maitreya is one of the more complex figures in the Buddhist pantheon. On the one hand, he is depicted and worshipped as the redeeming Buddha of the Future and, on the other hand, he is still active in the present epoch as a helpful Bodhisattva, who has renounced the opportunity of Buddhahood to enable people to trust in the future. The bent left arm of Buddha Maitreya with his palm facing outwards is in the abhaya gesture ("do not fear"). His right arm is dropped and outstretched with the palm facing downwards in the gesture of giving (vara mudra). The design of the central figure and of the pagoda-like pillars indicates the Indian-Afghan origin of early Buddhist art in China.

Mile Fo (Budai)

Stone, Tang dynasty, 618-907, provincial museum of Taiyuan, China

The adaptation of Indian Buddhist ideas to the cultural world of Eastern Asia led in China to radical changes to the "pure teaching," particularly in the area of popular devotional practice. This also applies to Maitreya (Chinese: Mile Fo), the future savior, whose Bodhisattva nature the Chinese see embodied in the kindly, laughing monk Budai who wanders the earth with his begging sack and prayer beads in order to offer help to the faithful. He tends to be found in the foyer of every temple, and he brings harmony, love, joy and well-being to the believers. The way Gautama's abstract teaching has become symbolically depicted in the Chinese environment is strikingly evident in Budai's huge belly, the centre of life being thought to lie behind his navel.

Mahayana emphasizes that it is not only the individual wise or holy person which is predestined for salvation but virtually all beings, which is why it is important to be concerned with the salvation of all.

The Bodhisattva Ideal in Mahayana

One of Mahayana's central concepts, apart from the void or emptiness, is the ideal of the Bodhisattva. If the Buddha is the enlightened one, then the Bodhisattva is a being of enlightenment, a developing Buddha. The Bodhisattva remains in the world solely for the benefit of other living creatures, in order to rescue others from the currents of suffering. Because he has long since overcome his own self, the Bodhisattva has compassion and empathy for all other living things and wants to do good for them. For Mahayana it is not just a question of assimilating into nirvana, but of putting his own "self" into nirvana in such a way that it will lead all living creatures to salvation. Tibetan Buddhism therefore translates Bodhisattva as "heroic being," and compares the Hinayana arhat to a person who gets lost with his family in the jungle and rescues only himself; by contrast, the hero (Bodhisattva) uses his strength to lead his family out of the jungle and into safety.

The Bodhisattva is universally compassionate because, although he renounces the world, he does not renounce the creatures who live in it. The Bodhisattva ideal owes a great deal to the practice of the "four states of the formless realm" which taught the monks to make no difference between themselves and others, and to learn compassion and empathetic joy in loving kindness and equanimity.

Mahayana distinguished between a number of different Bodhisattvas and Buddhas who in devotional practice are venerated as angels or helpers in times of need. The Bodhisattva Maitreya, the Buddha of the Future, enjoys particular popularity, as does Avalokiteshvara, who takes the boundless suffering of all living creatures upon himself and is called upon in times of distress: he is the personification of boundless compassion. Of all the Bodhisattvas, Vairocana, the "sun-like one," who is considered in parts of East Asia to be the Supreme Being, is particularly venerated, as is the "Original Buddha" (Ahi-Buddha), who has been enlightened for eternities and has created all other Buddhas through meditation so that they can act as protectors of all living creatures.

The Void

Developed by Nagarjuna, the Mahayana doctrine assumes that the Bodhisattva arrives at the insight that all things are empty, whereby "empty" is a synonym for "not-self." First and foremost, the doctrine says that all conditioned things, all things in the world, are "empty" and therefore not desirable. Nagarjuna often describes this emptiness as the mid-point between extremes and calls it the identity of yes and no as the mid-point between affirmation and negation, between being and non-being, between eternity and annihilation. Essencelessness and emptiness must exist in order for the changing world to come into being, and at the same time the correctly insightful approach to the void (the "emptiness attitude") permits one's own dissolution into nirvana or into the "suchness." The void is thus that which all opposites and contradictions have in common, and in this way it leads to the ultimate reality of the Absolute.

Of all the synonyms that Mahayana uses for the void, "non-dualism" is particularly important: all dualisms in the world are dissolved in the void or the suchness, such as the dualism between subject and object, between being and non-being, and particularly between the world and nirvana. The fact that this void is also described as "suchness" implies above all that the person who recognises this will leave things as they are and not force his own interpretations onto them. This, too, is an important step on the way to extinguishing the self.

Salvation in the New Doctrine on Wisdom

Salvation in Mahayana is characterized by three negatively defined and one positively defined attribute. The three negative ones are not-striving, not-affirming and not-leaning-on; the positive one is all-knowing. Not-striving means that, owing to his voluntary compassion with all living beings, the Bodhisattva will (for the time being at least) not reach salvation. But since the void has no definable characteristics we can never know when or where we will reach nirvana.

A great danger lies in thoughtless speech. Since every statement is a differentiation and represents an affirmation, not affirming is seen as characteristic of true salvation. Each affirmation delimits itself at least from its opposite, and therefore fosters dualism; furthermore a completely separate reality can never be in harmony with nirvana or the void, as the void is defined as eliminating the difference between yes and no, the affirmed and its opposite. The not-leaning-on means turning away from our reliance on the conditioned and impermanent things of this world which are the cause of fear. The positively defined attribute of all-knowing needs some explanation. For Mahayana, the historical Buddha was all-knowing in the full sense of the word, i.e. through his absolute thoughts he, as the enlightened one, had

unlimited knowledge of everything – not as a human being, not as the historical Gautama, but in his transformed body, in his "dharma body," which is the spiritual principle. The philosophical thinking behind that is as follows: if Buddha had not been all-knowing when he entered into the Absolute, then ignorance of things would restrict the realm of his knowledge, and if his knowledge were restricted he would not be identical with the Absolute as the All-Comprehensive.

Furthermore, all-knowing means extinguishing the self, and the dissolution of all ties to the self. Due to the fact that as an ego it constantly has to delimit itself from the not-ego, the worldly self (ego) can never reach all-knowingness. Only when "I" am no longer "I" is all-knowing possible. However, all-knowingness does not mean knowledge of the sum of all things but their totality which both includes and excludes every individual thing (individual knowledge).

FURTHER DEVELOPMENTS OF BUDDHISM

Bhakti: The Buddhism of Faith and Devotion

While in Hinayana Buddhism faith plays a completely subordinate role, Nagarjuna distinguished between the easy path of faith and the arduous path of wisdom. In the "bhakti" movement (which can be translated as faith or devotion), people began to worship deities as well as Buddhas and Bodhisattvas, which they ima-

The God of the North and of Wealth
Thanka (hanging scroll), 18th century, Yonghegong, Beijing

Buddha has 5453 names, and a particular iconography has developed for each one. They took a special form in Tibetan Buddhism and have been carefully handed down to preserve tradition.
One of the cosmic forces that has become personified is Mahasavama Vaishravana, the power of the north. He is depicted as an active force with the head decoration of a Bodhisattva, riding on a roaring snow lion, in his right hand the round banner as a symbol for the victory procession of Buddhism, in his left hand Mungo spitting jewels, which was what gave him the name "god of wealth." Sun and moon, two small circles in his halo, characterize him as the ruling deity among the guardians of the cardinal points and the deities who distribute wealth.

Jataka of King Sivi
Fresco, wall painting; Northern Wei dynasty, 5th century, Magao caves near Dunhuang, China

Jatakas are stories about the meritorious deeds of Buddha Gautama in one of his former existences, before he was born as Gautama into the House of King Suddhodana. The large number of jatakas that have been handed down over the years illustrate the Buddhist commandments and underpin the idea that collecting selfless deeds is enough to ensure liberation from the cycle of rebirths and retribution. The fresco shows how Buddha in the figure of King Sivi rescues a dove from the claws of a falcon. In return for the release of the dove, he cuts a piece of flesh from his body. Ultimately, however, he has to sacrifice himself completely in order to liberate the dove.

gined in human form. The paradises of the "Pure Lands" (Buddha lands) were also imagined in sense-based terms.

The bhakti movement brought three new strands of thought into Buddhism: 1) the theory of the transfer of (karmic) merit to others; 2) the conviction that the Buddha nature is present in all living beings; and 3) the creation of a great number of beings who have attained salvation. The theory of transfer actually contradicted the old Buddhist interpretation of karma prevalent in Hinayana, according to which each person is responsible for his own karmic fate; each person collects merit for himself. It was not until Mahayana that it was taught that Buddhists had to be prepared to share their merits with other living creatures. This now became a universal obligation, which incidentally does follow an inner logic: if the world and nirvana are ultimately identical in the void there can in truth be no difference between enlightened and non-enlightened beings. Furthermore, if compassion is meant to be unlimited, no living creature may be excluded from merit gained. The Buddhas and Bodhisattvas foster the virtue of believers and protect them from all dangers. They also guarantee tangible material advantages if they are invoked in certain undertakings. At the same time, in mystic thought they became objects of loving devotion, in other words – against the original intentions of Buddhism – a personal relationship to a personal Divine Being developed.

The bhaktis no longer thought of Buddha as having passed away into nirvana, but as living happily in a paradise (Buddha-land). The idea of the creation of a "Pure Land" through the karmic merit of a Bodhisattva illustrates the Buddhist confidence in the creative power of ethical actions. The believers attain rebirth in one of the "Pure Lands" through living a pure life and striving to attain Buddhahood. In prayer formulas they remember the Buddha or Bodhisattva they are worshipping by constantly repeating his name; their own mediation exercises are concerned with the beauty and perfection of the Buddha lands.

The Yogacarins

The school of the Yogacarins developed in the early centuries A.D. and dominated Mahayana thinking until around 500 A.D. Their theories are often very difficult to follow as the methods and effects of the trance state (samadhi) play a great part in their content. The school emphasises the high value of inner calm, and takes an approach that is more reflective, meditative and ascetic than intellectual.

The Yogacarins claim that the Absolute is thinking, basing this idea on certain statements of the Buddha. Unlike the prajnaparamita or Nagarjuna, they do not take the void (suchness) to be the ultimate reality. They do acknowledge the void, but describe it as thinking, connecting to the idea of the absolute "self-igniting thoughts." This says: when the human mind is confronted by the truth, the self-igniting spark of a thought is revealed, both in the inner depths of the self and in parallel in the inner depths of reality. It is thus a kind of "theory of correspondence."

The main theories of the Yogacarins are the teachings on the mind-only, storehouse-consciousness, the 3 ways of being oneself, and the three bodies of the Buddha.

Mind, thought and consciousness are synonyms in Buddhism. The Yogacarins see everything that can be perceived, including external objects, as "mind only;" things only exist in so far as they are part of the contents of consciousness, and all creations are pure creations of the mind. The Yogacarins also describe nirvana in positive expressions such as mind-only, thought-only, consciousness-only. They emphasize the dimensions of self-awareness (self-consciousness) as a "place" where the Absolute is to be found.

The Yogacarins confront the old problem that we cannot directly experience our consciousness (mind) as a subject; as soon as we (in an act of consciousness) turn towards the subject it becomes an object (of our consciousness), which is why an act of introspection does not present us with the subject as subject. The ultimate subject (mind) is therefore out of reach of our experience and not part of this world but transcends the structures of our consciousness. The Yogacarins try to approach this ultimate subject (mind, the Absolute) by a radical withdrawal from each object in an inwardly-directed state of trance. Where the subject is not opposed by an object, the innermost depths can be experienced in their purity; comprehension ceases where there is nothing outside the mind to be comprehended. The ecstatic trance states of the Yogacarins are therefore striving for a radical detachment from any identification with an object.

The theory of storehouse-consciousness says that a transpersonal consciousness is the basis of all (individual) thought activities. The mind thus has two layers: the store or basic consciousness, and individual thought consciousnesses. The difference between them is, however, one of function only. The storehouse-consciousness is the unchanging Absolute in which the changing individual consciousnesses sprout, as if in a kind of nourishing liquid, from the karma seeds of previous existences. All deeds and experiences of the past are preserved in the store or basic consciousness. The individual consciousnesses are not objective facts, but owe their existence to the store consciousness and are only erroneously (in the changing world) seen as separate individual consciousnesses.

For the Yogacarins all beings can be considered under three different aspects: first from the point of view of "common sense," which perceives real things and objects; then from the point of view of their reciprocal dependency and reciprocal conditionedness that early Buddhism also saw; and finally from the point of view of "actual reality," which is intuitively understood by the Yogi and in which a subject is no longer opposed by an object. According to this, all things form one single "such-existence" which is mind only, and in truth they are not differentiated.

With the theory of the three bodies of the Buddha the Yogacarins prepared the way for the transition to tantric Buddhism. They distinguish between the Buddha's "transformation body," which exists only in worldly imagination and went through all the stages of the Buddha legend, and Buddha's "enjoyment body," which reveals itself to Bodhisattvas and lives in the Pure Buddha Lands. These are distinct from the Buddha's "dharma body" in which Buddha realises his true Self and himself becomes the Absolute. This body is the primal one out of which the two other forms of body grew.

TANTRIC OR MAGICAL BUDDHISM

Forms of Tantrism

Tantrism has two goals: success (siddhi) in striving for complete enlightenment in this life, and success in striving for (worldly) health, wealth and power. It proves just as difficult for Buddhism as for Hinduism to trace the history of Tantrism, since its contents were originally handed down only in secret teachings to the initiated. It does not seem to have emerged as a clearly formulated system until after 500/600 A.D., but its origins reach back into the pre- Buddhist chthonic cults of the Mother Goddess and fertility rites. As in Hinduism, a distinction is made in tantric Buddhism between a more male "right-handed" and a more female "left-handed" tantra. As well as numerous sects, Tantrism has produced two significant schools: the left-handed form of Vajrayana ("Diamond Vehicle") and the right-handed form of Mi-tsung ("The School of Secrets").

The Pure Land of the West
Detail, fresco, Tang dynasty, 618-907, Magao caves Dunhuang, China

The "Pure Land School" developed into a separate Buddhist movement from the 4th century onwards. In the process, the Chinese ideal of immortality and the mythological tradition of the Jade Palace of the Queen Mother of the West, Wangmu, merged to form a western paradise, a place for the blessed, free of earthly misery, that everyone can enter by collecting merits. The Lord of the Pure Land is Amitabha, the Buddha of the West, symbol of original purity of mind, and untouched by earthly things. The Pure Land is also thought to be where Maitreya, Buddha of the Future lives, along with the Bodhisattvas. The picture thus shows the preaching Buddha Amitabha in an ideal Chinese-style palace under a canopy of honour and wearing the head decoration of a Bodhisattva.

Small Wild Goose Pagoda
Temple monastery Jianfu, 8th century, Xi'an, China

In China, which became the second home of Buddhism after northern India had been conquered by Islam, the Buddhist tradition of venerating relics met with difficulties because the Chinese believed that the intactness of the body was one of the prerequisites for being incorporated into the line of ancestors. China, a culture fascinated by pictures and writing, therefore accorded relic status to Buddhist texts, and the first stone pagodas were built to house scriptures. They also protected them better than the more perishable wooden structures.

Buddhist Ceremony in Japan

Buddhism has always had to reconcile a philosophical and speculative interpretation of the world with people's needs to make the metaphysical tangible. To this end stories from the Buddha's stages of existence and spiritual teachers, as well as ceremonial events and processions, mark special religious days (birth of Buddha, feast of Buddha's bathing, feast of the hungry spirits, feast of the incarnation of Avalokiteshvara etc.). Buddhist clerics also competed with the religions to gain favors from the heavenly powers for combatting epidemics, natural catastrophes and the like. Pilgrimages and also paid recitation of sutras in the home or temple are particularly associated with death, because people seek to influence the next rebirth of the deceased as well as that of the donor.

Vajrayana is derived from the sceptre or thunderbolt (vajra) that causes lightening to strike, which belongs to Indra, the Hindu god of war. It is itself unbreakable, but has the power to break everything else. In tantric teaching the vajra becomes a kind of supernatural substance that is as hard as a diamond, as clear as empty space and as irresistible as a thunderbolt.

Vajrayana is based on the Yogacarin premise that the world is mere imagination, "mind only," and identifies the void (suchness) in the ultimate subjective appearance with the vajra. The vajra is seen as tantamount to ultimate reality, the dharma and enlightenment. Through various practices, the pupils of Vajrayana are returned to their true "diamond nature" and receive a "diamond body."

The right-handed Mi-tsung is mainly known in China. This school combines two tantric systems, each of which is embodied in a magical circle (mandala): the circle of the mother's womb and the circle of the thunderbolt, which in a higher sense are identical. The Buddha Mahavairocana embodies the universe, and his body is made up of two complementary sides – the passive, spiritual element of the mother's womb (feminine) and the the active, material element (masculine).

Tantric Exercises and Meditations

Tantrism first of all distinguishes between the initiated and non-initiated, and in this makes a sharp distinction between exoteric and esoteric teaching. The methods of salvation cannot be learned from texts but arise only through personal connection with a teacher (guru) to whom the pupil unconditionally subordinates himself and who assumes the position of the Buddha for his circle of pupils.

Tantrism has three kinds of exercises: reciting magic formulae, carrying out ritual dances and hand movements, and self-identification with the deities through special meditation.

The followers of magical Buddhism expect the magic formulae to bring about direct material aid against things such as illness, accidents or demonic power. The magic formulae (Sanksrit: mantra) serve to protect life. For example, the utterance found all over Tibet "Om mani padme hum" (approximately: "O jewelled-lotus lady") is considered to be one of the most valuable gifts of the compassionate Bodhisattva Avalokitesvara to the suffering world; repeating the formula brings alleviation from suffering.

Tantric meditation has four stages: 1) an understanding of the void must be gained and the person's own individuality submerged in this void; 2) the "seed syllables" (bija) must be repeated and imagined; 3) the manifestations of deities as they appear in pictures, statues etc. must be visualized; and finally 4) through self-identification the person becomes a deity.

Mahayana's New Doctrine of Wisdom saw ultimate reality in the void while the Yogacarins identified this void with mind (only) and recognized nothing existing outside the mind. Vajrayana approaches this void through thoughts: in the ground of my being I have a

diamond nature. In tantric thought, individuality is renounced when a person is capable of identifying his self with the void. The syllables of the mantra correspond to the different powers and deities; a letter can conjure up the deities and is therefore called the "seed" (seed syllable) of the deities.

In magic there is no doubt about the fact that by identification with the magical power we can participate in the deity. But here, too, it is the void which in truth connects us with the deity, for it is only in the void that the subject may truly be identical with the object.

Tantric Philosophy and Mythology

Tantrism expects sacred acts to lead to salvation, since they bring about an alignment with the powers and aims of the cosmos. The Buddha is recognized only in his cosmic body (dharma body) and is seen as being omnipresent and no longer transcendental. The substance of the Buddha's (dharma) body consists of the six elements (earth, fire, water, air, space, consciousness): the actions of the body, language and mind are functions of this body. The world is a reflection of the Buddha's light and a manifestation of his dharma body, the Buddha being the hidden reality behind all things and their life principle.

In a further development of the Mahayana and Yogacarin teachings, nirvana and the world are seen as identical in the one absolute reality of the void. Tantrism also holds to the Buddhist need for elimination of the self.

Tantrism transposes its idea of humans onto the Buddha himself: the Buddha, too, (in his dharma body) is made up of five khandhas. These khandhas themselves are seen as identifiable Buddhas, and are called the five jinas (= victors, conquerors). The five jinas make up the body of the universe and manifest themselves in the five elements, the five senses, the five cardinal points etc. After 800 A.D. this doctrine was extended in that these five jinas, the tathagatas, were traced back to the Primordial Buddha, the Adi Buddha.

The teaching on the Adi Buddha was guarded as a special secret and amounts to a kind of monotheism or henotheism, which is contrary to the original Buddhism. The cosmos was traced back to an initial Godhead which was now described as the "womb of the tathagata." The world, too, was thought to have originated in this womb – an idea which also adopts monotheistic creation principles.

Left-handed Tantrism

Left-handed Tantrism has three main characteristics: 1) the worship of the shaktis as feminine deities, which are joined in an embrace and union of love with the masculine deities and give their energy to them; 2) the belief in numerous demons and awesome deities; and 3) the adoption of sexual intercourse and "immoral," or rather amoral, behaviour as one of the exercises which leads to salvation. The Buddha was originally thought of as a purely masculine principle and all higher gods and the inhabitants of the Buddha Lands were thought to be sexless. The first feminine deities in Buddhism were Prajnaparamita and Tara. The cult of Tara (the saviour) first appeared in popular Buddhism around the year 150 A.D. Prajnaparamita, whose cult probably originated in southern India, was called "Mother of the Buddhas" and placed at the side of the male Buddha as the feminine principle.

Shaktism, in both its Buddhist and Hindu varieties, sees the highest reality as the union of the active masculine principle with the passive feminine principle and calls the active principle "skill in means" and the passive principle "wisdom." Only the union of the two leads to salvation, and the Absolute itself is thought of as the final union of the two principles. Tantrism, like the rest of Buddhism, believes in the dominance of the mind over the body, which is to be controlled through consciousness. Tantra practices yoga exercises with the aim of transforming the weak human body into a "diamond body" and equipping it for the journey of the mind. Although Tantrism emphasises physicality more than other schools of thought and acknowledges that the body has its own truth, the ultimate aim is also to extend the capacity of consciousness.

DEVELOPMENTS OF BUDDHISM OUTSIDE INDIA

Ch'an and Zen Buddhism

All of the schools of thought mentioned so far developed principally in India. However, three schools of Buddhism developed in other countries and cultures: Ch'an Buddhism (in China) or Zen Buddhism (in Japan), Amidism in the coun-

Altar for Tsongkhapa
Ganden monastery, reconstruction, Central Tibet

An extreme environment with exceedingly hostile conditions has played a part in the development of the speculative, mystical Buddhism of Tibet which is both popular and autocratic. As long ago as the 7th century, Songtsan Gampo (617–649), who founded the first dynasty to rule the whole of Tibet, used the teaching on gentleness to resolve territorial conflicts. The Mongols, as rulers of Tibet, acted similarly when in the 16th century they declared the highest cleric of the Yellow Cap Sect (Gelugpa) as Dalai Lama, that is spiritual ruler and secular administrator of Tibet. The founder of the Gelugpa School was Lobsang Tsongkhapa (1357–1419). He reformed Tibetan monasticism, re-established Buddhist monastic orders, celibacy and the study of sutras, and imposed a democratic structure on the hierarchy of the monasteries. He did, however, retain the tantric mysticism of the "Diamond Vehicle" and tolerated numerous exorcist practices. Tsongkhapa, who founded (and died in) the Ganden monastery that was destroyed in the Cultural Revolution, is considered, like all Dalai Lamas after him, to be an incarnation of the Bodhisattva Avalokiteshvara and is therefore worshipped like all his successors. On the altar beside Tsongkhapa are his two favourite pupils, Gyeltsab and Khedrup.

The 14th Dalai Lama (Tenzin Gyatso) at a Ceremonial Assembly

The claim to the civil administration of Tibet has been disputed between the Dalai Lamas and the Chinese central government since the 17th century. Only between 1912 and 1949 was Tibet able to regard itself as a relatively independent state. This situation has given the spiritual leader of Tibetan Buddhism (in exile in India since 1959) a political as well as a religious role, and enabled the 14th Dalai Lama, to embody in a unique way the ideals of Buddhist spirituality and ethics in the eyes of the world and to offer these as an alternative model for the 20th century.

tries of eastern Asia, and Nying-ma-pa in Tibet. Buddhism did not arrive in China until 50 A.D., allegedly due to a dream of Emperor Ming-ti in the year 61, when he sent a study commission to India. And yet it was not until the year 355 that an imperial edict allowed the Chinese to become Buddhist monks. In Eastern Asia, Buddhism incorporated many elements of local religions, and in China and Japan, integrated the Taoist view that everything is an inseparable whole, the imperial state cult and ancestor worship, as well as the eastern Asian sensibility for nature and art.

Ch'an corresponds to the Sanskrit word dhyana and means meditation. Ch'an Buddhism is based on Mahayana metaphysics and also recognizes the meditation practices of prajnaparamita and the Yogacarins. It is essentially ascribed to the possibly legendary figure of Bodhidharma (around 520 A.D.), and since approximately 700 has been an independent school, quickly establishing its own rules and an independent organizational form.

Its most significant new departure is the reorganisation of physical work and introduction of the rule: "A day without work – a day without food." The Ch'an school survived the severe persecution of Buddhists that took place in the year 845, and since 1000 A.D. has been the leading Buddhist sect in China, along with Amidism. Its writings form a collection of dark pronouncements, riddles and paradoxes, and its teaching has penetrated all areas of eastern Asian culture.

In around 1200, the teaching arrived in Japan where it is called Zen Buddhism (Zen is also a word for meditation). With its simplicity and unperturbed heroism, it was very well received by the Japanese warrior caste. Zen Buddhism has had a strong influence on all areas of art and culture in Japan, in particular on painting and garden design, the art of fencing, and the tea ceremony.

The peculiarities of Ch'an or Zen Buddhism can be divided into four areas: 1) its radical empiricism, 2) its hostility towards theorizing of any kind, 3) the suddenness of insight or enlightenment, and 4) the significance as well as the negation of daily life. The traditional "construing" attitude of Buddhism is rejected in favour of radical empiricism. With rules such as "Don't think, try!" a great deal of scope is given to experimentation and attempts are made to

reach Buddhahood in ways not found in the scriptures. It is thought that the scriptures should be de-emphasized in favour of a practical attitude: "Recognizing one's own nature, that is Ch'an."

This attitude is accompanied by a hostility to all forms of theorizing and metaphysical speculation, because direct insight is held in higher esteem and it is thought that the truth should be depicted as concretely and practically as possible. The Ch'an masters are famous for their oracle-like pronouncements and original kinds of behaviour. They work on the assumption that enlightenment does not mature gradually but is a sudden act of recognition. This does not mean that preparation is superfluous or that recognition can be attained rapidly, but that enlightenment – like all mystical experiences – happens outside time in a timeless moment that actually belongs to "eternity." It is an act emanating from the Absolute and is not the result of human effort; enlightenment is a free act and not a karmic merit. Anyone who believes they can bring about enlightenment by an act of will, through ascetic living or meditation, is acting like someone who "polishes a brick to make it into a mirror."

Like Amidism and some schools of Tantrism, Ch'an Buddhism assumes that the fulfilment of Buddhist life can be found only in everyday things and their negation. Buddha is hidden in the unsightly things and events of daily life and the enlightenment to be found in life also consists in accepting this and attending to it.

Amidism

The name comes from the Buddha Amitabha, or Amida, revered in eastern Asia as the highest being. The cult of Amithaba arrived in China around 150 A.D. and around 350 A.D. developed these into an independent school, the "Pure Land School."

From 950 onwards, Amidism spread to Japan, and there, too, a school developed known as the "True Sect of the Pure Land." As the "Lotus of the Good Law" played a major role there, some scholars consider the Nichiren School (1222-1282) with its intolerant nationalism to be part of Amidism, while others see it in the context of Japan's national religion, Shintoism. The Amidism of the Far East became increasingly radical in socio-political terms, particularly the Shin sect (chin or Shin-shu), in which faith in Amida is in the foreground and morality is considered insignificant compared to faith, since all human beings will be admitted into paradise through Amida's goodness.

Nying-ma-pa

After 700 A.D., Buddhism came via Bengal to Tibet, where it encountered, and to some extent merged with, the native Bon religion. The strongly magical leanings of the old "Red Sect" were introduced into Tibet around 770 A.D. by the Indian Prince Padmasambhava. Padmasambhava's interpretation of Buddhism was a kind of Tantrism which was closely based on the Bon religion and developed its teachings between 750 and 850. Its followers call themselves Nying-ma-pa (= the Ancient Ones) and cultivate a secret magical teaching which stresses inspiration. The "Red Sects" and the teaching of Padmasambhava were constantly opposed by the reformist and more orthodox "Yellow Sect."

From around 1400, it can be said that the "Yellow Sect" has been dominant in Tibet. Since 1642, its leaders have been the Dalai Lamas, ruling as priest-kings. Following the occupation of Tibet by the People's Republic of China, the 14th Dalai Lama was forced to leave the country in 1959.

Nying-ma-pa is a branch of left-handed Tantrism. It worships 100 protective deities, 58 of them good-humoured and 42 evil. The true nature of the mind is nothing but emptiness. The magical nature of Nying-ma-pa is expressed particularly in the teaching of Thodgyal which says that there is a path to salvation or liberation in which the material body dissolves into the rainbow or passes into it like the colours of the rainbow.

Buddhism in Europe

Buddhism eventually entered European thinking, particularly through the influence of works such as Arthur Schopenhauer's (1788–1860) "The World as Will and Imagination," first published in 1818.

In his main work, Schopenhauer, who himself knew only one translation of the Uphanishads, emphasized the negation of the will and the idea of universal compassion. In 1875, Madame Blavatsky and Colonel Olcott founded the "Theosophical Society" which practised and propagated an esoteric form of Buddhism.

In the 20th century many enthusiasts of Buddhism have visited Asia, and Buddhist societies have been created in most western countries. In 1924 the German Paul Dalilke founded the first Buddhist Society in Berlin.

The Decline of the Teaching

The pessimism, particularly of Hinayana Buddhism, sees the course of the world as a story of decline, with Buddhist teaching itself included in this development. For example, Buddhism believes that the Law of the Buddha (dharma) exists only for a short time in full strength and purity, after which it declines until it reveals itself anew. It was initially estimated that the teaching would endure 500 years, but this figure was later increased to 1000, 1500 and 2500 years.

According to the prophecies, union with the dharma can only be achieved in the first 500 years, while the second 500 years are characterized by successful meditation, the third 500 years by erudition, and the fourth 500 years by conflict and criticism, until finally the Good Law is no longer recognizable.

The periods of time named differ, but the idea of progressive decline is widespread and means that in later ages the wisdom of the earlier times can no longer be attained. However, writings about the coming Buddha, the Buddha Maitreya (Buddha of the Future), who is kindness personified and follows his own cycles, have come into circulation. These speculations, which move salvation into a time in the future, bear similarities with the monotheistic religions' expectations of a Messiah.

Monks in Chamdo, Tibet

Again and again Buddhist monks go into areas of political crisis to carry out voluntary and peaceful work and to pray for peace. With their attitude of piety and serenity, they try to be role models for people to live together in peace, even in difficult situations.

"Whoever remains of steadfast mind when they come into contact with the things of the world and remains certain and free of worry and defilement, theirs is the highest blessing." (from the Nipata Sutra).

THE RELIGIONS OF CHINA

Chinese universalism emphasizes the universal harmony governing the entire cosmos, whereby the interaction of all elements is understood as something dynamic. The two basic principles of Yin and Yang, antagonistic yet complementary, are seen as driving the reciprocal movement of all forces, keeping everything in motion. The supreme cosmic principle is thought of in different ways, as the "Ruler on High" (Shang Ti), as "heaven" (t'ien) or as "the way" (Tao). The religious duties of the emperor have special significance. Taoism sees the Tao as the primal source and power of all being, out of which everything that exists has developed. With its concept of wu-wei ("non-action"), it propagates a contemplative attitude with a high degree of abstinence from worldly activities. By contrast, Confucianism, which can be called a state cult, demands respect for social traditions and the active participation of the individual for the good of the whole of humankind.

Yin and Yang

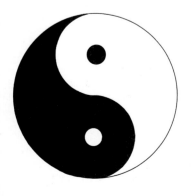

CHINESE UNIVERSALITY

Universal Harmony

Universality is an ancient metaphysical principle that underlies all Chinese thought: heaven, earth and humankind are seen as three components of one unified universe. For each phenomenon that appears in nature (macrocosm) there is a corresponding phenomenon in the human body (microcosm). The cosmic order is also considered to be the moral law governing human coexistence, an idea that is central to the philosophy of harmony. The inner connections between all components are seen as being dynamic, not static, and the highest wisdom consists in seeing the universe as one ordered whole. The elements, planets, cardinal points, seasons of the year etc. correspond to the different powers inherent in human beings. The five elements – wood, fire, metal, water, earth – are thought to be the changing and dynamic basis of everything: they are seen not as substances but as forces. There are fixed, in no way arbitrary, correspondences between them and the cardinal points, planets, senses and organs of the human being, animals, times of the day, seasons of the year and certain virtues and forms of government. It is not just the general correspondence that is emphasized, but the reciprocal conditioning or "destruction" of these elements, since one depends on the other for life. For example, earth absorbs water, water extinguishes fire, fire melts metal, metal cuts wood and wood ploughs the earth; the cosmos is seen as a universal mechanism in constant change. The two fundamental and antagonistic principles of Yin and Yang constitute the driving force behind all movement.

Yin and Yang

Yin and Yang are the two antagonistic forces at work in the cosmos and in nature. They have a wide range of attributes. Yang is seen as the masculine, active, procreative, creative and light principle; Yin is the feminine, passive, receptive, surrendering, enveloping and dark principle. They alternate in regular rotation, just as day and night, or the seasons of the year, succeed one another. They complement each other and are intricately interconnected, and it is their working together and against each other that produces everything that manifests in the cosmos.

Primal forces thus ensure the constant alternation of positive and negative, movement and rest, light and darkness, hot and cold, good and evil, etc. They are two sides of the Ultimate Oneness, and are symbolized by a circle divided by a curved line into a white half and black half. Each side contains the opposite principle in the form of a dot of the other colour. This figure is called t'ai-chi, which means "primal beginning," since the state of antagonism of Yin and Yang arose from a primal state in which the forces were undifferentiated.

Heaven is seen as a masculine Yang phenomenon, earth as feminine and Yin; heaven is spirit, earth is body, heaven is ceaseless movement, earth is at rest, heaven is blue and spherical, earth is yellow and square. The square corresponds to the four cardinal points, to which is added a fifth point, the centre, which is thought to form a link to heaven in the form of the tree of life or axis of the world. It is concern for this connection that essentially determined the religious duties of the Emperor.

The Highest Principles of the World: Shang Ti and T'ien

The universe is envisaged in Chinese thought as a gigantic, ordered, living organism. The question of whether ancient Chinese thought should be called naturalistic or pantheistic, and to what extent belief in a personal creator God or a creative principle can be assumed, poses problems.

The central term for that which rules the world in cosmic order and preserves the universe is "Shang Ti" meaning "Lord on High." Shang Ti first appears in early testimonies as a Supreme God, who is also identified with the pole star, as the Supreme Lord and controller of the world. He is described as a human-like being but never has a clearly defined shape. It is said of him that he issues orders to the kings and is the creator of everything. He is connected with ruling the world, but is not a being that is personally worshipped.

In many texts, for example those of Confucius, t'ien (= heaven) is also named as the Supreme Ruler. Heaven is thus seen as the primal ground of all things, from which everything else proceeds, and which rewards with good fortune and good harvests and also punishes with natural catastrophes. Sometimes it is seen as God, sometimes in an impersonal sense as fate. It was not until later, under the influence of Confucius, that t'ien was also described as father and educator of mankind, and allocated natural forces.

The third term for the Supreme Being is "Tao." Tao means "path," originally the path of the stars in the sky. Some thinkers describe the Tao as a primal substance possessing magic power. For Confucius, Tao meant the law of order in nature and the life of mankind. For Taoists the Tao is the rational, transpersonal natural law and at the same time being itself, from which the bipolar division heaven and earth and all other polar distinctions emanated.

The practical attainment of universal harmony is important in Chinese thought, and the most important element of this is to know the future trend of the course of the world and to exercise a favourable influence on it. The most famous testimony to this is the I Ching, the "Book of Changes," ascribed to the mythical Emperor Fu Hsi (2950 B.C.) and supposedly put into its current form by King Wen (around 1000 B.C.). The changing states of the cosmos are described and depicted by the hexagrams of the I Ching, each composed of trigrams in varying combinations.

The most noble science in ancient China (as in the ancient Orient and India) was astrology, particularly the theory of good and bad times (chronomancy). There is a complicated system of number, shape and colour symbolism, and people should direct their actions ethically according to the cosmic order.

Ancestor Worship and the Role of the Emperor

To the Chinese the world seems to be populated by numerous gods and demons, good and bad spirits, who are derived from Yin and Yang. The gods of the state religion are as a rule cosmic powers, but there are also a number of local household gods and family gods. In popular faith they were thought to bring good fortune and ward off harmful magic.

From time immemorial, ancestor worship has played an important role. The Chinese cult of the dead includes complicated rituals that begin at the funeral when the spirit of the deceased is recalled. Ancestors belong to the family, and are integrated into family life.

The official religious cult has always been administrated by the state. For this reason there was no separate priest class in the religion of Ancient China, and the ceremonies were performed by the emperor and civil servants, the duties of the emperor being principally of an ethical and religious nature. It was up to him to bring about the connection to heaven and cosmic harmony, and the art of government and the entire state system were connected with these religious duties. At the solstice, the emperor always offered a sacrifice to Shang Ti, the Lord of Heaven, which is why he was also called "Son of Heaven" and seen as the sole representative on earth of heaven.

The religious duties of the emperor or king are linked to a complicated system of prophecy

Guandi, the God of War
Silk embroidery in a temple shrine, 18th century, Shanxi Province

As with many popular Chinese deities, a historical figure has over time gradually taken on the functions of warding off danger and disaster – in this case the god of war. Guan Yu, a general from the time of the Three Empires (3rd century) is one of the most popular of the deified folk heroes, and until recent times there was a temple to the god of war in every district town. At the same time he was worshipped as the god of justice, and court was held in the hall of his temple. A specific feature of popular Chinese religion is the way it has incorporated Buddhist and Taoist ideas into its belief system. This is expressed here by the symbolic figures who are accompanying Guandi but also seeking his protection.

Household Altar
Southern Chinese farmhouse, Fujian Province

A traditional farmhouse in southern China is often one large room dominated by the household altar. The family tree and offerings are placed on the altar table. The choice of deities, whose (paper) images are placed on the altar is a matter of family tradition or personal preference. Often an image of the kitchen god is found there, along with his wife and the entire court. As god of the house he is responsible for all that goes on within the family. Sacrifices are made to him on fixed dates and special occasions. At the end of the year his image is burned (the kitchen god goes to the Lord of Heaven to report on the family) and after the great house-cleaning at the beginning of the New Year a new image is placed on the altar (the kitchen god returns).

A Local God
Gilded statue in a village temple, 18th century, Zhejiang Province

Every larger settlement had a "Temple to the City God," which served religious purposes (such as processions and prayers for protection against epidemics) and provided space for general assemblies of people (for instance temple markets). Historical figures from the town's history usually acted as city gods. In larger villages, the temple was often on the edge of the village in the middle of the fields in order to ensure that the crops were protected as they were sown and harvested.

that can be seen in the earliest religious relics in China, the oracle bones. The emperor assumed care for the welfare of the people by establishing the "will of heaven" (t'ien-ming). This illustrates the belief that it is heaven's responsibility to take care of the welfare of the earth and humankind. This paternalistic principle had probably been predominant since the time of the early agricultural societies in China, and it ascribed shamanist powers to the emperor. Through this knowledge he aligned himself with the powers of nature and was able to curry their favour by prediction, or rather by a predictive imitation of what was to come, in complicated and secret rituals.

Most notable among the sages and mediators of divine powers were the mythical Emperor Fu Hsi and the five "exalted emperors" who came after him. The task of the emperor was thus principally astrology and a precise establishment of the calendar (using his knowledge of what was to come). The calendar had to be set up to permit human life to be regulated by heaven.

A Brief History of Religious Development

According to tradition, the history of China begins with Emperor Fu Hsi, who is thought not only to have compiled the I Ching, but also to have created the beginnings of culture. He is thought to have introduced hunting and fishing, agriculture, domestication of animals, calculation of time and the principles of administration of the empire.

Fu Hsi and the five "exalted emperors" were succeeded by 22 hereditary dynasties. During

the 3rd dynasty (Chou Dynasty), around 1100 B.C., China developed a fixed and ordered state system with refined religious customs. Service to the imperial ancestors moved into the foreground and the state was imagined in patriarchal terms, modelled on the family.

From 490 B.C. onwards, state power rapidly weakened and there was a corresponding rise in the power of local rulers. The epoch of the "Warring States" (480/403–221 B.C.) saw power struggles and to some extent states of anarchy, and in religious terms was also a time of great turbulence. The ancient Chinese religion's loss of certainty was brought about by Confucianism's attempts to renew in particular the state religion.

The Ch'in Dynasty (221–206 B.C.) saw the rise of a strong central power once more. The Han Dynasty (206 B.C.–220 A.D.) promoted Confucianism, and after 61 A.D. Buddhism advanced into China. The Tang Dynasty (618–907 A.D.) gave China a period of cultural glory, while the Sung Dynasty (960–1260/78) represented the heyday of Chinese art and science, and once more promoted Confucianism. The Mongolian Yuan Dynasty (1260–1368) promoted Buddhism, while the Ming Dynasty (1369–1644) attempted to bring about reciprocal influences between Confucianism, and Taoism as well as Buddhism in China. The syncretistic ideal of this epoch was to attain the humanity of Confucius through Taoist and Buddhist meditation.

The final Manchu Dynasty (1644–1911) saw a time of political and religious unrest beginning in the early 19th century. The subsequent

Dragon Dance
Dragon Boat Festival in Leshan, Sihuan Province

The symbol of the dragon unites mythological and cosmological elements. The dragon is a symbol of Yang, the masculine, generative power, and as such is the symbolic animal of the Emperor and Son of Heaven. It is connected to water which ensures fertility, to rain, rivers and the East, since the sun rises out of the Eastern Sea and the summer monsoons ensure growth. At the beginning of this season (early June) the "Festival of the Dragon" takes place. Dragon dances (the dragon "plays" with a pearl) are performed in honour of the poet Qu Yuan (died 278 B.C.). The tradition of the festival as a tribal event goes back to early times when the dragon was the totem animal of the Yue tribes.

civil war and new regime sought a partial restoration of old religious ideas, but since Mao Tse-tung took power in 1946–49, religion in general, and Buddhism in particular, was forced into the defensive. Maoism is generally anti-religious, but has at times has made unusual links to some forms of Ancient Chinese thought.

TAOISM

The Personality of Lao-tzu

The name Lao-tzu means "old master" and refers to a mysterious and historically controversial personality. Tradition has it that he lived between 604 and 517 B.C. and that he was born in the village of Chu Jen (Hu province). His real name is thought to have been Li Erh Tan and he is said to have spent some time as curator of the imperial archives at the court of the King of Chou in what was then the capital Lo-yang. Modern researchers doubt whether he really lived at this time, and if the name Lao-tzu does not refer to a philosopher who lived in the 4th century B.C. His writings, however, the Tao-te Ching, have been attested as dating from the 3rd century B.C.

A great number of legends surround his life and his personality, including the story that at the end of his life he tried to leave China for the west riding on a black ox. At the border the guard asked him to write down his thoughts before leaving the country, which is how the Tao-te Ching came into being.

The Tao-te Ching

The name "Tao-te Ching" means "The Book (king or ching) of the law of the world (Tao) and its power." It is said to be the only extant piece of writing by Lao-tzu, and is one of the most original works of Chinese thought. This mysterious work has been translated into more European languages than virtually any other work in the Chinese language.

It contains 81 short sections or chapters, some of them in rhyme, that convey his thoughts in the form of aphorisms, in no particular sequence. The language is impressive, and full of highly poetic imagery. Chapters 1 to 37 offer definitions of the Tao, chapters 38 to 81 definitions of the te (= "the power of the Tao," sometimes also translated as the "Virtue of the Tao") and the relationship of Tao and te, which is why the book is actually entitled "The Book of Tao and Te."

The Theory

In the centre of Lao-tzu's thought is the concept of the Tao, which is seen as the eternal source of all being and the force underlying everything. At the same time the Tao is also seen as the law governing the world and the ethical guideline for correct action. It is an eternal Ultimate Oneness and the highest principle of the natural and social world. It is translated as path, life, God, law or natural order, but at the same time it is described as nameless and indefinable. It can be understood as the universal law or the will of God, but it is definitely an active force, not a static ideal.

Thinking of the Tao as the Absolute implies assuming an impersonal principle, but in some places in the "Tao-te Ching" is referred to as God or the "Mother Goddess." With this, Lao-tzu, or the author, no doubt sought to make a connection with ancient Chinese images. Its indefinability as a cosmic and ethical authority is described in countless paradoxes which later became the most popular stylistic tool of the Taoist school.

The Tao is also the primal source of the world from which everything was formed. Out of the purely transcendental non-being, being emerges, the Tao, as undifferentiated Ultimate Oneness, and this unity then generates within itself the duality of Yin and Yang. From the dualism of this principle, the breath of life is formed, which brings about harmony between the two antagonistic forces. This triad of Yin, Yang and the breath of life then generates the Many ("the ten thousand beings").

In this way the Tao is the source of all beings, nourishes them with its power and brings

Lao-tzu
Stone sculpture, Song Dynasty, 11/12th century, Qingyuan Shan near Quanzhou, Fujian Province

Lao-tzu was the legendary teacher and philosophical founder of Taoism. When Taoism was expanded into an initially esoteric and then popular religion, Lao-tzu was taken into the trinity of the supreme deities (Taishang Laojun). This sculpture in the grounds of a Taoist temple (destroyed) shows the god Lao-tzu as the "old sage" with a bald head, flowing beard and long ears which were seen as a sign of wisdom. This 5 meter high and 7.3 meter wide figure is one of the few examples of large Taoist sculpture.

The Sign of Change, I Ching

Old form of the sign "I," or "change" taken from a stone engraving, Song Dynasty, 960-1278

The Pictogram "Shou" ("Longevity")

Calligraphy by an unknown master, probably 17th century, stone rubbing

The striving for immortality, or at least for longevity, goes back to the beginning of Chinese high culture. It is connected both to the cult of ancestors and to the Taoist ideal of not intervening in the course of things. The cult of old age (and thus of health, correct eating and wisdom) has ensured a place for all time in popular culture both for the sign "shou" and for the god of long life, Shouxing, particularly as veneration of age was something agreed upon by all the schools of philosophy and religion.

Hermitage in an Idealized Landscape

Engraving on a stone stele, Eastern Han Dynasty, 25–220, Temple of Confucius, Qufu, Shandong Province

them to completion through its workings. Through the fact that the Ultimate One, the Tao, becomes the Many, opposites appear in the world which did not previously exist (good/evil, heavy/light, long/short, high/deep, before/after, etc.). They are mutually dependent on one another, i.e. none of them can exist without its opposite. The same is true of human virtue. Taoist ethics are based on the fact that the opposites that exist in the world illustrate how the world and humanity are separated from the original natural unity. This is why one must give up worldly striving and try to attain freedom from all earthly ties, including social ones. The Tao is the only permanent thing in the changing world and one should immerse themself completely in the Tao and dissolve into it.

In this the Taoist ideal is ultimately a quietist ideal: the action of a wise person who is permeated by the Tao is ultimately "non-action" (wu-wei), i.e. working through mere (exemplary) existence and refraining from any short-term worldly action. Wu-wei is the soft, gentle principle that in the end nothing can resist and which ultimately asserts itself; it is not merely the absence of action, but an attitude of non-intervention in the course of things and the art of being in harmony with the workings of the Tao. The ideal of Taoism is the immortal being (hsien) who withdraws from the world and immerses himself in the Tao. Activity directed towards existence is constantly contrasted by the contemplative immersion of oneself in the peaceable and conciliatory calm of self restraint.

And yet the claim of Taoism is similar to that of Confucianism: its ideal is not simply the wisdom of the individual, it also sees its path as serving the moral renewal of the community, the state, and ultimately the world. All evil in the world arises from the fact that people have distanced themselves from their earlier natural state and morality. The political ideal of Taoism consists (in contrast to Confucianism) in a sceptical attitude to all political action. What is considered desirable is a small society in which people can live peacefully and in an easily understandable system according to their tradition without wars and without relationships with neighbouring countries. The good Taoist leader does not actually rule through action and powerful assertion but

works solely through being a sage and thus an ethical role model; he too allows the Tao to work (wu-wei).

The School of Lao-tzu

Lao Tzu's pupils, particularly Lieh-tzu (Latin: Licius; 4th century B.C.) about whose life no further details are known, elaborated on his short and obscure phrases, wrote commentaries on them and systematized them. He wrote the "True Book of the Flowing Primal Source" which elaborates Taoism metaphysically using a well-developed cosmology. According to this, the Tao is the primal generator that itself was not generated and is constantly changing although it itself is unchangeable. From the primal One the forces of Yin and Yang are formed, from Yin and Yang the five elements proceed, which change into the Nine, which constitute the cosmos. The unceasing changeability of the world is described by a theory of metamorphosis that in places sounds very modern. Lieh-tzu claimed that through years of contemplation he had experienced the elimination of the difference between I and not-I – an ideal that Buddhism later adopted, particularly in China. With his strong mystical leanings, Lieh-tzu prepared the way for later popular Taoism.

Popular Taoism

Magic played no role for Lao-tzu himself, but in time it became a dominant theme in his school. The great attraction of this changed form of Taoism for the religious masses led to the rise of a popular Taoism that is more religious and magical than philosophical.

Central to it is a belief in the ability to make an elixir of eternal life. A kind of Taoist church grew up headed by a "heavenly master" (T'ien-shi). These heavenly masters formed their own dynasty and were referred to in Europe as "Taoist popes." The dynasty of the heavenly masters resided on the "Dragon and Tiger Mountain" in Kiangsi between 1016 and 1930. The heavenly masters were regarded as heads of the church, and a separate hierarchy of priests with monks and secular priests grew up and was dedicated principally to prediction and weather forecasting. Many of the heavenly masters gained a great reputation due to their power to make talismans and their secret ceremonies of invocation. They inspired countless legends about their mysterious abilities.

Eventually a separate Taoist hierarchy of gods was formed, at the head of which was the "Trinity of the Three Pure Ones" consisting of the god of heaven Yu Ching, the primal beginning T'ai-chi as the personified Tao, and the deified Lao-tzu. The Taoist pantheon is complicated and strictly hierarchical. It adopted a large part of the Chinese cult of the emperor, such as the cult of the "Jade Emperor" as the Lord of Heaven and the "Great Emperor" as ruler of the earth, to whom countless gods are subordinate. Three gods of good fortune help people who trust in them and, in the underworld, the ten "Kings of Hell" reign, whose hells are described very graphically.

A pronounced belief in an after-life developed, promoting a strict ascetic attitude amongst the monks. The monastic ideal of "creative non-action" (wu-wei) was seen as meditation on the Tao and the concept of wu-wei was interpreted in a broad variety of ways, including as "emptiness" and thus including seen as a parallel to the Buddhist ideal of nirvana.

Some schools increasingly interpreted the Tao as a Mother Goddess and linked it to a marked nature mysticism. The desire for immortality took the form of a search for a magic mushroom that would bestow immortality. Magical powers were also used to bring about a balance between Yin and Yang. The wealth of Taoist literature led to a first canon of Taoism, containing 1200 works, being compiled in 471 A.D. By the year 748 the canon contained as many as 7300 writings, and in 1444 the last Taoist canon was compiled, which, with 5318 works, is the largest religious canon in the world.

CONFUCIANISM

Confucius

The name Confucius is the Latinized form of K'ung-Fu-tzu which means "Master Kung from Fu." Catholic missionaries reporting back to Europe about China used this name, and it then became popular in the Western world. Confucius' personal birth name was Ch'iu (= hill) and Chung-ni (= central Ni). He was born in 551 B.C. in Ch'u-fu, a provincial town in Lu (today Shantung). He was the son of a military commander and came from an aristocratic but impoverished family. He had a good education

Pine Trees and Cranes
Stone engraving by an unknown master, 17th/18th century, stone rubbing

The pine is the archetypal Chinese tree. Since it can withstand cold without losing its needles, it is a symbol of persistence, endurance and long life. The traditional symbolism of the pine was well developed as early as the "conversations" handed down from Confucius ("by its stillness it lengthens its life").
The same applies to the crane, which brings into the symbolism of long life the relationship between father and son. When he calls, his young answers. When a Taoist priest dies he is transformed into a feathered creature (crane) and ascends to heaven. Expressions such as "celestial crane" or "blessed crane" point to the wondrous characteristics that are ascribed to the crane as an animal symbolizing wisdom. The combination of the two symbols expresses the highest wish for wisdom and longevity.

and from an early age showed great interest in China's spiritual traditions. He worked at the court of the ruler of Lu but, due to quarrels with government officials, frequently moved to different places, working mainly as a teacher and counsellor. In 501 B.C. he became the administrative head of a district and rose to minister of justice to the ruler of Lu. However, in 496 he resigned and wandered the country with his disciples for 13 years. In 483 he was allowed to return with honours to his home in the dukedom of Lu where he died in 470 B.C.

His character was described as unprejudiced, gentle and dignified. He is said to have been respectful yet self-confident. He had no interest in magic and led the modest and abstemious life of a sage, without being an ascetic. He was very concerned with the principles of order and undertook historical studies which he used in his efforts to renew culture and morality.

After his death he was quickly honoured as the state teacher in conservative and official government circles. He received the highest state honours posthumously, and in 174 B.C. the first emperor of the Han Dynasty visited his grave. In 120 B.C. the first temple to him was erected and in 555 A.D. the order was issued to erect a temple to Confucius in each prefecture of China. In 1086 he acquired the rank of a Chinese emperor, and in 1906 Confucius was accorded by imperial decree the same status as the deities of heaven and earth.

The Hall of Harvest Prayers

On the grounds of the Altar to Heaven, early 15th century, reconstructed 1889, Peking

The special role of Chinese emperors grew out of the traditional identification of the highest secular and religious representative in the figure of the ruling "Son of Heaven." As ruler, he was the supreme and sole priest, offering, on behalf of state and people, prayers to the old nature gods (heaven, earth), gods of the land and grains, the sun and moon, patrons agricultural, the planet Jupiter, imperial ancestors and Confucius, and made sacrifices and offerings (food, silk, jade etc.). The grounds of the Altar to Heaven was the most religious place in the kingdom. In the "Hall of the Harvest Prayers" the Emperor twice a year asked the Lord of Heaven, Shang Ti, for a bountiful harvest at new year and the beginning of spring.

Forest of Steles Engraved Texts from Confucian Classics

Temple to Confucius, 14-18th century, Peking

Confucius' Writings

Confucius mainly wrote works on moral philosophy and state theory. The authorized writings of Confucianism consist both of his writings and those of his direct pupils, along with some works of later Confucians.

There are 5 canonic books that Confucius is said to have written himself: a) the I Ching ("Book of Changes"), whose origins are thought to go back to the mythical emperor Fu Hsi; b) a collection of 305 early songs (Shih Ching); c) the "Book of History" (Shu Ching), which contains edicts and speeches made by different rulers; d) "Spring and Autumn Annals" (Ch'un Ch'iu), a book written by Confucius describing the history of his home state of Lu, to which he adds his moral criticism; and e) the "Book of Rites" (Li Ching) which looks at different religious and social rituals and is from the Confucian school.

In addition to these are 4 classic books: a) Lun Yu, a collection of conversations between Confucius and his pupils; b) Ta Hsueh (Great Learning), moral commentaries, some thought to have been written by Confucius himself; c) Chung Yung ("Doctrine of the Mean"), the description of the inner serenity of the sage, thought to have been written by Confucius's grandson Tsu Ssu (Kung Ki), who was a great Confucian scholar; and d) writings about the philosopher Meng-tzu (Latin: Mencius) (372-289 B.C.), the most significant thinker of later Confucianism. In addition to this there is a wealth of secondary literature. Confucianism does not see itself as a closed system, but favours the form of discussion and anecdotes.

The Teaching

Confucius' philosophy of ethics, further developed by Meng-tzu, starts with the assumption that man is by nature good and that all evil is the result of lack of insight. Educating people to virtue and harmony is therefore the supreme commandment. The holy and wise men of history are considered to be role models, which is why respect for parents and ancestors is obligatory. The goal of Confucianism is to educate people to love truth, goodness and generosity, nurture family relationships and maintain polite social manners. It aims for a certain ideal of moderation without asceticism and holds the "Golden Rule" (reciprocity of treatment) in high esteem. People must bear in mind the whole, the cosmic interconnections and always look to the needs of the community and the interests of the state.

Confucianism develops these high moral standards without evoking divine commandments or revelations. For this reason it has often been criticized by religions for having developed an autonomous ethical system devoid of any metaphysical underpinnings. Although Confucius was not an opponent of religion – he was a conservative aristocrat and expressly affirmed the traditional (religious) rites – he did not advocate any particular beliefs and made no statements about life after death, but he did affirm ancestor worship. He avoided all speculation on the transcendental and the term he used for the highest principle was not "Shang Ti" (Lord on High) but t'ien (heaven). He thus left it open to the individual whether they envisaged the highest principle in personal terms or not. He did, however, place particular emphasis on cosmic harmony. As Confucianism makes no statements about a divine being, it is considered by many not as a religion in the proper sense of the term but as a philosophy of state and morality. However, the cults and rites and worship of Confucius as a deity have turned Confucianism into a religion, and Confucius himself believed in the power of ritual to bring insight to the human heart.

Chinese thought distinguishes between "chia" (= philosophy) and "chiao" (= religion), but emphasizes the connection between the two. The Chinese consider Confucius to be a "Ju" (= scholar, man of letters), and thus as an expression of China's intellectual culture.

Confucian social theory revolves around the central concept of "jen," which means "humanity," and consists of the 5 virtues: dignity, generosity of view, loyalty or integrity, hard work, and charitable nature, and is particularly concerned with people fulfilling their social and political obligations in a state in which communal life is viewed as an organism. Integrity of the heart goes hand in hand with a striving for personal perfection. The principal virtues are considered to be moderation, equanimity and honesty. Respect for rites (Li) thus regulates the social order by linking the present to ancestors and the realm of history.

The Confucian School

Meng-tzu (also known as Meng K'o) is considered to be the greatest interpreter and organizer of Confucian thought. His life was similar in many ways to that of Confucius. He had a gift for dialectic thinking, and is spoken of today as the "Second Sage" of Confucianism. Meng-tzu elaborated the theory of the natural goodness of human beings, which states that philanthropy (humanity) and fairness (sense of duty) are innate qualities. He also set great store by goodness as the principle to be embodied by rulers.

Confucianism soon became the essential philosophical pillar of the Chinese imperial and state cult and at times displayed intolerance towards the budding Taoism of Lao-tzu, and later towards Buddhism. It sought to assert itself as the sole legitimate "state religion" of China. Later some Taoist and Buddhist ideas did seep into Confucianism, making it more metaphysical and speculative. The human being was seen as the battle ground of good and evil forces, concieved of as the non-material (good) principle and material (partially good, partially evil) principle. According to this theory, human beings are made up of matter and reason.

Confucianism was repeatedly reformed and elaborated, particularly by the two neo-Confucian schools – the "Doctrine of Principle" and the "Doctrine of the Mind," which taught the "Study of Things" as a way to attain wisdom, and described a path of direct enlightenment. The Confucianism School also produced a number of important jurists and experts in constitutional law. As a result of the early position of monopoly held by Confucianism, Europeans for a long time saw the entire Chinese state philosophy as being Confucian.

Through the cult of the state and emphasis on the sacrifice to heaven by the emperor, Confucianism gained distinctly religious features. Even just before the Civil War in 1910, a separate Confucian Church was formed in China. As the embodiment of the sober and practical life, Confucianism was, and still is, held in high esteem by emigrant Chinese, particularly by those living in the U.S.A. and in other East Asian countries such as Vietnam and Korea. There is also a special Japanese variety of Confucianism which takes the form of several different schools, and harmonizes well with Japan's state and imperial cult. Confucius is seen by many Chinese as guarantor of the continuity of Chinese culture.

There are a number of other Chinese thinkers, sages and philosophers who had quite widespread influence for a time in China, but in the end could not match the significance of Confucianism and Taoism. After blossoming in China, Buddhism incorporated many aspects of early Chinese religion that were originally foreign to it such as the cult of the ancestors and the dead, or the cult of the emperor and the state. The Buddha Amitabha (Amida) enjoys particular veneration in China because he is linked with the ancient Chinese idea of a moral world order. A number of eclectic thinkers have repeatedly attempted to synthesize China's great religious and philosophical systems.

Confucius
Idealized portrait in statue form, stone, Tang Dynasty, 618- 907, Taiyuan Provincial Museum, Shanxi Province

There is no portrait of Master Kung that is even approximately historical. Although the Confucian state and moral doctrine developed over centuries into the most popular of the "Hundred Schools," its standards were based on a noble attitude to life and inappropriate as standards of correct moral behaviour. During the Han Dynasty (206 B.C.-220 A.D.) people began to reflect once more on the teachings of Confucius. These were elevated to the level of a state doctrine, and the veneration of the master in his home town of Qufu and at the imperial academy took on the status of an act of state. Since then Confucius has mainly been depicted in a dignified posture with the robes of a high court official or chancellor, his beard indicating old age and great wisdom. This oversized monumental sculpture in Taiyuan probably dates from the 9th century, a decisive time for the revival of Confucianism (neo-Confucianism).

THE RELIGIONS OF JAPAN

Shintoism, Japan's original indigenous religion, can be described as an animist nature religion. With its veneration of the beauty of nature, its admiration of outstanding events, people and actions, its myths surrounding the descent of the Emperor from the sun goddess Amaterasu, and its cult of ancestors and the souls of the dead, it has had a decisive and lasting influence on the Japanese way of thinking. Shintoism is rooted in the pragmatic needs of daily life, and has played varied roles in Japan's history, particularly as it places no value on dogma and has taken on very diverse forms. As the state religion between 1868 and 1945, it also had a decisive influence on Japanese politics. Buddhism spread throughout Japan from the 6th century onwards, taking on a unique character and merging in many ways with Japanese thought. Today Japanese Buddhism is very active in the world peace movement.

SHINTOISM

Origins: Primal Religion and Ancestor Cult

The archaic primal religions of China, Japan and Korea have a number of common elements, namely the cult of ancestors, shamanism and agricultural magic. Their beliefs centre around the idea that the lower soul remains connected with the body even after death, staying close to it and returning as a demon or a ghost to harm the living, if not pacified with offerings and by paying respects.

These ideas are closely connected with the cultivation of the land that is so vital to life. The land was cultivated by local farmers who lived in dependence on the forces of nature and vegetation cycles, which needed to be favourably influenced or controlled through magic and ritual. Weather forecasting and geomancy played an important role, and the recurring cycles were honoured in cyclical religious practices, and in Japan also in the form of ritual drama (No theatre).

People strove to attain magical power, which was seen as the cause of the unusual and powerful achievements of human beings. Control of the forces of nature was gained (on behalf of the people) by the shamans or later by the Emperor who was accorded the functions of a high priest. For example, the Japanese Emperor (tenno) still prays to all four cardinal points on New Year's Eve in order to re-establish the order of the universe and ensure that all will go well in the year to come. The traditional power of the Emperor in China and Japan was thus not primarily political but "ethical" in origin; he was the preserver of the cosmic order.

The idea that the world and humans were created out of the sexual union of the gods means that the gods, humans, the forces of nature and the world differ not in essence but only in the degree of power they hold. For this reason, in the magical agricultural ceremonies held in Japan on New Year's Eve time is suspended and the cosmos is re- established – under the influence of man.

Similarly, the rituals of the ancestor cult, which vary greatly from one region to another, have direct success as their aim: the objective is to ward off danger, ensure good fortune and prosperity and heal the sick. Food offerings are intended to make the shadowy existence of the dead person (ancestor) well disposed and his name is commemorated in recurring rituals. In this way the bond with ancestors is preserved and constantly renewed through the religious meal. In Japan it is said that the ancestors live in the mountains in winter, come down to the rice fields in spring to watch over the harvest and then, after receiving the offerings, go back to the mountains.

Shinto: Basic Concepts and Myths

Shintoism may be described as an animistic nature religion. The name means literally "Way of the Gods" but was not used until the 6th century A.D. to designate the original religion of Japan and to differentiate this specifically Japanese faith from the "Way of the Buddha"

Shinto ceremony
Priests during a ceremony of devotion at the Shrine of Ise

The Shrine of Ise is Japan's national shrine, dedicated to the sun goddess Amaterasu. The innermost shrine of the complex, which is surrounded by a copse of cedars, houses the octagonal mirror, the "original source of the pure heart". Since each generation wants to re-build the shrine, the 65 buildings that make up the complex are demolished and rebuilt every 20 years. At the same time the ritual objects are renewed. According to tradition, the sun goddess Amaterasu herself expressed the wish to live in Ise, the "Land of the Divine Winds" and specified to the people who built the shrine how she wanted it to be. The designs of the main Shinto shrines in Ise and Izumo are based on the traditional Japanese house.

Japanese high priests

Shinto is to a high degree a cult of purity and avoidance of breaking taboos, which includes shedding blood and anything connected with death. Before a ceremony the priest undergoes extensive cleansing rituals and ablutions (misogi, harai) in order to re-establish the "purity of heart" that is innate to human beings. After the cleansing, during which the gods are greeted like guests of honour and treated with great respect being present in particular religious objects (shintai), the ritual offerings are made: twigs from the sakaki tree as a symbol of the first fruits of the field or of the deity himself, then rice and rice spirit (sake). The ceremonies are often accompanied by religious dances (kagura) and ritual prayers (norito). Most Shinto festivals celebrate the harvest.

that had come into the country with Buddhism. Shintoism is the basis of the Japanese view of life and is a deeply rooted part of the national identity.

The ancient Japanese myth of how Japan was created plays a particular role in understanding its national identity and the significance of the Emperor in the religion of the country. The myth has it that the primal pair of deities, Izanagi and Izanami, emerged from a supreme godhead. They were commanded to create and order the world (with Japan at its centre) and to erect the celestial pillar, the axis of the world, to connect heaven and earth. The country is formed out of the sexual or conjugal union between the two gods, who embody the dualism of universal principles – comparable to the Chinese Yin and Yang. During a religious ceremony of cleansing in the river, the sun goddess Amaterasu is born, out of the eye of Izanagi. She is considered to be the progenitrix of the oldest dynasty of Japanese emperors, who still reign today. The legendary first Emperor Jimmu was her great-grandson and to this day the Japanese emperors consider themselves direct descendants of theirs.

Shintoism sees the universe as an interplay of indestructible energies, which manifest themselves in the constant changes in natural phenomena. All these phenomena are thought of as divine beings, and require respect to make sure they bring good fortune. They are countless and constantly growing in number as ancestors and heroes of cultural and historical significance become deified. For example,

Robert Koch, the discoverer of the tuberculosis bacterium, has been included amongst the Shinto deities.

Religious practice includes bringing offerings, particularly of food and fruit, and reciting prayers (norito) asking for a good harvest, protection from illness and danger and for a peaceful home life. Shintoism has no concept of reward and punishment in another life (after death) nor any system of dogma and doctrines; it is expressed and realized through religious practice and ritual.

Connectedness with nature is central to Shintoism, especially in the "harmony" brought about by an intense feeling of being connected with nature. This feeling is especially sensitive to the aesthetic beauty of nature and is intended to ensure that people, in all their activities, do not come into opposition to nature. "The basis of Shinto is a feeling for the sacredness of nature and life" – Thomas Immoos once said.

The powerful invisible beings that are venerated are called "Kami," the ancient Japanese word for deity (the word makes no distinction between one God or several gods) or the divine, which was probably originally thought of not as a personal God but as a principle or force that can be translated by "the Supreme." Every deity, spirit of a dead person, or natural phenomenon possesses a soul in which two opposing forces are at work – one good and gentle, the other evil and wild. The religion aims to make the sinister evil powers kindly disposed. Shintoism (originally) had no belief in

Shrine on the island of Miyajima

Central to Shinto is the belief in divine beings (kami) which traditionally inhabit heaven and earth. Divine status is attached to anything which is striking, elevated and beautiful or possesses outstanding qualities: in brief, anything which awakens a sense of awe. In this way, things of natural beauty, mountains and seas, human beings, plants and animals can become gods. The gods are imagined as spirits that live in shrines or go to shrines to be venerated. Symbols of every Shinto shrine are the gateways (tori-i), which in their simplest form are two pillars topped by a cross beam. There are often several such gateways on the path to a shrine lined with stone lanterns, and there is always at least one directly in front of the shrine itself.

revelation or in any purely transcendental power, but believed in the power of human beings. For this reason, the rituals and customs are essentially concerned with mastering life and increasing personal achievement, a fact which is indispensable for understanding the Japanese achievement ethos.

Peculiar to Shintoism is the fact that it initially had no developed system of ethics, but to a large degree adopted that of Confucianism. An integral part of the very earliest origins of this religion was, apart from the role of nature, a respect for ritual purity and its reflection in the human soul in the form of the highest value of "makoto" or inner purity. Purity appears to be the essential point of life, so that Shintoism has even been called the "religion of purity."

Along with the lack of a system of ethics – which incidentally does not mean a lack of morals – all metaphysical speculation takes second place to the sense of aesthetics and pragmatic functionalism. With inner purity Shintoism is striving for simplicity of life and harmony with nature. There is no clear philosophy on life after death, apart from the idea that the dead need to receive offerings of food.

In modern Japan, ancient tradition and modern life are juxtaposed in a way that is difficult for Europeans to understand. For example, modern building projects are always accompanied by traditional religious ceremonies. A quite natural part of this "religion of national optimism" is therefore not just prayers for fertility and protection against evil, but also requests for professional success and financial profit. Through hard work man participates in the effect of divine forces in the world. Thus the Japanese work ethos and sometimes expansive Japanese nationalism are firmly anchored in Shintoism, as is unconditional loyalty to the Japanese Imperial Household. However, the latter is now waning considerably.

Religious Buildings and Shrines

The original religious buildings consisted of only a square marked out with bamboo stakes and linked by straw ropes. The gods took up residence in a tree or stone within this space. The structure was re-erected before each festival and was usually sited on a mountain because the gods came down from the sky. In time permanent structures were constructed, initially in the form of enclosures of stone walls (iwakura), in front of which a place for religious dances was marked out.

Later, permanent buildings or shrines were constructed in order to house religious objects; these were primarily objects that symbolized the presence of a deity, such as a mirror, sword or shaped stones. This developed into the sanctuary (honden), the innermost building or area of the shrine which, like a tabernacle, became the real symbol of the god, and the site of offerings. A larger building immediately in front of the building housing the inner sanctuary was used by the priests to perform religious rites. A separate free-standing building for religious dance is placed in front of the larger shrines.

The whole complex is usually surrounded by a hedge to separate the sacred space from the profane. A wooden gateway with two cross beams leads into the sacred precincts: it is called "tori-i" (literally: "bird house") and is derived from the idea that the spirits of the dead go into birds and can find a resting place here. Shintoism's most important religious place is the Shrine of Ise, which historically has often been Shintoism's spiritual centre. It is dedicated to the sun goddess Amaterasu as the progenitrix of the imperial family.

Shinto Rituals and Festivals

One of Shintoism's most important festivals is called "Matsuri" (from "matsu" = to wait, namely for the arrival of the gods). The essence of Matsuri consists in constantly renewing the vital force that connects the gods and humans. The gods manifest during the festival and possess the actors during the ritual drama, which then serves as a kind of "predictive imitation" of natural events. Its prototype is religious dance. The Matsuri ritual drama unfolds in five acts: 1) ritual cleansing, 2) evocation of the gods, 3) sacrifice, 4) uniting (humans with the gods), and 5) leave taking (of the gods). The aim is to renew the vital force for the gods, humans and natural powers by a ritual return to origins. Connected to this are very important New Year's rituals in East Asia as well as Japan, which serve to reconstruct the cosmos and give new birth to life. In Japan, this is traditionally carried out by the "predictive" prayers of the Emperor.

Every Shinto festival begins with the establishment of the Sacred Area: four bamboo trunks are rammed into the earth in a square and joined together by straw ropes on which ceremoniously cut strips of white paper flutter. The white paper symbolizes divine presence, which is why the word for the gods, Kami, also means paper. This area is usually in a clearing; clearing, forest and path are important Shinto concepts. The fenced off precinct is called "niwa" (= garden).

It is important that (in harmony with Chinese thinking) a fifth point is added to the four cardinal points, symbolized by the bamboo stakes. This is the centre, which symbolizes the celestial pillar or world axis and is therefore called "yama" (= mountain). This is often symbolized by the "tree of life" (matsu), and in Shintoism is connected with the mountain spring because the "life source" rises from the peak of a mountain, making it the world mountain.

During the festival, the mountain or tree becomes the seat of the god, illustrating its connection to the celestial pillar erected by the primal divine couple. As in Chinese thought, this acts as a world axis connecting heaven and earth. The main feature of both the dance and ritual drama is a circling around this central point. As the life source belongs to the world mountain or axis, primal Shinto was closely connected to a mountain cult and water rituals. Water is the elixir of life and symbolizes flowing, potential, cleansing power, regeneration and creation.

The Matsuri festival also commemorates the two antagonistic principles in nature which are similar to Yin and Yang. That is why "agon", competition, is an integral part of Shintoism,

Competitive games
Jidai festival in Kyoto

Ritual competitive games between two guilds (za) are an integral part of Shinto, and are held according to traditional rules. These usually take the form of a race between festively decorated religious floats in a "competitive festival" (kenka matsuri). Both parties make reference to the same shrine, and the competition is seen as a way of ascertaining the will of the deity. The ritual abandonment of daily order in the festival and competition play a great part in these events. In the earliest collection of Shinto texts dating from the 8th century, there are reports of battles between the gods themselves. For example, the wild god of storms Susanoo drives the peaceable sun goddess Amaterasu into a cave, from which she is able to escape only with the help of "800 myriad gods" to let the sun shine on the earth once more.

Samurai, 1870
Historical photograph

From the 13th century onwards the members of Japan's hereditary warrior caste were vassals to the powerful provincial princes with whom they had a feudal relationship requiring absolute loyalty. Their strict code of honour ("bushido" the way of the warrior) had a religious and nationalist vein and supported the Japanese class-based state right into the 19th century.

No mask
Puppet of a No actor with lion's head mask

No is the Japanese form of theatre, classically severe in gesture, word and music which developed out of the religious plays that were performed in front of the shrines. The essence of No, in which monologue predominates as a revelation of the inner struggles of the actor, is achieved through the unity of actor, word, music, place of action and costume. The stage and all props are based on the ideal of concentrating on the essential. All the figures who appear in No, including the women's roles, are played by men, and each role has a precisely specified gesture language. The fixed characters in No dramas include the gods, demons and priests or monks. There are several highly renowned, traditional No schools which interpret the spirit of No in very religious and philosophical terms.

taking the form of competitive sport or No competitions, for example. Races and competitive games also take place between the various guilds who organize the festival. In some areas the competitions include a quite dangerous race between two decorated religious carriages pulled at great speed through the streets by young people. The ritual dramas and No plays are often performed with the famous Japanese masks, which are intended to be real symbols of the deity depicted, each god being personified in a different mask. The religious actors are always men, who also play the feminine roles. The oldest known No masks date from the 7th century, and they are sometimes kept during the year in the shrines as symbols of the gods. The very expressive masks are supposed to make the invisible gods visible. The purpose of the masks is thus not to disguise, but on the contrary, to facilitate a ritual manifestation of the gods or the spirits of the dead. The No mask is the site of the sacred (divine) in ritual drama.

The History of Shintoism

Shintoism developed in the early days of Japanese history from a merging of indigenous customs with the beliefs of immigrants from Asia and the South Sea Islands. The earliest recorded Shinto practices were in the Yayoi period (250 B.C.–300 A.D.). In the Konfun period (300–710 A.D.), a tribe of horsemen from Central Asia introduced the three most important symbols into primal Shintoism: the

longsword, the sun mirror and the curved jewels. The imperial dynasty then emerged distinctly, and the first Shinto shrines were built. The people were divided up into clans, Shintoism incorporated ideas from Confucianism and Taoism, and the political rituals surrounding the imperial household developed. From 645 onwards the imperial office supervised the rituals for the Shinto religion. The Yamato Empire was created on the basis of noble lineage. Chinese philosophy, in particular ideas about the Yin-Yang polarity, usually expressed in Japan by the image of light and shadow, began to predominate.

In the 10th century, Shintoism appeared for the first time as a comprehensive religious system with myths, rituals, clans of priests and 3,132 shrines. The shrines were under imperial administration and the Emperor became the sole supreme representative of the religion, whilst the duties of government passed increasingly to the princes of the imperial household, and later to the shoguns (imperial administrators or deputies). The 50-volume Shinto collection, the "Engishiki" was compiled. From the 6th century onwards, Shintoism was radically transformed by the advance of Buddhism. Buddhist monks took over many Shinto shrines in Japan and re-interpreted religious practices, but without overturning or destroying previous belief. Buddhism itself identified the Shinto gods with Buddhas and Bodhisattvas. Ryobu Shinto ("Two-Sided Shinto") developed, according to which the cosmic Buddha Vairocana was identical with the sun god Amaterasu.

As early as the 13th century, massive opposition to this developed amongst the old Shinto priesthood, who strove to liberate the primal Japanese Shinto from all extraneous religious influences. The centre of this opposition was the Shrine of Ise. In the 15th century, Yoshida Shinto turned the tables and declared Shintoism to be the origin of all religions, and the basis of Confucian, Taoist and Buddhist thought. The cult of a central god that had been slowly developing, now took centre stage in the form of the cult of the Daigen Sonshin, the "Great Lord," which had its own purity rituals. In this time of political and religious confusion, Kitabatake Chikafusa (1293–1354) wrote his famous book on the supremacy of God and the Emperor (Jinno Shoto-ki), creating a uniform national consciousness and political ideology rooted in Shintoism.

In the Edo period (1600–1867), nationalistic tendencies led to a strong synthesis of Shintoism with Confucianism, and to a state and imperial cult. At the same time, Shintoism moved away from Taoism and Buddhism. The "Japanese soul" was defined in contradistinction to everything that was foreign, in particular Chinese influences, leading to a policy of deliberate isolation.

In the Meiji epoch (1867–1912), the Emperor once more assumed responsibility for government, and Shintoism now became the spiritual basis for a programme of modernization within the country and for military and economic expansionist foreign policy. In 1868, Shintoism and Buddhism were separated by law, symbolizing a "national cleansing", and Buddhist monks were driven out of the Shintoist shrines. As early as 1869, the Kashikodokoro Shrine was built in the imperial palace where the Emperor acted as the sole high priest of State Shinto. The Japanese state appeared as the "imperial family" in a close-knit entity of nation, people, Emperor and the gods. These ideas characterized Japanese imperialism from 1890 onwards, leading to the belief that the Japanese had been chosen by the gods to dominate the world – or at least Asia. The Shinto state cult demanded loyalty and willingness to sacrifice oneself for the Emperor and the nation, an ethos which contributed to Japan's tyranny in Asia and the country's catastrophe in World War II. Since State Shinto was tainted in this way, the Allied Occupying Powers ordered that it be dissolved in 1945.

Forms of Shinto

Shintoism can essentially be divided into 4 basic types:

1) Popular Shinto (Minkan Shinto) is the folk religion as practised in families and in the villages. Natural phenomena and vegetation cycles play an important role, as do "places" – arable land, water, mountains and forests. Central to popular Shinto is a cult of fertility magic and warding off demons that is locally rooted and takes on many different forms.

2) Shrine Shinto (Jinja Shinto) is a strictly organized religion which took shape mainly in the Meiji period when the imperial office once more became active in the Shinto cult. By 1945, 218

state shrines and 110,000 local shrines had sprung up, of which around 80,000 still exist. They were supported by the state and had strong nationalist tendencies. As 'official Shinto," shrine Shinto also developed (in particular after 1945) into "academic Shinto" (Fukko Shinto), developing a carefully elaborated theology and carrying out literary research.

3) The national forms of Shrine Shinto developed into State Shinto (Kokka Shinto) with very close links to the Shinto of the imperial household (Koshitsu Shinto). The tenno was celebrated as a descendant of the sun goddess Amaterasu and the great imperial ancestors. Loyalty to the Emperor and the nation was equated with obedience to the gods. State Shinto had strong monotheistic leanings and emphasized the direct line of descent from the sun goddess to the imperial household, and therefore the divinity of the Emperor. Japan was considered the spiritual and cultural centre of the world.

The Shinto "Matsuri" festival was linked to the word "matsurigoto" meaning to rule. Shinto was expressly defined not as a religion but as a "national cult" and attempted to emphasize the ethical purity and integrity of the "true heart." After the death of Emperor Meiji (1912), the Meiji Shrine was founded in Tokyo. This became politically as important as the Yasukuni Shrine at which the Japanese war dead from World War II are commemorated. Since State and Imperial Shinto are seen as partially responsible for Japanese tyranny in Asia in the 1930s and 1940s, the Allies ordered its dissolution in 1945, along with the separation of state and religion. Since the 1950s,

Zen monks playing bamboo flutes (shakuhachi) and asking for donations (komuso)

Since the end of World War II, Buddhists in Japan have been particularly active in the area of social work and the peace movement. The donations collected by monks are used to support social projects such as hospitals, nursery schools and educational institutions. In their pronounced pacifism and practical acts of charity, the otherwise very different Buddhist schools and sects in Japan are in total accord.

Zenkoji temple in Nagano

Buddhist temples are richly decorated, particularly with precious Buddha statues and devotional images. Since its introduction by Prince Shotoku in the early 7th century, Buddhism has adapted to the pragmatic character of religious thought in Japan. Buddhist temple ritual focuses on the here and now, with healing components ("Medicine Buddha") and petitions to the "Merciful Kwannon" for good harvests or commercial success. The public ceremonies performed by the monks have changed the character of the original doctrine, taking on many popular folk practices. At the head of the Buddhist pantheon are the Primal Buddha Vairocana, Arida who helps bring about salvation, and Yakushi the doctor of body and soul.

The helpful Kwannon

The highly venerated feminine Kwannon corresponds in Japan and China to the Bodhisattva Avalokiteshvara, who postponed his own salvation to help other living things attain that status.

this form of Shinto has taken a distinctly religious direction which strives for life in harmony with awe for nature and the gods.

4) Sect Shinto (Kyoha Shinto) currently comprises 13 (recognized) new groups and countless sub-groups which have emerged from popular Shinto since the 19th century. Some of them are very esoteric in character and were brought into being in times of crisis by charismatic figures (often from a rural or farming background). The "New Religions" that are strong in Japan today grew up as offshoots of the same trends after World War II.

BUDDHISM IN JAPAN

Zen Buddhism

Zen Buddhism arrived in Japan in the 6th century (538) and soon gained favor with the imperial court and high aristocracy. It quickly adapted to the indigenous Shinto religion, and became part of the official state religion. Japanese Buddhists were mostly eminent scholars with considerable education and high status. From the 8th century onwards, Buddhism in Japan disintegrated into a number of different schools, of which the two main Tendai and Shingon schools were great rivals.

The founder of the Tendai School was Saicho or Dengyo Daishi, a Japanese Buddhist monk (767–822) who adopted from Mahayana Buddhism in particular Nagarjuna's theory of the void and the doctrine of the Lotus Sutra ("The Lotus Sutra of the Wondrous Law") from China. His teachings were generally very close

to Chinese thought and assumed several levels of illumination and meditation. Tendai Buddhism was strongly favored, and protected by the emperors.

The founder of the Shingon School, Kobo Daishi (744–835), introduced Tantric Buddhism into Japan and also taught magical practices in his esoteric school. He adopted the doctrine of the three bodies of the Buddha and propagated veneration of the cosmic Buddha Vairocana. Amidism has existed in Japan since the 11th century in four schools, who called themselves the "Pure Land Schools." Based on Amidism's doctrine of grace, they claimed that transition into the "Pure Land" was possible on earth and not solely after death, an idea to which Japanese thought was very amenable. From the end of the 12th century, Buddhism in Japan became a broad popular movement, particularly through the influence of the Amidist schools.

Zen is a path of meditation aimed at attaining salvation by virtue of one's own power. Its ideal of enlightenment originally grew out of the Tendai School. Zen Buddhism became the decisive religion for the Japanese warrior caste with its teachings on physical and mental discipline, the courage to sacrifice oneself, and disregard of physical pain. For this reason it was linked very early on to Bushido, the "Way of the Warrior." Zen has to be seen more as a meditation technique and "attitude" than as a substantial doctrine; the value of silence, hard practice, composure and concentration, and the overcoming of all passion is particularly

Buddhist fire ceremony

Because any contact with corpses, which are subject to decay, bring about ritual impurity in Shinto, funeral ceremonies and rituals for the dead in Japan are the domain of Buddhist monks, who earn their living in this way, and cemeteries are often attached to Buddhist temples. During the annual Obon Festival in August, in which families and relatives commemorate their ancestors and deceased relatives, Buddhist priests pray for their souls, although Buddhism had no original rituals concerning the souls of the dead. During the Obon Festival, fires on hillsides or in front of houses invite the souls of the ancestors to come to their old home, where they celebrate a reunion with their descendants for two days before being given a festive send off.

emphasized, while proliferous speculation and magical practices are rejected.

Zen subscribes to the ideal of simplicity and directness and claims to be pure Buddhism, untainted by magic. Its teachings were developed particularly by the Zen Masters Eisai (1141–1215) and Dogen (1200–1253) who understood Zen as a striving for direct enlightenment based on self-discipline under the guidance of a Master.

The meditation exercises (zazen) have the objective of reaching sudden enlightenment (satori). This existential transformation is known as "Death and Rebirth" and is more a practice than a doctrine. Zen Buddhism loves using paradoxes and contradictions to underline its scepticism towards the mere intellect. The goal of the individual is to attain his own liberation for the good of the Great Universal Law – the "Buddha Heart" of the world thus becomes active in the heart of the individual.

Nichiren

Nichiren Shonin (1222–1282) was a character full of contradictions who gave Japanese Buddhism a strongly nationalistic flavor. He was an energetic, active and combative reformer who originally wanted to purify Tendai Buddhism of all its magical and mystical ingredients. He saw himself as a manifestation of Bodhisattva energies, and regarded the Lotus Sutra as the key to all salvation. However, he did not stress meditating on it but demonstrated that reciting its title ("Veneration of the Lotus Sutra") like a formula was the way to salvation.

Nichiren placed himself at the centre of an apocalyptic revelation and interpreted his time as an age of decline. Each word of the Lotus Sutra is, by virtue of its magically charged "word soul" (kotodama), regarded as an incarnate Buddha. Nichiren attacked all other schools of Buddhism with zeal and intolerance, and demanded state persecution and destruction of his opponents. Caught up in the conflicts of his time, he was initially condemned to death, but this was later commuted to exile. His strongly nationalist direction accorded Japan an historic mission to save the world. The Nichiren school became the third main movement in Japanese Buddhism, along with Amidism and Zen.

Religions in Japan Today

Today, Japanese Buddhists – along with Buddhists from other East Asian countries and the Dalai Lama from Tibet – are leading lights in the ecumenical movement, seeking peaceful dialogue with other religions, and working in the religiously motivated peace movement.

From the end of the 19th century, but increasingly since the end of World War II, Japan has seen the development of an unmistakable diversity of so-called "New Religions," virtually all of which have adopted and modified different elements of Shinto and Buddhism, but in which the influeces of Christianity and other religions are also clearly recognizable. Their founders have often appeared as charismatic prophets, claiming to re-interpret an original truth.

JUDAISM

A fundamental part of Judaism, to which people belong both by descent or by choice, is the acknowledgement of the covenant of the One God (Yahweh) with humankind, whom he created and to whom he gave his commandments. The original covenant with Abraham and then Noah was elaborated by Moses, to whom God gave the essential teachings of Judaism and the law in the form of the Torah. For Jews, being the chosen people implies a particular obligation to follow God's commandments. God has repeatedly spoken to humankind through the prophets. The connection in dialogue between God and his people runs through daily life, and is reflected in the religious cycle of festivals in the Jewish year. It has also provided comfort and strength in the various experiences and sufferings that Jews have had to endure throughout the course of history. The Jewish view of history is characterized by a notable messianism, and by the divine promise of the Holy Land.

GOD AND HIS PEOPLE: REVELATION AND THE COVENANT

The Covenant Tradition

In Judaism, the creation of the world serves as a prelude to the covenant God made with humankind, beginning with Abraham and the patriarchs. God enters into a relationship with the people he has created, as a personal partner in dialogue, and announces his real presence (Yahveh: "I am who I am"). The covenant is understood in very pro-active terms in Judaism: people are not simply passive objects of divine grace or divine action, but are called to responsibility and partnership, having to work at their salvation by the way they leads their lives. Creation thus seems to be designed around the two poles of God and mankind. This tradition of dialogue, on which the covenant is based, leads to an awareness of repeated encounters between God and man throughout history, requiring no intermediary figures to act as special advocates before God (such as Jesus in Christianity or Mohammed in Islam).

God made the covenant with Abraham as the head of a family, (Genesis 17:1–8) and the Jewish people see themselves as the descendants of Abraham. God's covenant with Moses is more broadly defined, and includes the entire people of Israel (Exodus 6:2-8). In so far as Noah, as sole survivor of the flood, is the father of all mankind, however, the covenant is ultimately between God and all people, which means that all who follow the law will find salvation.

The covenant is regarded as unbreakable, even though man often enough fails to meet God's requirements. Since God in effect "gave something in advance" and led the people of Israel out of slavery in Egypt to the Promised Land, Jews believe that their faith will be judged more severely and that they will be punished more severely than other people for transgressions. Thus, the covenant is both a reward for the faith of their forefathers – particularly Abraham and his descendants – and an honor, but it is also a burden and an obligation.

The Chosen People

Since Biblical times, the reference to the "chosen people" has been a mystery – particularly for Jews themselves, because this state of being chosen cannot be ascribed to any innate merits of the people of Israel, but solely to the unfathomable will of God. As with the tradition of the covenant, being a chosen people has to be seen in its two aspects: first, that God as creator of all things is the creator and father of all people; but, second, as the God of the Hebrew Bible (or to Christians, the Old Testament), is the God of one people, namely Israel, whom he has freely chosen.

The state of being chosen is seen as being "in a relationship of trust" with God, and does not imply any kind of national superiority, but rather Israel's particular obligation to fulfil God's commandments. Thus the misfortunes that the Jews suffered during the time of exile (from 70 A.D. onwards), and still suffer, is linked in Jewish tradition to the idea of being chosen. The people of Israel have not sinned any more than other people, but are punished more severely for transgressions. Unlike in Christianity,

The animals leave Noah's Ark
Coloured copper engraving, 17th century

The first book of the Bible tells the story of the flood, which God sent over the earth as a punishment for people's disobedience. God ordered Noah to build an ark for himself and his family and to take at least two of all other creatures with him on his journey. After the flood and the salvation, a new covenant, signified by the rainbow, was made between God and humankind. This covenant guarantees, through God's pledge, the continuation and order of creation. Thus, humankind is in a sense given the chance to make a new beginning. This is not, however, a re-establishment of the state of paradise, but a starting point for history.

guilt is seen not in terms of original sin but as a historical failure.

THE JEWISH CONCEPT OF GOD

The One and Only – Yahveh

The central statement in the Jewish concept of God is the absolute oneness and uniqueness of God. The most important verse in the Bible on this is the Shema Yisrael (Deuteronomy 6:4 "Hear, O Israel, the Lord our God, the Lord is One") which is seen in Judaism both as a profession of faith and as a central prayer. This is the dialogue-seeking God of the covenant who communicates with his people and obliges them to hear.

One of God's names is "the Eternal," describing his omnipresence, but in all his different manifestations it is one and the same God who is encountered. The fact of being without beginning or end emphasizes what Yahveh says of himself, that he is both the First and the Last (Isaiah 44:6). As such, he is not only the Creator God who created everything from nothing (beginning), but also the saviour at the end of time, and the omnipresent actor in history.

At the same time, however, the commandment to make no image of God has to be heeded. The original purpose of this was no doubt to make a distinction from the heathen worship of images, but it also served as a protection against the temptation to try to use or divert God into an image, or to try to intervene in the creative power which is God's alone. God can be invoked by people, but cannot really be named, since each act of naming fixes him and thus would be tantamount to limiting the absolute Being of God. Thus the Bible contains not only the name Yahveh (YHVH) for God, but also other names such as Jehovah ("Lord"), Adonai, El or Elohim.

The oneness of God arises for Judaism out of Yahveh's statements about himself, and is not deduced philosophically. Abraham is seen as the first person to bear witness to the oneness of God in a polytheistic environment. The actual sin against God is seen as the act of falling away from him and praying to other gods or idols, which includes praying to any pictorial image of God. This is expressed most unequivocally in the story of the "Dance around the Golden Calf (Exodus 32)."

The Bible depicts monotheism as the result of a development. The Hebrew Bible (and Old Testament) repeatedly tells of Yahveh's dispute

The Fall and the Expulsion from Paradise
Book illumination, around 1360, Darmstadt, Hessische Landesbibliothek

The story of paradise and the Fall, described in the third chapter of the book of Genesis, deals with humankind's fundamental susceptibility to the temptation to listen to voices other than God's, and to distrust God. After Eve had herself been lured by a serpent into going against God's commandment and eating of the forbidden fruit of the Tree of Knowledge of Good and Evil, she also gave Adam some of the fruit. After they had both eaten of the fruit, they realized for the first time that they were naked, and were ashamed. They joined fig leaves together and made them into loincloths. They were then both expelled from paradise (the Garden of Eden) by God, and all living things forfeited their perfection and immortality. Yet, at the same time, God equipped human beings for their newly-gained life. He sent cherubim to stand outside paradise with swords of flames to guard the path to the Tree of Life. Paradise is still used as a metaphor for ideal conditions, and the expulsion from paradise, linked to the wish to regain what had been lost, is a frequent motif in literature and art.

with the gods of the surrounding ancient oriental cultures, in particular against the Babylonian god Baal and the gods of the Egyptians (for example, Exodus 12:12, where Yahveh announces that he will execute judgement on the gods of Egypt). It is not until the prophet Isaiah and King Josiah's religious reform at the end of the Babylonian exile that worship of one god develops into the true monotheism propagated by Moses.

Elohim, the term for God used in the Hebrew Bible, appears both in the singular and the plural – there simply is no other name for God any more. God's claim to universality was the logical consequence of this monotheism. God reveals himself in different manifestations, but is nevertheless eternally the same and indivisible. As an imperious God, he presents mankind with ethical commandments and demands that they be followed. An ethically indifferent cult of routine sacrifices (which was the case with the pagan gods) is not sufficient to fulfil his commandments.

Nevertheless, Jewish theology has few dogmatic principles. In the 12th century, Moses

Moses proclaims the Ten Commandments
Misrach plaque, oil on canvas in neo-Gothic wooden frame, around 1900, Vienna, Max Berger's Judaica Collection

The two tablets with the Ten Commandments are the core of the religious and moral statutes which were revealed to Moses on Mount Sinai, and an expression of the covenant established between God and Israel.
What happened on Mount Sinai is seen as God's revelation of the covenant, with Moses proclaiming God's commandments to the people of Israel, gathered at the foot of Mount Sinai.

The Judgement of Solomon
Giorgione, around 1505, Florence, Uffizi Gallery

According to tradition, King Solomon was the second son of David and his wife Bathsheba. While David was still alive, Solomon seized the throne from his older brother Adonia in a coup. Traditionally he is thought to have written several books of the Bible. The most famous story is recorded in the first Book of Kings, and tells of his judgement in a dispute between two women. Both had given birth to a child, but only one child had survived, and both claimed to be the mother. Through King Solomon's seemingly hard judgement that the child should be divided in two, the identity of the true mother was rapidly revealed, since she preferred to renounce her claim to the child than see it killed.

Maimonides summarized these in 13 principles of faith. The central message of the Jewish belief in God is: God is the creator of all things, he is the prime mover and directs all things; there is one God and nothing is any way comparable to him; God has made the free decision to reveal himself and has communicated his commandments (laws) to humankind through Moses; the words of the prophet are the truth; God knows all human actions and is good to those who follow his commandments, punishing those who transgress his commandments; furthermore, that one day the Messiah (sent by God) will come and one day the dead will rise again.

THE JEWISH VIEW OF MANKIND

Man Recognized by God

The statement in the Bible that man is created in God's image (Genesis 1:27) forms the basis for the Jewish view of humankind. The difficulty with the idea of "being made in his own image" is that the believer is not supposed to form an image of God. Apart from this idea of being made in God's image as described in Genesis 1:26/27, there is also the statement in Genesis 2:7-8 that man is made from the dust of the earth (clay) and that God breathed life into him. Genesis 2:21-25 also depicts humankind as having been created as man and woman. To counteract the temptations of anthropomorphism, attempts have been made to translate "in God's own image" with "similarity" or "shadow." Jewish theological anthropol-

ogy defines mankind as "recognized by God" ("the recognized man," Schalom ben-Chorin), thus as man in a "situation of dialogue" (Martin Buber, Frank Rosenzweig) or in "correlation" with God (Hermann Cohen).

Dialogue is ensured by the personal natures of both God and humans; (inner) openness to the action of God plays an important role. People are dependent on God to order creation justly and are part of that creation. Man has to prove himself as "God's partner" in the creation by acting according to God's moral laws. People are subject in life and the world to many temptations of evil and fail repeatedly in concrete historical situations – beginning with Cain's fratricide – but, since we are made in God's image, humans are fundamentally good, loved by God and will be led to salvation. There is no concept of original sin in Judaism.

Yet despite the omnipotence and omniscience of the Creator God, people are responsible for their actions. They have the possibility and the capacity to make choices, and are thus free to do something or to refrain from doing it. People also have the power of reasoning, the ability to understand the ethical order of the world and to direct their actions in accordance with its laws. Since all people are made in the image of God and are God's children (creatures), the rights of the individual are limited by the rights of others. Mankind's task is to act, to actively shape the world according to God's laws. High value is placed on (physical) work, but times of rest and reflection (sabbath, holy days) are also prescribed. People are known, measured and judged by their actions. As a rule of behaviour the "imitation of God" (Imitatio Dei) has to be the fundamental principle behind human striving, which does not mean wanting to be like God, but living according to God's commandments.

Sin is a rebellion against God and the divine order, but in Judaism it is always seen as also being a degeneration of the true nature of humankind. The purpose of punishment is thus not retribution, but to be a reminder of the true nature of humankind. Thus the Hebrew word for remorse, "teshuvah," actually means "returning" in the sense of man returning to his true nature. The Hebrew Bible recounts a number of situations that represent thoughtless rebellion against God and these are followed by God exacting judgement.

Suffering

In the Jewish understanding of God, nothing is as characteristic as the famous theodicy question, namely why righteous and holy people also have to suffer in this world. The story of Job, whose firmness of faith God put to the test, is a prime example of this. The believer may not interpret his suffering as direct punishment for transgressions he has committed, but he needs God's help to endure them. A Hasidic prayer thus says: "God, do not tell me why I am suffering, for I am without doubt not worthy of knowing, but help me to believe that I am suffering for your sake." This prayer expresses the request for recognition that suffering is neither arbitrary nor meaningless, even if the meaning often remains hidden from us. Suffering is considered to be a particular mystery of Jewish faith; again and again it is said that God rewards and punishes whomsoever he will.

The suffering that afflicts a person is the consequence of his moral freedom: he is not indifferent, but capable of doing good or evil. A person can experience suffering in three ways: as a punishment, as a test, or as the atonement suffering of the righteous. It is easiest to understand rationally as a form of punishment; as a test it is clearly described in the interrupted sacrifice of Isaac (Genesis 22) and in the Book of Job. Suffering as a means of atonement of the righteous is a collective interpretation of the fate of the people of Israel. For modern Judaism, the question of the meaning of suffering is posed once more in an acute form by the experiences of the 20th century (for example expulsion and annihilation, Auschwitz, and the general events of the Holocaust).

The Prophets

The prophets are seen as having been chosen by God to proclaim his true word. The Hebrew word "navi" means the prophet of the word, "calling out" on behalf of or "called" by God, who has the task of passing on God's message to the people. He speaks to the people on God's behalf. The rabbinic tradition distinguishes the "three major prophets" – Isaiah, Jeremiah and Ezekiel – from the "12 minor prophets" ("dodeka prophets").

The high degree of significance accorded to the prophets can be seen from the fact that the scriptures about them, which include a large number of the later books of the Hebrew Bible, including the history books, are ranked directly

after the Torah in order of importance. The gift of prophecy is seen in Judaism as particular proof of God's grace, and the prophet is therefore always more than a mere clairvoyant or soothsayer; he is someone who has been enlightened by God's spirit, which also accounts for his prominent position. In describing the way most of the prophets experience being called, the Hebrew Bible emphasizes the suddenness and unexpectedness of being chosen. Abraham is regarded as the first of the prophets (Genesis 20:7).

The prophet always brings about a situation of decision-making for the community or the people: when he appears they have to decide for or against the word of God and take upon themselves the possible consequences of their decision. Examples of prophetic pronouncements have been requiring Israel to profess their belief in the one God who is Yahveh, strengthening God's covenant with mankind and protesting the decline in moral standards, and warning against worshipping idols. Many prophets had apocalyptic visions of an imminent execution of God's judgement and use an admonishing tone. They appear in concrete historical situations and require the community to take immediate action. Here, too, Judaism emphasises human freedom: if people did not have the possibility to decide for or against the word of God as mediated by the prophet, the whole class of prophets as warning and calling people to convert would be superfluous. Often

The Temple of Solomon in Jerusalem
Model, 20th century, detail

In the 10th century B.C., King Solomon constructed the first temple in Jerusalem, on a site determined by King David, on Mount Moriah in the northeast of Jerusalem. It took seven years to build this magnificent temple with the palace complex adjoining it to the south. In accordance with the sequence of rooms laid down in the tabernacle, there was a court with two columns called Jachin and Boaz in front of it. Behind that was the main holy place with the table for the shewbread, ten candelabra and an altar of incense. Beyond that was the Holy of Holies, with the Ark of the Covenant and cherubim. The temple, which was surrounded by a number of courtyards, was destroyed by Nebuchadnezzar in 588. The second temple was built in the early 6th century B.C. It was simpler and was modified several times, including by King Herod the Great. In 70 A.D. it was destroyed by the Romans.

Misrach Plaque

Watercolour thought to be by Naum Gutman, around 1900, Vienna, Max Berger's Judaica Collection

Jews turn to face the east when praying, and wall plaques such as this indicate the correct direction in Jewish homes. This one is made of parchment and is quite artistically crafted. In general, such plaques contain calligraphy of Psalms framed by various symbols and ornamentation.

Misrach (Hebrew: "East") is also the name given to the east wall of the synagogue.

the words of the prophets are linked to the Jewish history of salvation, in the form of promises handed down, such as Isaiah and Jeremiah promising that a new time of salvation would come.

Moses

Moses plays the outstanding role in Judaism of handing down the law (Torah) and leading Israel out of slavery in Egypt. No later prophet teaches anything new in Judaism that was not already contained in the Torah of Moses (Sab. 104a), and he is considered to be Judaism's great teacher. Maimonides calls him the "Father of the Prophets," who came both before and after his time. Many traditional Jewish stories are concerned with the life and legends of Moses. His prophecy, recorded in the five books of Moses (Pentateuch), is seen as the root of all other prophecy. Yet although he is seen as Judaism's greatest law-maker, the tradition constantly stresses that he is actually only the bearer and pronouncer of God's commandments.

Moses is the charismatic figure par excellence: he is a prophet, proclaimer, judge, and even

leader of an army, leader of his people into the wilderness, liberator and law-giver. He delegated the priestly and preaching functions largely to his brother Aaron. The title Jews give to Moses is usually "Rabbejnu" = our teacher, and later Jewish tradition also gives him philosophical abilities. The Jewish prohibition on making images is also ascribed to Moses. Martin Buber sees Moses' significance mainly in his "theopolitics," i.e. the direct exercise of God's supremacy in and via a community who in this relationship of covenant with God became one people.

THE TORAH

Teaching and Law

The Torah is seen as God's law, which Moses brought to the people of Israel as handed down in the five books of Moses, the Pentateuch. But the Torah is not only the law, it is also the "basic teaching" or the "written teaching" (as distinct from the later "oral teaching" of the rabbinic tradition). Belief in and reference to the Torah are fundamental elements of the Jewish faith; among the few "dogmas" of Judaism are the belief that the source of the Torah was God and that it was fixed by Moses, whereas its written form and its transmission over time are points still disputed by scholars of the Jewish scriptures.

While strictly Orthodox and fundamentalist Jews believe that the entire Torah was given to Moses at one time, and that Moses alone handed it down, research by Biblical critics has identified temporal and stylistic inconsistencies and emphasizes that, although the spirit of the Torah is the same, namely that of Moses, it involved several writers. This approach distinguishes between the sacredness of the scripture, which it acknowledges just as much as the Orthodox groups, and the literary process by which it was created. The Pentateuch is essentially a combination of four source texts – Yahvehist, Elohist, Deuteronomist and priestly scripture – between which connections have been made.

Judaism believes in the immutable and irreplaceable nature of the Torah, which is thus seen as the complete revelation of God's commandments. This statement, which was not formulated in this way until later Judaism, serves to distinguish Judaism from Christianity and

Islam, which each make reference to the Torah in their own way. However, a question posed by scholars of the Jewish scriptures asks to what extent the commandments of the Torah, such as the laws governing clothing, diet and marriage, have an eternal character, and whether some of them may be interpreted only in the context of a specific historical time.

Post-Biblical rabbinic scriptures attempted to codify and interpret the religious laws, taking into account changes in society. It is important to note, however, that the later scriptures (the Talmud – Mischna and Gemara) are never seen as new Torahs, but always as interpretations of the original Torah. The immutability of the Torah is always emphasized, as are its numerous ritual and ceremonial prescriptions, as stated in Deuteronomy 4:2: "Add nothing – and take nothing away." This immutability is also expressed in a reverence for the letters and the typography of the Torah. Copiers of the Torah undergo a long and rigorous training and must observe certain purity rituals. Reading from the Torah must similarly be without error. During each expulsion that the Jews were subjected to, the Jewish communities rescued their Torah scrolls as their most precious possessions.

In rabbinic tradition the Torah is said to have been given to the people as a "means of purifying themselves." Tradition (Rabbi Simlai) assumes that Moses originally received 613 commandments, comprising 365 negative prohibitions and 248 positive commandments. The numbers have symbolic value, the year having 365 days, and Judaism believes there

are 248 parts of the human body. All these prohibitions and commandments together constitute the basic belief in God. The 613 prohibitions and commandments also correspond to the 613 letters of the Decalogue (Ten Commandments).

In rabbinic terms the Torah is the "order of creation" and the entirety of the sacred tradition. For this reason the "Written Torah" is always complemented by the "Oral Torah" (the tradition). Again and again, the scriptures call for the laws to be kept – particularly in times of diaspora or persecution. The intention is to translate the law into living action, rather than slavishly follow the letter of the law. It is said that God will forgive virtually everything before he forgives failure to study the Torah.

Judaism as a Religion of Learning

Learning is a religious duty and general ideal that applies not only to scholars, and Judaism and (religious) education go hand in hand. It is the principal task of parents, and particularly of the father, to pass on knowledge to the children (especially to his sons). The teacher plays an important role in Judaism, as does the rabbi, who is the religious teacher in the Talmud school.

From an early age education is an obligation, and is primarily dedicated to learning the Torah, yet a high value is also placed on learning in secular fields. The Hebrew language is important in this, as the exodus from Egypt also represented linguistic liberation, with Hebrew being seen as the language of God and the

Torah Shield
Silver, gilded in parts, 1806, Vienna, Max Berger's Judaica Collection

The Torah is written on a parchment scroll and kept in a special shrine, decorated with a curtain. The Torah scroll itself is also decorated, for instance by a mantle, which at the same time protects the Torah, with a crown, finials and a plate. The artistically worked shield marks the scrolls that are needed for the readings of that particular week, or for the Holy Days.

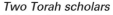

Two Torah scholars
Painting by Mane-Katz, 1943, oil on canvas, private collection

For Judaism, learning and education are of central importance, with study of the commandments of the Holy Scriptures (Torah) a sacred obligation of every Jew.
From an early age, children are introduced to elementary reading and writing skills, to the prayers and to weekly extracts from the Holy Scriptures that are read in the synagogues each sabbath.
The Hebrew word "Torah" originally meant teaching or instruction, and comprises considerably more than the law.
The Torah is the divine order of the world and creation, so that learning the Torah and the later tradition ("oral Torah") includes learning the laws and inter-connections of this world.

Bar Mitzvah
Etching signed "Ben Ary," Vienna, Max Berger's Judaica Collection

At the age of 13 a boy is considered to be an adult in religious terms and is obliged, or rather entitled, to fulfil all the commandments. This is usually marked by a special celebration. The "Bar Mitzvah" ("Son of the Law") is now allowed to put on the tefillin for certain prayers – as shown in this picture – and is called upon during the act of worship to speak the blessings on the Torah. Today there are also similar ceremonies for girls, called the Bat Mitzvah.

creation, practically as the primal language prior to the confusion of Babel. The promise therefore also speaks of the re-establishment of Hebrew as the original sacred language of all people at the end of time. Nevertheless, early on in the diaspora, translations of the scriptures were made, notably the Greek Septuaginta, although since the Middle Ages there has been a return to Hebrew even in the diaspora.

Commitment to the Law

A Jewish boy becomes an adult in the religious sense at the age of 13, a girl at 12, events which are marked with the celebration of the Bar Mitzvah (= "son of the law") or Bat Mitzvah (= daughter of the law). A boy's Bar Mitzvah involves him being presented to the elders of the community, after which he is allowed to read from the Torah in the synagogue. The celebration for girls originated in Reformed Judaism during the 19th century. The Jewish boy or girl places himself or herself under the authority of the Torah. The celebration of this act of coming of age in religious terms is a sign of rejoicing in God's laws, which is more than mere obedience to the law, and expresses gratitude to God, who guides people. The laws concerning everyday behaviour in accordance with the instructions of the Torah are called "Halakhah" (from the Hebrew "halak" = to go, thus pointing the way).

Difficulties are posed by the question of to what extent the laws of the Torah apply to everyday life and how they can be brought into harmony with political laws, or with the laws of specific countries. At least since the French Revolution, Josephinism and the Napoleonic Code, when Jews received full rights of citizenship in various countries in Europe, this question has become more acute and has focused on the degree to which Jews are integrated in the civic life of a state. In the 19th century, Neo-Orthodox and Conservative Jewish circles recognized the danger of Jewish views of the law being watered down if there was too much Jewish assimilation. When Jews became politically emancipated, the question of integration became increasingly urgent and provoked various attempts to define Jewish identity and tradition.

The Synagogue

The synagogue is the religious centre of a Jewish community, at least since the diaspora. Previously this function was exercised by the central temple in Jerusalem, which was destroyed in 70 A.D. The Greek word "synagogue" means "assembly or community," and the synagogue was originally a place for gatherings of any kind. Today it is primarily a place of worship, which revolves around the central reading from the Torah. The Torah Scrolls have long been kept in a special cupboard called the Ark. These are always handwritten copies, rolled around two wooden staves, and protected by a mantle and shield. The tops of the rods are decorated with finials (rimmonim), silver pomegranates or crowns, which express the regal dignity of the scripture. The synagogue has a podium or lectern (bima) as a special place for readings. Before it is read, the Torah Scroll is carried in a solemn procession to the lectern and unrolled there. The reading is in Hebrew, and is traditionally read by a succession of men. Today the prayer leader has a special role in the worship, but not the rabbi. Originally anyone who had studied the Torah intensively and was recognized by the community as a pronouncer of the law was seen as a rabbi. The special role of the community rabbi, who is above all a teacher and arbitrator and who performs marriages, funerals and circumcisions, has only existed since the Middle Ages.

Prayer

It is the Jewish belief that God hears people's prayers and always answers them, although often not in the way people expect. Prayer is seen as speaking to God, as an expression of supplication and gratitude. It must always be said with inner conviction, but at fixed times and on special occasions prayer is said according to particular rules (in this there are similarities with Islam). There are three times for prayer: morning, noon and evening. The core of the daily morning and evening prayer is called "Shema" (referring to Deuteronomy 6:4-9 and 11:13-21, and to Numbers 15:37-41). In the rabbinic era the Amidah or Tefilah were also said mornings and evenings with the Shema. The beginning of the Shema is always "Hear, O Israel …" Apart from ritual prayer there is also personal prayer, and in Judaism prayer is described as "the heart's worship." The heart refers not so much to feeling as to the seat of understanding and insight. In prayer as a dialogue with God, the person goes beyond the monologue and moves towards dialogue as the counterpart to God speaking to people.

JEWISH LIFE

The Jewish Year, Festivals and the Sabbath

The Jewish year is based on the lunar calendar of 354 days, being adapted to the solar year by adding a month in leap years. The fixed calendar has 7 leap years every 19 years. In Biblical times, the beginning of the year could fall in spring (Pesach) or in autumn (Harvest Festival), but autumn (1 Tishri) later became established as the date for the New Year. Since the Middle Ages, the Jewish calendar has begun with the creation of the world, and the Christian year 1240 corresponded to the Jewish year 5000. The year begins with the ten "Days of Awe," the days of reflection, from New Year's Day (1 Tishri) to the Day of Atonement, Yom Kippur (10 Tishri).

The Jewish New Year (Rosh Ha-Shanah) was recorded for the first time in the Mishnah (Torah commentary). New Year is the day of divine judgement; the books in heaven are opened (Talmud) and each creature is judged. Reference is made to this in the New Year liturgy, which includes blowing a ram's horn (shofar) as a reminder of judgement and repentance, and of the final judgement.

Yom Kippur, the Day of Atonement on 10 Tishri, is described in detail in the Bible as a day of strict fasting and rest on which people should serve God as do the angels. It is a day of changing one's ways, repentance and atonement. As a sign of inner change many people wear a white smock when praying on this day, and the synagogue is usually also decorated in white. The liturgy consists of repeated confession of sins and prayers for God's forgiveness (Selichot). The day ends with the closing prayer ne'ila ("to close") and the sounding of the shofar.

A few days after Yom Kippur, the seven day Feast of the Tabernacles (Sukkot) begins. This was originally a harvest festival, and is followed by the feast of "Rejoicing in the Law" (Simhat Torah). People erect a booth with a roof of leaves or twigs in the garden or on the balcony and move into it for the duration of the feast days. It is a particularly joyful festival. Similar to it is the Feast of Weeks (Shavuot), which was originally a festival celebrating the wine harvest. Shavuot is also celebrated as the anniversary of God giving the Torah to Moses on Mount Sinai. The Feast of Pesach, or Passover, out of which the Christian Easter arose, is a very family-centred festival with an elaborate liturgy in the home. It was originally a spring festival (from the Hebrew "pesah" = to leap, lambs gambolling) at which unleavened bread (matzos, flat unleavened cakes) was eaten for seven days, and a sacrificial lamb slaughtered. It is particularly a festival when pilgrimages are made in memory of the exodus of the Israelis from Egypt. As all leaven has to be removed from the house, these rituals gradually developed into thorough house cleaning as a preparation for the feast. The feast includes elaborate customary food and rituals that take place around the table, such as eating bitter herbs and matzos, and reciting the Hallel (Psalms 113 to 118).

Hanukkah, an eight-day Feast of Lights around the winter solstice, goes back to the time of Judas Maccabaeus. In 167 B.C. the Syrian King Antiochus IV desecrated the temple at Jerusalem, but in 164 B.C., following the Maccabean Revolt, it was re-consecrated with a celebratory sacrificial fire. The Feast of Lights commemorates a miracle in which one small jar of oil that had remained ritually pure burnt for 8 days throughout the entire temple consecration festival. Throughout the feast days lights are lit and placed in windows, and the use of candlesticks with 8 candles (menorah) has developed to commemorate the miracle.

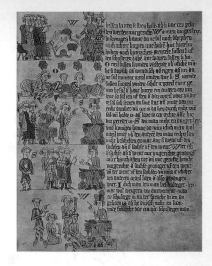

Jews in the Middle Ages
from: Sachsenspiegel, Heidelberg, book illumination, around 1300/1315, parchment

The custom of forcing people of different religious beliefs to wear a mark on their clothing to distinguish them from the majority was first recorded in the 7th century, under Islamic rule. In the western world, Pope Innocent III ordered use of this kind of distinguishing mark in 1215. The pointed hat, originally a normal article of Jewish clothing, was increasingly seen as a stigma. From the 15th century, Jewish men also had to wear yellow patches on their chests and women blue threads on their headwear. The enlightened absolutism of the 18th century abolished these distinguishing marks. As part of their measures to persecute Jews and deprive them of their civil rights, the Nazis issued an order in 1940 requiring Jews to wear the yellow Star of David.

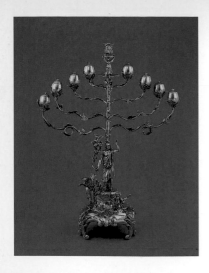

Hanukkah Candleholder
Georg Wilhelm Marggraff, around 1776, solid silver, cast, engraved, Berlin, Stadtmuseum (Jewish Museum)

Hanukkah candleholders, called minorah, are used to commemorate the miracle which occurred when the desecrated temple in Jerusalem was re-consecrated in 164 B.C. Tradition has it that the tiny amount of oil remaining would only have provided enough fuel to keep the temple lamps burning for one day. But the oil lasted for 8 days until new oil was found. For this reason one candle more is lit on each evening of the joyous 8 day festival until all 8 candles burn the final night.

Traditional Jewish Wedding
Contemporary photograph, Israel

The Feast of Purim commemorates the Jews being rescued by God. The Book of Esther tells how, with God's help, the plan of the Persian Wesir Haman to massacre all Jews on a day that would be determined by lot (pur) was sabotaged by Esther, the Jewish wife of the Persian king, and her foster-father Mordecai. The feast days are celebrated by abundant eating and drinking, masked processions and Purim games. Purim gifts are exchanged.

The observance of the sabbath as a day of rest is particularly characteristic of Judaism. The sabbath as the 7th day of the week is a sacred day of rest, like the Christian Sunday and Muslim Friday, linked to God resting after creating the world. For Judaism it also has the additional significance of commemorating the liberation of Israel from slavery in Egypt. It is still a matter of controversy exactly which activities are forbidden on the sabbath and which are exempt from the ban. What is of fundamental importance on the sabbath is not outwardly doing nothing, but rather taking time for self-examination, pausing and reflecting on Jewish tradition; the sabbath is a strength-giving symbol of Judaism. The sabbath meal is prepared the day before, and is meant to be eaten with special solemnity. At the end of the day, a solemn ceremony with benedictions is performed to mark the end of the sabbath (Havdalah = "separation" of the sabbath from the weekdays).

Home, Dress and Dietary Laws

The traditional Jewish house has on the right door-post of the entrance a small case containing parchment scrolls, the mezuzah (literally "door-post"), bearing the text of Deuteronomy 6:4–9 ("Hear, O Israel …) and Deuteronomy 11:13–21. There are very early records of the use of the mezuzah.

The clothing especially typical of Eastern European Jews, and still worn predominantly by strictly Orthodox Hasidic Jews, consists of a black caftan and fur hat (streimel). Pious Jews also wear a small prayer shawl (tallit) over a robe. For particular prayers in the synagogue or at home the men wear tefillin (from the Hebrew "tefillah" = prayer), leather straps attached to small leather boxes containing texts from the Bible. The headwear during prayer is a small, usually black, skull cap called a kippah. In Orthodox circles, the religious hairstyle, consisting of a long beard and sidelocks

that are not cut (as specified in Leviticus 19:27) is meant to emphasize the eternal validity of God's commandments.

The Jewish dietary laws are elaborated in the kashrut (which means "suitability, ritual aptness," and from which the Yiddish term "kosher" is derived). They prescribe a strict separation of clean and unclean animals, and place a special ban on pork. This was probably originally for hygiene reasons (to avoid parasites), but also served to make a distinction between Judaism and other religions.

Cleanliness does not, however, refer to the animals themselves, but to purity before God. Only the meat of clean animals may be eaten and only clean animals may be sacrificed to God. There is also a strict ban on consuming blood, because blood means life and was even once considered to be the seat of the soul. For this reason, animals have to be slaughtered by a special cut to the throat and the blood allowed to drain completely. Islam has adopted these laws in their entire stringency.

Furthermore, consumption of or financial gain from meat and milk together is prohibited. The dietary laws were for a long time extended to reject certain foods that had not been prepared by Jews (were not "kosher") and led to Jews taking their meals separately. It is important that hands are washed before meals, and that the food is blessed by the father of the house. A prayer of thanksgiving is also said before meals.

Rites Surrounding Birth, Death and Burial

In addition to their first name, each child is given a specifically Hebrew name, by which he or she is called to the Torah, and which is used in all religious ceremonies including the prayers said by relatives to commemorate the dead. Eight days after the birth of a boy, the ritual circumcision (B'rith Milah: "Covenant of Circumcision") is carried out in the presence of ten members of the synagogue (previously the whole community) by a specially trained circumciser, the Mohel, who has a high status. The circumcision takes place as a sign of entering into covenant with God, following the pattern set by Abraham (Genesis 17:10 ff; Leviticus 12:3). It is accompanied by prayer, expressions of good wishes and benedictions. Judaism has great respect for the peace of the dead and the intactness of the dead body, and therefore actually prohibits autopsies. Today, however, this rule has been relaxed. Due to the "return to the earth" whence people came, burial is the only possibility in Judaism. Traditionally, the funeral (according to Deuteronomy 21:23) takes place on the day of death or the day after, though this too is sometimes extended nowadays. At the funeral relatives rent their clothing – today usually a symbolic armband – as a sign of grief, and say the Kaddish, an Aramaic prayer which particularly requests the salvation of the deceased.

Reward and Punishment

Judaism developed the idea of divine justice as a system of reward and punishment, and this was later adopted by Christianity and Islam. Behind it is the idea of belief in a compensating and retributional justice, which in turn arose from the concept of a just God, but also God as judge. This, of necessity, led to ideas of the after-life which are not found in older parts of the Bible. They go back to what God said to Moses, i.e. that he would "blot out of his book those who had sinned against him" (Exodus 32:33). Judaism is conscious of the difficulties presented by the diversity of ideas about what form salvation for the righteous will take – paradise, the coming of the Messiah and living in his kingdom, the resurrection of the dead, or reward in this life.

In addition to this, life in the Promised Land is fundamental to Judaism. The ideal of just retribution in this life on earth for actions carried out is borne by the hope that runs contrary to much earthly experience, where, for instance, it is seen that the righteous may suffer and sinners prosper. The hope is fed by the certainty that God examines hearts. The fact that Judaism affirms the "righteous who suffer" in this world is also a contributory factor.

The Afterlife and Resurrection

The belief in a life after death as a permanent connection between God and the righteous has crystallised over time. Early Jewish literature contains no systematic ideas or dogma on life after death, nor to what extent resurrection is to be imagined physically. The idea of resurrection is linked to participation in the Messianic kingdom. Where this was understood in "material" terms, such as living in the Promised Land, people believed in physical resurrection. More sober tendencies concentrate on the spiritual joy of the resurrected.

It is also a matter of controversy whether all people will participate in the resurrection, or whether sinners and the damned will not be resurrected, and the biblical passages which refer to this are inconsistent. Originally there was no doctrine of two natures or double predestination in Judaism. The Pharisees believed that only the righteous will be resurrected, and the Talmud names groups who will not participate in the resurrection: the arrogant and ignorant, the race of the deluge, the clan of Korah and certain individuals. In rabbinic literature, the idea emerges that those who deny the resurrection will not themselves be resurrected.

ESCHATOLOGY AND MESSIANIC EXPECTATIONS

Hope of Redemption

Eschatology and messianism are closely connected in Judaism, although they do not necessarily always concur. Eschatology is characterized by the idea that God is the First and Last, and that history unfolds between creation and completion. Through history God has led the people of Israel out of slavery and will continue the process through to redemption. Judaism is the historical religion par excellence, and under God's guidance history becomes the history of redemption. For this reason, Judaism, unlike Christianity, makes no distinction between secular history and the history of redemption. The knowledge that God was the First engenders hope in God as the Last.

Teaching about the Messiah is at the centre of the Jewish religion of hope. This belief gives the strength to hope, and the devout Jew can be characterized as a "hopeful person." The question as to the historical moment when the messianic age will "enter into" history is a difficult one. The relationship between the coming of the Messiah and people's readiness for his coming has concerned Jewish thinkers throughout the ages, and in this century Ernst Bloch, Walter Benjamin and Gershom Scholem in particular.

According to Schmarjahu Talmon, it is possible to distinguish in Jewish thought between a "restorative messianism," based on the idea of a "golden age" at the beginning of the history

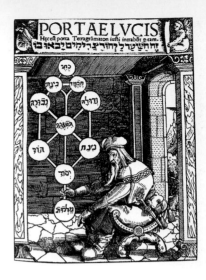

The Sefirotic Tree (Kabbalah)
from: Paulus Ricius, Porta Lucis, woodcut, Augsburg, 1516

Kabbalah is the term used since the 13th century for Jewish mysticism. Its aim is to achieve mystical union with God, and knowledge of the last hidden things. Using a code of letters and numbers, a hidden meaning is found in each sentence and symbol in the Bible. Central to kabbalah is the doctrine of the 10 sefirot or spheres which are often depicted in the form of a tree or a human being.

The 10 spheres of the sefirotic tree represent the 10 primal numbers or powers of creation or, in the kabbalistic "Book of Bahir," the 10 Divine Emanation powers. These are arranged in a particular pattern, and interact with one another to determine all that happens in the world. Through faith and obedience to the Torah they can be positively influenced by the people of Israel.

Gravestone of Rabbi Löw in the Old Jewish Cemetery in Prague

Masada, Aerial View of the Fortress
Photograph, 1980

The former hill fortress of Masada is on the western shore of the Dead Sea, and is one of the national symbols of Israel. Here recruits are sworn on oath and communal Bar Mitzvah ceremonies are celebrated. After the Holy City of Jerusalem and the temple had been destroyed in 70 A.D. by Roman troops and the population driven out of the city, over 900 men, women and children fled to this fortress, according to the reports of Flavius Josephus. For three years they put up tough opposition, until the Romans finally managed to penetrate the fortress. The resistance fighters killed themselves to avoid captivity.

of Israel, approximately during the reign of King David, and a "utopian messianism," which awaits a universal kingdom of peace, love and justice, with features that have not yet existed in history. But there is also a merging of the two positions, for instance in the teaching on the "coming of the prince of peace." Restorative messianism began to express itself particularly in Zionism and the State of Israel Movement; utopian messianism expressed itself particularly in the different variations of socialism and communism with strong elements of salvation (to some extent as early as Karl Marx, but more especially with Leo Trotsky, Rosa Luxemburg, Gustav Landauer, Kurt Eisner, Ernst Bloch and others).

Messianism is a fundamental element of post-Biblical Judaism, although it does refer to the statements made in the Bible. The Talmudic tradition distinguishes two types of Messiah figure: the Messiah Ben-Joseph, who is a suffering and subservient Messiah, and the Messiah Ben-David, the son of David, who is a triumphant and victorious Messiah. It is thought that the Messiah Ben-Joseph will prefigure the Messiah Ben-David. Judaism expects the Messiah to bring salvation from all suffering and evil. Salvation has to be a publicly visible and perceptible process, and after the Messiah has come, history cannot simply go on as before with its wars, injustices and suffering. According to Schalom Ben-Chorin, Judaism expects the Coming, not the Second Coming (as Christianity does for example in the figure of Jesus Christ).

Particularly since the 19th century, Jewish messianism has undergone a process of secularization in the form of Zionism and Socialism or Marxism, although without entirely sacrificing its specific beliefs. Jewish messianism has to prove itself by the kingdom or society that results from it. Thus Moses Hess (1812–1875), for example, speaks of the arrival of the messianic day as the "Sabbath of History." Also for thinkers such as Hermann Cohen (1842–1918) and Walter Benjamin (1892–1940), messianism is a category of historical philosophy.

Eschatology and messianism belong together because for Judaism, history and the history of redemption belong together: the "Kingdom of God" (Martin Buber) has to be a visible kingdom. The Kingdom of the Messiah is thought of as a kingdom of the "Anointed King" (Ha-Melech Ha-Maschiach), regardless of the fact that the historical kings of Israel – with the possible exception of David – were not ideal characters. Generally speaking, messianism is one of the central elements of Jewish faith, but it is nevertheless not so clearly and obviously fixated on a particular historical figure (such as Christianity is on Jesus Christ for example). This can be seen in the fact that in Jewish scriptures the messiah has different names.

THE HISTORY OF THE PEOPLE OF ISRAEL

Biblical Times

The history of Israel is inextricably linked in time and place to the Middle East, particularly to Palestine. The culture of the land of Mesopotamia and of the "fertile crescent" with its highly developed societies (Hethite, Sumerian, Babylonian, Assyrian and others) is central, although there was also a special connection with Egypt and the Nile. And yet the nomadic tribal culture that was early Israel – with its history of acquiring land, moving on and being driven out – was also characterized by the desert. The proximity of Egypt, Assyria and Babylonia led to Israel being repeatedly invaded by these dominant kingdoms.

The story of Israel's development is linked in the Hebrew Bible with the legend of the flood, in which Noah survives to become the founding progenitor or father of a new mankind. His eldest son, Sem, is regarded as the father of the Semitic peoples named after him, including the

Arabs. Abraham, whose grandsons Jacob and Esau again founded different tribes, also descended from Sem. The 12 tribes that made up "Israel" were founded by Jacob's 12 sons. The so-called "Age of the Patriarchs" is historically difficult to comprehend. What is important is that in this period the people settled in one place and turned away from local gods to worship Yahveh, the One God of the Covenant. The link to Egypt stems from the fact that, of the 12 sons of Jacob, who represent the subsequent 12 tribes of Israel, Joseph was sold to the Egyptians. The time in Egypt came to an end when Moses led the people of Israel out of slavery, an event strongly linked to the "identity" of the people of Israel as documented in the Decalogue and the idea of the Promised Land (Book of Exodus). God confirmed the bond of the covenant and himself "settled" in the divine Mount Sinai. The tribe of Levi became outstanding as the tribe of priests (Levites).

The territory was marked out by the tribes of Israel advancing into West and East Jordan (Palestine), which involved conquering or driving out other tribes (Book of Joshua). The authority of Joshua as the successor of Moses safeguarded the distribution of land. The battle against the Canaanites was always depicted as the victory of Yahveh over the enemy's gods. The division of the people of Israel into 12 tribes with different territories was retained, the period in which the tribes lived together before an actual state was formed being known as the "Time of Judges." Outstanding individuals emerged in different tribes, the most significant of whom was the charismatic leader Gideon (Book of Judges).

The organizational difficulties of tribal culture led to a single kingdom being formed under the great kings Saul, David and Solomon. The kingship of Saul, who was actually a warrior king, came about both by Yahveh's designation (the will of God) and by the acclamation of the people, or rather the tribes. David is seen as embodying the ideal king, who consolidated the kingdom by excellent organization and gave Jerusalem special status, including religious significance, as the centre of the kingdom, although he actually ruled two kingdoms: the Northern Kingdom of Israel and the Southern Kingdom of Judah. David is said to have ruled for 40 years, probably between 1004–964 B.C. His son Solomon is known as the king of peace and justice (the "Judgement of Solomon") who built up trade relations with neighboring kingdoms and built the Temple in Jerusalem. His reign is thought to have been around 964–926 B.C.

The time that followed is characterized by confusion and internal power struggles. The kingdom was divided into the Kingdom of Israel in the north, and Judah in the south, each having its own line of kings. The kingdom of Israel was, generally speaking, less stable than the kingdom of Judah. Both kingdoms were ruled at times by kings with dubious abilities (heredi-

Pogroms: Plundering the Judengasse in Frankfurt in 1614
From: Johann Ludwig Gottfried, Chronica, coloured copper engraving by Matthäus Merian, Frankfurt, 1619, re-coloured.

Throughout history false accusations were repeatedly made against the Jews. As a result, they were expelled from German cities, where they were forced to live in slums or ghettos. Although most people knew it was untrue, they were accused of ritual murders, desecrating the host, poisoning wells or spreading the plague. Their opponents used every opportunity to take bloody revenge on them. For example, the rumor was spread that the Talmud demanded the murder of Christians, and the disappearance of a Christian child was held as "proof" of this. Jews were also made responsible for economic crises. In 1614 members of guilds in Frankfurt accused them of usury, and plundered the Judengasse.

Theodor Herzl
Portrait around 1900

The journalist and writer, Theodor Herzl, was the founder of Zionism. The Dreyfus affair in France made him realize that the Jews had to form a nation and found their own separate state. His work, "The Jewish State," published in 1896, was the inspiration for the founding of the Zionist Movement. As president of the World Zionist Organization, he conducted numerous negotiations with politicians and thus created many of the essential requirements for the founding of the state of Israel in 1948.

tary dynasties), which is why many prophets appeared in this period, predicting disaster.

Both kingdoms were overshadowed by the up-and-coming Assyrian (Syrian) Empire and were drawn into its policy of expansion. Thus, in 733 B.C. the state of Israel came under military occupation and became in effect a province of Assyria, with the last vestiges of autonomy disappearing in 722 B.C. Judah was able to maintain its independence under difficult conditions, but was under constant threat from the Assyrians. At the end of the 7th century B.C. the gradual decline of Assur began, accompanied by the rise of Babylon, which led initially to Judah being liberated from Assyrian clutches (period of restoration under King Josiah, 640-609 B.C.). Under the Babylonian King Nebuchadnezzar (605–562 B.C.), the Kingdom of Judah and its capital, Jerusalem, were conquered, in 587/86, and the Jews taken into "Babylonian captivity."

The time of Babylonian exile until 538 B.C. brought about a grave identity crisis for Judaism, with the prophets urging the people to maintain their faith in Yahveh. With the supremacy of the Persians (from 539 B.C.), the Jews were allowed to return to their homeland. The entire region remained under Persian rule, but the Jews were allowed religious autonomy. The Temple of Solomon in Jerusalem, destroyed by Nebuchadnezzar, was rebuilt and consecrated in 515. Internally, the leaders Ezra and Nehemiah worked to re-establish the orthodox faith and reorder social conditions.

The early days of Greek supremacy and Alexander the Great are hardly documented at all in the Hebrew Bible. However, the Jews, despite being caught between Persia and Egypt, did manage to assert themselves. In the meantime the country was divided into two administrative provinces, (Jerusalem-) Judah and Samaria. As there were no longer any royal dynasties, the high priests gained in importance, formed their own dynasties and were responsible for the fact that the legal regulations took on a certain rigidity. When the Alexandrian Empire was divided after 323 B.C., Israel was caught between two rival dynasties who were fighting each other, the Egyptian Ptolemites and the Seleucids. The Book of Daniel chronicles the confusion of this time. Eventually the Seleucids occupied the country and the city of Jerusalem. The Jews were initi-

ally granted religious and cultural autonomy until Antiochus IV Epiphanes (175–164 B.C.) attempted to forcibly impose Hellenistic practices on Jewish culture and religion. This provoked the Jews to a revolt which is known as the Maccabean Revolt, after the leading family of high priests. It was sparked off by the prohibition of sacrifices in the Temple of Jerusalem. In the warfare that followed (168–164 B.C.), particularly led by Judas Maccabaeus, the Jews were victorious and resumed their religious practices.

In 142 B.C. the supremacy of the high priests and popular leaders (including kings) was established from the Hasmonean dynasty (until 40 B.C.), while the entire region gradually became a province under Roman rule. The Jews were caught up in constant warfare and revolts. In literature, a number of apocalyptic visions date from this time and had lasting influence which extended to John's Apocalypse in the Christian New Testament. Numerous sects grew up, such as the Essenes of Qumran. The high point of this cultural epoch was the rule of Herod the Great (37–4 B.C.) and his successors with the approval of Rome. Uprisings against the taxes levied by Rome and Rome's religious demands, such as making sacrifices in front of the Emperor's image, led to a punitive expedition under Titus, in which the temple and large parts of Jerusalem were destroyed in 70 A.D. and the "scattering of the Jews into all countries of the world" (diaspora) began. Judea's last great rebellion against Roman rule took place in 132–135 A.D. under Bar Kochba.

Post-Biblical Times

Post-Biblical Judaism is characterized by its spiritual conflict not only with Hellenism but also with Christianity and Gnosticism, and later with Islam. It must be said, however, that the mutual influences are complex. The Jewish Apocrypha and apocalyptic texts were written in the 1st and 2nd century A.D. and the expectation that the coming of the Messiah was nigh inspired the Bar Kochba revolt. The rabbinic tradition (Mishnah, Babylonian Talmud) ensured spiritual coherence under the conditions of the diaspora. Even in the Classical Age, under the Greeks and Romans, there was some strong resentment against Jews. The Jewish population was accused of religious autonomy and reproached for the radicality and exclusiveness of their monotheism. Towards the end of the Classical Age a large number of Jews still leaved in the Near East, but many had emigrated to the Mediterranean area and Southern Europe.

In Europe the Jews were subjected to waves of increasing intolerance, and in certain epochs to the missionary zeal of Christians, and as early as the late Middle Ages they were living in ghettos in the cities. By contrast, early Islam, particularly in Spain, was in general tolerant towards Jews who were allowed to hold various state posts (since the 10th century there had been official "court Jews" in Cordoba), were held in high esteem as doctors and scholars, and participated actively in the philosophical discourse of the (Islamic) Middle Ages. Their most significant thinker was Moses Maimonides (1135–1204), who made a great contribution to systematizing and formulating the Jewish faith.

The Jews underwent great suffering in Europe and the Middle East at the time of the Crusades from the end of the 11th century. There were pogroms, sacking and pillaging, forced baptisms and persecutions in many central European cities. In 1205 the Pope wrote a clearly anti-Jewish statement in which he declared the Jews to be "eternal slaves" in order to "atone" for the murder of Jesus Christ. This was followed by clothing regulations and other discriminatory measures (Emperor's protection in return for paying a tax, regulations on

compulsory baptism) and many cities financially blackmailed their Jews. In Medieval Europe the Jews, having been excluded from public office and many occupations (guilds), worked mainly as moneylenders, pawnbrokers and merchants. From the 14th century, and particularly after the expulsion of the Moors in 1492, persecution and oppression of the large Jewish communities in Spain increased, with many of the Jews living there forced to emigrate to the Maghreb or Orient.

Between the 16th and 18th centuries, inspired by the mystical tradition of the medieval kabbalah, a number of messianic movements grew up with charismatic leaders, the most famous of which was the "Messiah" Sabbatai Zwi (1626–1676) from Smyrna. "Sabbatianism" was brought to the west by pupils and follow-

Jews at their Market Stall in Lodz
Photograph around 1915/16, taken during the German occupation of Poland in World War 1.

The Jews who emigrated to Lodz in the mid-19th century must take most of the credit for the rapid development of the textile industry there. They soon set up their own small businesses or traded in textiles, and Jewish workers were also employed in the hand weaving trade.
Eastern European Jews developed their own culture and tradition in cities such as Warsaw, Lodz, Lublin, Kaunas, Riga, and Vilnius. German troops, working with local anti-Semitic forces, destroyed most of this during World War 2.

The Railway Gate to the Death Camp of Auschwitz-Birkenau
Photograph, 1945

Auschwitz, the largest German concentration camp, has become a synonym for the racist Nazi program to annihilate the Jews of Europe. This death factory, unprecedented in history, was built, steadily extended and modernized with the sole aim of wiping out human lives in the most barbaric way. In 1942, the mass murders began. In gas chambers camouflaged as showers, up to 6,000 people were murdered each day, and more than a million people were killed here in Auschwitz-Birkenau alone. They came from every corner of Europe that was occupied by Germany during World War II. Today the complex is a museum and a place of remembrance, ensuring that the crimes perpetrated against the Jewish people in the 20th century will not be forgotten.

Wailing Wall in Jerusalem
Western retaining wall of the
Temple Square, built after 20 B.C.

The Western Wall, also known as
the Wailing Wall, is all that remains
of the wall that surrounded the
temple built by Herod. Since the
16th century it has been a place for
Jews to assemble and pray, but also
to lament the destruction of the
temple in 70 A.D. The Wailing Wall,
at which Bar Mitzvah celebrations
are still held, became a national
symbol when, after the Six Day War,
the Israeli government demolished
the adjoining buildings and re-
designed the area in front of it to
create a holy site.

ers of Zwi and spread particularly throughout
Poland and the Hapsburg Empire. In Eastern
Europe Hasidism grew up in the 18th century,
a movement towards more feeling, emotion
and piety. Separate communities were formed
within Judaism which met with opposition
from Orthodox rabbis. Nevertheless, Hasidism
exercised a great attraction on Judaism in
Eastern Europe.

From the end of the 16th century until the 18th
century, the Viennese courts and some
German courts entrusted so-called "court
Jews" with the management of their financial
affairs. The Age of the Enlightenment brought
equal rights for Jews in public and legal matters above all through the civil legislation of the
Napoleonic Code. Opposition to Jews being
integrated and having equal legal status arose
after the Congress of Vienna in 1815, but initially only took the form of a media campaign.
Vicious anti-Semitic pamphlets and racist theories were distributed, supported in France and
Germany by numerous members of universities and conservative intellectuals. The emancipation of Jews never established itself in
Eastern Europe, and the Jewish populations in
the Polish and Russian areas of influence were
subjected to repeated pogroms.

In Germany, Austria and France various political parties took up the cause of anti-Semitism.
It was in these countries, in particular, that

since the turn of the century anti-Semitism had
been ideologically underlined by equating
Jews with the Bolshevists (communists) or
"international finance Judaism" and a "Jewish
global conspiracy" was construed.

Anti-Semitism reached a horrendous climax of
unprecedented dimensions from 1933 to
1945 during the Nazi regime in Germany
under Adolf Hitler. Malicious anti-Semitic campaigns, notably propagated by the magazine
"Der Stürmer" (stormtrooper), were intended to
prepare the way for the German people to tol-
erate and perpetuate the marginalization and
persecution of the Jews. Measures escalated
from targeted discrimination (boycott of Jewish
businesses from 1933, Nuremberg Race Laws
in 1935) to pogroms ("Kristallnacht" in 1938)
to systematic massacre after the outbreak of
World War II. From 1939 onwards, Jews
within the German sphere of influence, particularly in Eastern Europe, were systematically
recorded and marked out for annihilation. At
the Wannsee Conference in January 1942 the
SS and various branches of the police insti-
gated the decision to organize the annihilation
of the Jews (in Nazi terminology described as
the "Final Solution to the Jewish Question").
From March 1942 onwards, extermination
camps were built in the east, with Auschwitz,
Majdanek, Sobibor and Treblinka being lasting
symbols of this horror.

At the same time, the annihilation of the last
remaining Jewish Ghettos in the east (such as
Warsaw and Vilnius) began. In the same year
the deportation of Jews from the occupied
countries in the west to the extermination
camps in the east started, continuing until the
collapse of the reign of terror (end of 1944
until May 1945).

The Promised Land

There is scarcely a passage of any length in the
Torah that does not refer to God's promise to
Abraham and his descendants concerning the
land of Canaan. Rabbinic literature describes
the Holy Land as the "centre of the world," yet
even the Bible is aware of the fact that other
peoples lived in the country. Judaism has two
answers to this problem: a) the tribes living in
the country have committed so many sins that
the land has become desecrated; or b) no people
has a right to possess a country, since the earth
belongs to the Lord alone. The idea is thus that

the land was lent by God and was only "on loan." The concept of being God's chosen people is considered to be one the mysteries of Judaism, but so too is the idea of God "residing" in the Holy Land. The concepts of being God's chosen people and the promise of the Holy Land are intimately connected in Judaism.

Even after the temple of Jerusalem had been destroyed and the Jews scattered in foreign lands, the holiness of the country and the promise of it remained. Many Jews see living in the Holy Land as a religious obligation, comparable to the commandments of the Torah, and accepted the rule of a succession of foreign powers (Seleucids, Romans, Arabs, Crusaders). Nostalgia and yearning for the Promised Land are a thread running through the entire Jewish scriptures; the exodus from Egypt is also linked to the arrival in the Promised Land as a "homecoming."

Exile (Galuth)

In Biblical times the people of Israel were led out of the Holy Land into Babylonian captivity. But even in exile, God never abandoned his people. This is an important conviction in the faith of all Jews, the only thing which made it at all possible for them to live in exile. Even after the second great expulsion of the Jews in 70 A.D., the conviction remained that God allowed the faithful to suffer in exile only to ultimately lead them back after these tests.

Exile was, and still is, seen as a test of faith of the "suffering servant of the Lord," which leads not only to the atonement of the sins of their own people but of all who were chosen to bear this heavy fate. The task of Jews in exile is to remain true to God and never forget the Promised Land. Many documents of exile bear witness to the fear of the Talmudists and scholars that in the diaspora the Jews could merge with or be submerged in the culture of the country of exile or could despair of there being any hope of a return to the Promised Land.

Returning Home: the Zionist Movement and the State of Israel

Zionism was the response to the failed civic emancipation of Jews. It was, however, also a revolutionary movement in 19th century Eastern Europe against the lethargy and fatalism of the Jewish communities there to anti-Semitic attacks and pogroms. A consideration of a state of Israel began, accompanied by the idea of letting the economic and social achievements of Jews benefit the Jews themselves. The fact that Jews belonged together regardless of national origins was also emphasized.

Preparatory work was done by the Jewish emigration or rather immigration movements and the establishment of Jewish colonies (settlements) in Palestine. From the mid-19th century, Jewish settlers bought plots of land there. More people joined the movement after the Jewish pogroms in Russia in 1881/82.

The outstanding figure of political Zionism was the writer Theodor Herzl (1860-1904) who convened the First Zionist Congress in Basle in 1897, drew up a settlement programme for Palestine and negotiated with the British mandate authorities. The Zionist efforts were given political impetus by the British government's "Balfour Declaration" of 1917, in which Great Britain supported certain settlement programmes in Palestine.

Jewish settlement in the country became acute during and directly after World War II, after which British and Arab powers tried to place quotas on the number of Jews immigrating into Palestine, or even to stop it all together. The young combative kibbuzim movement grew up, which founded settlement colonies and energetically went about the task of making the land fertile. In 1947, after bloody conflicts, the UN passed a resolution which divided Palestine into a Jewish and an Arab state. This was followed by the Jewish National Council in Palestine declaring the founding and independence of the State of Israel in May 1948. In its dramatic history to date it has tried to maintain a balance between self-assertion vis-a-vis its neighbours and a policy of dialogue with the surrounding Arab countries.

Yad Vashem Memorial

In August 1953 the Israeli parliament passed a resolution to set up a central national memorial for the heroes and the millions of victims of the Shoah. Yad Vashem contains a library, archives and a museum. The name Yad Vashem comes form a verse in Isaiah (56:5) "... to them I will give in My house and within My walls a monument and a memorial." Leading up to the memorial is an avenue of trees planted for the "Righteous amongst the Peoples," for all those who in times of persecution and oppression preserved their humanity and helped those who were persecuted.

CHRISTIANITY

As the world religion with the greatest number of adherents, Christianity, through its extensive missionary work, has spread across all continents. Its concept of God is rooted in Judaism, but the centre of its faith is Jesus Christ, Son of God and Son of Man, and his unique act of salvation. Christianity's trinitarian concept of God was, however, only formulated after long debates. The Christian church was formed after the Pentecost experience of the apostles. During the Middle Ages, the church attained an unprecedented position of power – both spiritual and secular – mainly through the institution of the Roman papacy. The Reformation led to an inner renewal of the religion, but also to a schism within the Christian church. Today the stronger self-confidence of non-European Christianity is beginning to have a more marked influence.

Adoration of the Kings
Rogier van der Weyden, c. 1455
Central panel of the altar of the three kings, Munich, Alte Pinakothek, detail

In line with the early Christian community's conviction that Jesus had a divine mission, even the oldest of New Testament records re-interprets the birth of the Saviour as a supernatural mystical event (virgin birth), and transform it into a miracle. Central elements of the Christian message were integrated into the birth legend: Jesus's turning to the poor and disempowered (circumstances of the birth, stable, manger); annunciation and witness of the community (annunciation to the shepherds); the message's claim to universality (adoration of the Magi); and persecution (infanticide in Bethlehem).
With the rise of the cult of the Virgin Mary in the late Middle Ages, the "event at Bethlehem" became a central motif in Christian art.

THE CHRISTIAN CONCEPT OF GOD

God the Father

In its concept of God, and particularly the idea of God the Father, Christianity has a great deal in common with Judaism (and Islam), partly due to the fact that the Hebrew Bible was incorporated into the canon of Christian scriptures as the Old Testament (OT). God revealed Himself and described himself ("I am who I am"). He is the creator of all things, including humankind, with whom he has made a covenant. He announced his commandments to humankind, and is the Lord of history and of judgement.

However, where Christianity differs from Judaism is that in the New Testament (NT) God the Father repeatedly speaks of Jesus Christ as his son (e.g. Matthew 3:17, Mark 1:11, Luke 3:22). Furthermore, when he is dying on the cross, Jesus commits his spirit into the hands of the Father, and with his resurrection proves that the Father is the God of life. St John's Gospel and the apostle Paul, in particular, deal with aspects of God's revelation of himself, and link God the Father with Christology.

Christian thinkers, particularly during the patristic age and from the Middle Ages through early modernity, have wrestled with many problematic issues: God the Father who was in the beginning, the questions raised by the oneness of God (monotheism despite Jesus Christ and the Holy Spirit as further

aspects of the divine), God's omniscience and whether he predetermines all events (predestination), and God's omnipotence. Another debate is the paradox of theodicy, that is, how and to what extent a good and just and omnipotent God is responsible for evil in the world. Evil (personified) is depicted as having been created by God – in the form of the fallen angel Lucifer, who fell from grace as a result of his own arrogance – but also as God's "partner" and opponent or rival in designing the order of salvation. Satan takes advantage of human freedom and tempt an individual to turn away from God or do evil.

God the Son: Jesus Christ

Before looking at the historical Jesus, we must first of all look at the divine functions of Christ. Jesus Christ is the central leading figure and, as is evident from the name, the "centre" of Christianity. His manifestation is directly connected with the salvation of creation and the redemption of humankind. In his Sermon on the Mount he gave his followers a new ethos, the religion of love, which at one and the same time fulfils and replaces the old (Jewish) religion.

For a long time the question of how to understand the person of Jesus Christ caused difficulties: as "begotten" of the Father from the beginning, as the Word of God (logos) that was always with God – as the prologue to John's Gospel puts it – or merely as an outstanding person "adopted" by God. At any rate God

becomes incarnate in humankind in the person of Jesus Christ ("The Word became flesh," John 1:14) who voluntarily takes upon himself the suffering of earthly existence, is largely not recognized, and is finally executed, taking upon himself, with his death and resurrection, the sins of humankind: Jesus as the "new Adam" or "last Adam." The historical uniqueness of this act of salvation determines the entire Christian view of history. Alongside rational and historical features (Jesus as a charismatic itinerant preacher), Christology contains a number of highly speculative, messianic and ascetic ideas. Jesus's claim to prepare the way for God's kingdom of justice, which he described as being more in the next world than this ("My kingdom is not of this world"), was initially a disappointment to the more political messianic tendencies in the intellectually restless Jewish milieu around him, where the coming of a king from the House of David was expected. This transcending of the old expectations was linked in early Christianity to Jesus (physically) resurrecting the dead, and led to the apocalyptic expectation that the kingdom of God was imminent, a belief that was only gradually abandoned.

Jesus's crucifixion was incorporated into the idea of the Son of Man as the "suffering servant of God" or "suffering Son of God" which go back to Old Testament Jewish examples of the suffering righteous (Job). The early Christians chose the cross as their symbol of identification, and in so doing transformed the instrument of humiliating death into a "symbol of victory" – something which their milieu at the time had difficulty in understanding. By venerating the cross and the crucifixion scene a cult grew up around Mary the mother of God, and later the "sorrowful mother." Ancient Oriental mother deities and ideas of purity important in the mystery religions played a role in this cult. This can be regarded as an emancipation of the feminine element within an otherwise entirely male concept of God, particularly through her connection to the wisdom of heaven (Sophia).

The Holy Spirit

Of the three persons of God, the Holy Spirit is the most difficult to comprehend, yet it can be recognized through its actions. In Catholic doctrine proceeding from the Father and the Son (filioque), in Orthodox doctrine proceeding

from the Father alone, the Holy Spirit is seen as the actual creative element in the lives of Christians and the church. It produces order and tradition and yet can also have revolutionary effects. It is the living and "life-giving" spirit (Paul) whose power first became evident at Pentecost when the disciples, despondent after Jesus's ascension to heaven, were inspired by the spirit to go forth in the world and spread the gospel. This event is seen as the birth of the church. The church takes or derives its authority to bind and loosen ties on earth, with the power of the sacraments and the continuity of its development, from the Holy Spirit.

By contrast, the revolutionary element of the Spirit shows itself mainly in the actions of all Christian charismatics, from Joachim of Fiore and the radical Franciscan spirituality, through Savonarola and Thomas Müntzer, up to the later reformers and saints who invoked its power. They understand the revelation of the Holy Spirit as a charismatic continuation of prophecy, which repeatedly collides with the more conservative power of the Holy Spirit, controlled by the church, working through tradition, continuity and service to God.

The Holy Trinity: Speculation and Dogma

The early professions of faith in the NT mention the Trinity of Father, Son and Holy Spirit (e.g. Matthew 28:19, 2 Corinthians 13:13 or Romans

Crucifixion
Mathias Gothart Grünewald, ca. 1513/15, side panel of the Isenheim altar, Unterlinden Museum, Colmar

The crucifixion of Jesus, interpreted as his sacrifice and suffering (passion) for the sins of humankind, is a liberating and joyous message at the centre of Christian doctrine. Starting with the meal shared with his disciples (Last Supper) and the night vigil in the Garden of Gethsemane, followed by arrest, derision, sentencing for blasphemy and carrying the cross, the passion ends in Jesus's agonizing abandonment on the cross, and shows the Son of God in the darkest hour of his human existence. Reflection on the central significance of his death on the cross for the Christian faith was one of the points of departure for the Reformation. To his depiction of the crucified Christ, famous for its expressiveness, Grünewald adds the figure of Mary Magdalene, accompanied by the "disciple whom he loved" (John 19:26), the Old Testament symbol of the sacrificial lamb, and John the Baptist as the one who pointed the way to the Messiah. John the Baptist's facial features in this painting are possibly those of the painter.

Altar of the Resurrection
Hans Memling, c. 1485/90, Paris, Musée du Louvre

The belief that Jesus Christ rose from the dead after he had been laid in the tomb accounts for the certainty of early Christianity that Jesus of Nazareth, who overcame death, was without doubt the Messiah prophesied in the Old Testament, and the incarnate Son of God. Although he did not establish the kingdom of God on earth, for believers his victory over death ended the bondage to existential anxiety and fear of death. Attempts to find natural explanations for the disappearance of the corpse were not able to diminish this faith, although they did contribute to the resurrection story being embellished (the tomb being guarded). Since the victory over death and breaking through the supremacy of natural laws gave Christ omnipotence over time and space, nature and psyche, Memling surrounded the picture of the victorious, resurrected Christ with scenes from legends of the saints.

1:3 f), but without clearly formulating the oneness of God. In other words, the NT contains no doctrine about one God in three persons. However, the statements of the New Testament on the revelation, and particularly the statements of Jesus himself, are steered in a direction that is then formulated as a unity of revelation: God reveals himself in the Holy Spirit through Christ. Early Judaeo-Christianity had no explicit doctrine on the Trinity.

Later formulations of dogma on the Trinity incorporated not only the thinking of Paul, but also Greek-Hellenistic speculation, taken particularly from neo-Platonic philosophy (Plotinus, Proclus). Corresponding questions were discussed by the Church Fathers in a complex and often very controversial form. The main issue concerned the position of Jesus Christ: was he truly God or only half God, and did his divinity not jeopardize the oneness and transcendence of God the Father.

The Adoptionists, for example, assumed that Jesus was originally an outstanding human being who at his baptism was "adopted" by God as his son. The Arians sparked off a grave crisis of direction in the early church: the presbyter Arius claimed that Jesus was not of one being with the Father but only of a similar being (homoiousios). After arduous struggles, the Christian dogma that the son is of one being with the father (homoousios) was adopted. Against the Monophysites, who wanted to recognize only one nature in Jesus, namely the divine nature, the dogma of the two natures – the divine and the human in the one person of Jesus Christ – asserted itself in the 6th century: Christ is "truly human and truly divine."

The Council of Nicaea (Nicaea, 325 A.D.), headed by Emperor Constantine, was important for the drafting of an ecumenical creed (Nicene Creed) intended to be binding for all the regional churches. At the same time, during its period of transition to becoming a state church (392), the early church developed increasing intolerance to people within its own ranks who held divergent opinions, and involved state authority in its theological arguments.

The Council of Constantinople (381) formulated for the first time the Christian dogma of the Trinity and the "Niceno-Constantinopolitan Creed" which is essentially still valid today. However, in the following centuries there were repeated vehement controversies about various points of the dogma of the Trinity. The Latin Church Father, Augustine (354–430), can be regarded as one of the most significant formulators of the doctrine of the Trinity as it is valid today, by placing the Trinity of God at the centre of Christian dogma.

THE CHRISTIAN VIEW OF MANKIND

Freedom, Sin and Grace

The point of departure for Christianity, as for Judaism and Islam, is the statement that God created humankind in his own image (Genesis 1:27). Thus God recognizes himself in humankind, and human beings are partners in God's revelation of himself. Two ideas follow from the belief that man was made in God's image: a) human beings are entirely dependent on God; and b) human beings, because they are made in God's image, are different from all other creatures. Human beings have a spirit (soul) and body, which originally, in the legacy of Judaic thought, were seen in unity or connection. Due to the influence of Greek-Hellenistic thought on Paul and the Church Fathers, a certain body-soul dualism developed which led to a devaluation of the body (the "flesh").

Despite affirming God's omniscience and the theory that all events have been predetermined by God, Christianity stresses the freedom of human beings, which also allows them make a choice which is morally bad or which goes against reason. Human beings thus have the freedom to turn away from God, which is why the idea of the sinfulness of human beings plays such a major role in Christianity. It is the only one of the major monotheistic religions to link evil in the world since Adam and Eve's fall from paradise to the idea of the "original sin" of humankind, from which the universal role of savior for Jesus Christ as the "last Adam" evolved. Disorder, evil and suffering in the world are caused by the misuse of human freedom. Through original sin, all human beings and the entire world are in need of redemption – which is why the act of salvation Jesus Christ performed when he became man (incarnation) applies to all people. And yet human freedom in Christianity is also the prerequisite for human love. In the spirit of the Sermon on the Mount, people are called upon to love their neighbors as themselves and to do good for them, to forgive and make peace with them, since it is possible to encounter Christ in one's neighbor ("What you have done for the least of my brothers you have also done for me").

Since early Christianity knew no body-soul dualism, the resurrection idea has a material aspect, Christianity believing not only in the immortality of the soul, but also in the resurrection of the body. The very idea of the incarnation of God in human form and the personhood of Jesus Christ has meant that the personhood of all human beings in their physical and spiritual aspects gains a unique status. This view has fundamentally influenced the entire thinking on subjectivity and individuality in the western world.

Christianity is committed to the universal ability of human beings to love as the path to perfection of the individual. The Christian idea of being chosen is in many respects similar to that of Judaism, and is in Christianity also linked to the interpretation of history as the history of salvation. Acceptance of Christ's sacrificial death is the prerequisite for salvation of all people who know the story.

For the church, correct belief is a prerequisite for redemption, in other words the believer's agreement with the teachings of the church.

In Protestantism, faith is strongly linked to the grace of God that forgives sins, while for Catholic doctrine God's grace is an important prerequisite for salvation, but the individual also has to participate in his own salvation to the best of his abilities. For Protestantism, human beings can do nothing without the grace of God, they have to surrender completely to divine grace. However, the practical consequences of this attitude with regard to human capabilities and actions in the world are interpreted very differently by the individual Protestant churches. While Luther conceded that human beings have autonomy, Calvin, with his idea of "double predestination" (to salvation as well as to damnation), saw people as being able to change only very little of their predetermined fate.

Christian Eschatology and Ideas of the Afterlife

God as the just judge considers the deeds of human beings, rewarding the righteous and punishing sinners. Final retribution for deeds performed in this life does not take place until life on this earth is over, with the righteous going on to eternal life. Yet the NT gives only a few details of paradise, such as the bliss of looking upon God, eating at the Lord's table or claiming that God rules from eternity to eternity (Matthew 19:28). It was only later that authors began to embellish ideas of heaven and hell. Those who died having committed unpardoned cardinal sins go to hell when they die, and stay there forever. They suffer a threefold punishment: the loss of the sight of God, (physical) agony, and the permanent reproaches of their own conscience. The doctrine of the eternity of punishment in hell is, however, a moot point, as some people see it as contradicting the goodness of God. The resurrection of the dead will – like Jesus Christ's resurrection – be

Rose Window Depicting the Day of Judgement
Chartres Cathedral, west facade, c. 1220/30

As the appearance of the Son of God on earth did not lead to the founding of the kingdom of God's righteous on earth, as had been expected, the idea of a final judgement of people's beliefs and deeds was transposed to a transcendent sphere at the end of earthly time. The impressive stained glass windows, flooded with light, were a warning to believers, as they left the house of God, to constantly bear this in mind.

Thomas Aquinas (1225–1274)
Ideal portrait by Joos von Wassenhove (van Gent), c.1470, Paris, Musée du Louvre

Thomas Aquinas, a member of the Dominican Order, taught at the universities of Paris, Rome and Naples, and from 1259 was court theologian to Pope Urban VI. By synthesizing the philosophical tradition of antiquity (Aristotle) with ecclesiastical doctrine, he created a comprehensive theological system of values, order and knowledge that became known as Thomism. His rational explanations of church dogma, the subordination of knowledge to faith, the distinction between essence and existence, the categorization of the world and the inherent capacity of reason to recognize and prove the existence of God, represent the apogee of "Christian philosophy" in the Middle Ages (Scholasticism).

Celtic Crosses
Cemetery of a monastery in Cashel,
7/8th century, Ireland, Cashel,
County Tipperary

In the wake of the Christianization of
the Celts, who had emigrated to
Ireland around 600 B.C. (Latene era),
Irish Christianity developed in the 5th
century in a way that was both
intense and had its own specific
cultural form. As Ireland had never
belonged to the Roman Empire and
its culture had not gone through any
period of Latinization, Christian art
made connections to the ornamental
world of images of the Latene era
and adopted much of the symbolic
language of the peasant clan system
(sun symbol, for example) which was
characteristic of Ireland until well into
the 9th century. Similarly the early
Irish Church, which was primarily
monastic, fitted into the clan system.
A particular feature of Irish
monasticism was the tradition of the
itinerant monk (peregrinatio), as a
consequence of which enthusiasm
for education, scientific inclinations
and study (e.g. of the Classics)
became widespread in almost all
monasteries in the Irish and Scottish
region, triggering intensive
missionary work in England and
Central and Northern Europe
(including, for example, St. Gallen,
Regensburg, Würzburg and Vienna).
Irish clerics were considered the
most highly educated of their time,
and they taught for example at the
courts of the Frankish emperors.

physical; the resurrected body is envisaged as
immaculate and incorruptible.

For a long time there were different interpretations of the time when the Day of
Judgement and resurrection would take place,
as well as of the finer details. In particular, different groups of "Chiliasts" and "Millenarianists,"
i.e. followers of the teaching of the thousand year
kingdom (in the biblical sense), often made complicated calculations which got mixed up with
impatient and revolutionary expectations of salvation. These groups were particularly strong at
the end of the Middle Ages and in early modern
times, and were almost always in opposition to
the official church, which usually persecuted
them as advocates of "Adventism." Sections of
the Reformation, the Anabaptists for example,
also belonged to these groups.

John's Revelation or Apocalypse, which all
Christian-Messianic groups refer to as their
"basic text," is very closely modelled on the
Jewish apocalypse of the Old Testament, as
described in the Book of Daniel. The essence of
the message is that just before the dawning of
God's kingdom, decline in morals, injustice,
wars, plague and general depravity will culmi-
nate in the "supremacy of the anti-Christ." The
kingdom of divine justice will stand out all the
more clearly from this chaos. With the renewed
appearance of Christ as the one ushering
in God's kingdom, "time fulfils itself." John's
Apocalypse assumes that only after the
Thousand Year Kingdom, in which only the
privileged witnesses to the faith will reign with
Christ, will the general judgement and resurrection of the dead occur.

JESUS AND THE EARLY DAYS OF THE CHURCH

The Historical Jesus

In accounts of the life of Jesus, historical
descriptions have become mixed with legendary, transfiguring elements. While the existence of the historical Jesus is not generally
disputed, his divinity is disputed by non-
Christian sources (Judaism, authors of the
antiquity, Islam). The sources for the life of
Jesus are divided into two groups: the four
Biblical gospels, and the apocryphal scriptures
that were later removed from the canon by the
church and which deal principally with Jesus's
childhood.

The first three gospels (Matthew, Mark and
Luke) are known as the synoptic gospels
because they have a great deal in common.
They transmit more biographical and historical
events from the life of Jesus and are Greek
elaborations of original texts that were presum-
ably written in Aramaic. John's gospel, by contrast, which was written somewhat later,
poetically transfigures the life of Jesus, and
enriches it with metaphysical reflection and
speculations about the history of salvation.
The sources are probably Jesus's immediate
circle.

Jesus (the name is a diminutive form of
Joshua, actually Jehoshua = "God's help") was
the eldest son of the carpenter Joseph and his
wife Mary; he had a number of brothers and
sisters (Mark 6:3). His parents lived in Nazareth
(Galilee), yet according to Matthew and Luke
Jesus was born in Bethlehem, thus fulfilling the
Old Testament prophecy of Micah. The year of
his birth has been long disputed, but is now
generally thought to have been a little before
the year 0, between 6 and 3 B.C. Jesus probably worked initially, like his father Joseph, as a
carpenter, but his outstanding qualities are
mentioned in the story of the 12-year-old Jesus
in the Temple (Luke 2:42 f.).

Jesus was baptized in the Jordan River by
John the Baptist, who prefigured and prepared
the way for Jesus. After John the Baptist was
imprisoned (and subsequently executed on the
orders of Herod the Tetrarch), Jesus returned to
Galilee. According to Luke, Jesus started his
public work, which lasted only three years at
most, when he was about 30 years old (Luke
2:23). Accompanied by his disciples, Jesus
travelled through the country as an itinerant
preacher, healed the sick, and relied on the
hospitality of his followers, as documented by
his frequent presence at feasts. Thus Jesus was
not an ascetic who turned away from the
world.

His way of life and religious message soon
aroused the suspicion and hostility of the traditional Scribes and Pharisees, who feared his
growing support. They took advantage of his
visit to Jerusalem to arrest him, try him for blasphemy (Mark 14:64) and, with the approval of
the Roman Procurator Pontius Pilate who held
office between 26 and 36 A.D., finally to have
him crucified. As Jesus died in agony, there
was an eclipse throughout the country (which

is why April 3 of the year 33 has been calculated as the probable day of his death).

Jesus was a man of the people, who preached in a simple and clear language, which was nevertheless full of imagery. He used allegories and parables from the craft trades and farming worlds of his audience. He set no store by formal study of the scriptures and taught a practical and active gospel of love of one's fellow human beings, promising the coming of the kingdom of God and countering his opponents and non-believers with a mixture of understanding and threat of future judgement.

The Sermon on the Mount

The Sermon on the Mount contains the core of Christian ethics, and thus the entire ethos of Christianity, since Jesus does not primarily require of his followers insight, but obedience. Christianity requires people to follow a pro-active ethical path in life.

The Sermon on the Mount, recorded by Matthew and Luke in the form of short, pithy sayings and comparisons, demands not an increased obedience to the law as advocated by Judaism, but obedience to the God of love. It is not so much an appeal to reason as to generosity and people's hearts. Jesus made radical demands, calling for people to renounce the exercise of power and violence, even in retaliation. The Sermon on the Mount is perhaps the greatest challenge to Christianity itself. There have been countless attempts, including by church institutions themselves, to weaken the Sermon's message or make it politically less contentious. In the Sermon on the Mount, love is depicted as being the fulfilment of the Law, and as a noble ideal is contrasted with the Law that had thus far applied, which love both fulfils and supercedes.

The "Holy Scriptures"

The canon of the Christian faith, compiled by the church – the Holy Scriptures – comprises the books of the OT, which are also the basis of the Jewish faith, with the addition of the canon of the New Testament, which consists of the four gospels of Matthew, Mark, Luke (with the Acts of the Apostles) and John, as well as the 21 letters of the Apostles (13 by Paul, 2 by Peter, 3 by John, 1 to the Hebrews, 1 to Jacob and 1 to Judas), and finally John's Revelation (Apocalypse).

While Protestants see the Holy Scriptures as the only true source of faith, the Catholic church teaches that the transmission (by the church) is the continuation of a tradition of teachings revealed by God with binding authority. For this reason its dogmas, the teachings of the Church Fathers, resolutions of the councils etc. are regarded as "rules of faith" that are binding for believers. The creeds of the early councils are the principal symbols of this faith. They are also widely recognized by other Christian churches.

Early Christianity and the Apostles Peter and Paul

Jesus's appearance came at a time of great religious unrest and millenaristic expectations. Jesus's crucifixion, as well as his resurrection and ascent to heaven, left the twelve disciples and the small original community, consisting of different Jewish groupings from the lower social classes, in great confusion. They initially expected the end of time to begin (apocalyptic Adventism). According to the account of Pentecost in the Acts of the Apostles, the Holy Spirit came over them and constituted the messianic community around the central message of Jesus.

Luke records the ideal image of the original community with regard to sharing of possessions and mutual help. These Jewish Christians were in many respects rooted in ancient Jewish messianic faith, and yet differed fundamentally in their Christology and the initiation ritual of baptism. The community was held together by the celebration of the Holy Communion in remembrance of Jesus's last supper before his arrest, with the symbolic sharing of bread and wine. The "Lord's Supper" became, along with baptism, the second fundamental symbol of early Christianity.

The experience at Pentecost, which ultimately induced the apostles to travel to all countries to spread the gospel, is today seen as the date the Christian church was "founded" as the community of those gathered together in faith. Yet its structures were initially very provisional in nature and differed from one place to another, and the hierarchy of an overall church did not exist at that time. There are different interpretations of the extent to which it can be assumed that the early church had the same ecclesiastical offices as the later church.

The Apostle Peter
Mosaic, 6th century, Ravenna, Baptistry of the Arians

The New Testament suggests that Peter played a leading role among the disciples and he may be considered the first leader of the earliest Christian community in Jerusalem. For that reason he is traditionally depicted as the eldest of the disciples, and described as the "rock" on which Jesus said he would build his Church (Matthew 16:18). Since Peter was martyred around 65 A.D. in Rome, the bishops of Rome, as successors to the "See of Peter," claim the sole leadership of the Church, basing this claim to Papal primacy over the entire church on Jesus's words: "I will give you the keys to the kingdom of heaven" (Matthew 16:19). The dispute over the primacy of Rome, which was contested both politically and theologically, led in 1054 to a definitive schism, the church splitting into Roman Catholicism and Greek Orthodoxy.

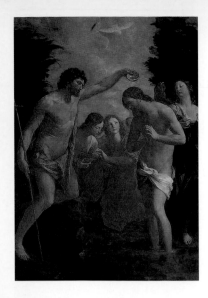

The Baptism of Christ
Guido Reni, c. 1621/23, Vienna,
Kunsthistorisches Museum

Baptism as a symbolic act of
purification by water was
widespread in the ancient world.
Christian baptism is not based on
Jesus's baptism by John the Baptist
but on Jesus's command to be
baptized in the "Name of the Father,
and of the Son, and of the Holy
Spirit." Thus, the person being
baptized (originally adults) was not
only subjectively taken into the
Christian community, but also
objectively entered into the
community of the Saviour and the
redeemed, and was freed from the
burden of original sin.

The Monastery of Monte Cassino

This, the original Benedictine
monastery founded in 529 by
Benedict of Nursia, was for many
centuries a centre of art and science.
In its prominent position on a steep
mountain in Campania, the ideals of
hermitage are united with those of
the monastic community.

The Sacraments

The church sees the sacraments as bearing witness to the mystery of Christ. The Catholic and Orthodox Churches recognize seven sacraments: baptism, confirmation, Communion (Mass or Liturgy), confession, ordination, matrimony and extreme unction (now called the anointing of the sick). Protestantism has only two: baptism and the Eucharist. Their derivation from holy acts as they are described in the gospels is controversial. The most important sacrament is baptism, symbolically carried out by moistening with water. The Catholic view is that baptism cancels out original sin, whereas the Protestant view is that it cancels out only the guilt of original sin which leads to damnation, whereas the desire to sin remains part of human nature. Baptism is regarded as "re-birth in Christ" and was originally performed only on freely consenting adults, which is why radical groups such as the Anabaptists reject infant baptism. For the official church, baptism of children is necessary for the salvation of souls in case a child dies without having been baptised.

Confirmation means "confirming faith" and is meant to strengthen young people's belief. For the Catholic and Orthodox Churches it is a sacrament, although not for Protestants. The Eucharist (or Mass) is for Catholics just as important a sacrament as baptism, due to the actual presence of Christ in the bread and wine, while Protestant churches tend to see the Lord's Supper symbolically.

The sacrament of confession, which Luther originally wanted to keep, links Christ's power to forgive sins (Matthew 9:2, Mark 2:5, Luke 5:20 f.) with the granting of this power to the apostles (Matthew 16:19 and 18:18 and John 20:23) and the position of the church as the legal successor to the apostles. The church, or rather its priests, can by proxy grant forgiveness of sins (absolution) and require penance. The abuse of the system of absolution was one of the main factors leading to the Reformation, which deprived priests of this right. Extreme unction, normally carried out only on the death bed, has now been extended in Catholicism to include ministry to the sick, which has long been the case in the Orthodox Church. Catholicism also recognizes ordination and marriage as separate sacraments. Other church acts of consecration are not considered to be sacraments in the full sense.

Christian Monasticism and Holy Orders

Monasticism as an institution developed out of the early Christian ideal of perfection, according to which the perfect life of a Christian was to be found in renouncing the world and loving God and one's fellow human beings. Even the early church recognized male and female ascetics as a separate class of people, making reference to Paul, who in his epistles had praised Christian celibacy. In the 2nd and 3rd centuries a close link between mysticism and asceticism grew up, particularly in Syria and Palestine.

Early monks (coenobites, from the Greek "koinos" = communal) shunned the decadence of urban life, and sought solitude and calm in the desert (desert monasteries), where monks lived in cells or caves largely as hermits, even if they did live in communities of some kind. The most extreme form of hermits were the famous stylites who lived at the top of pillars. These early ascetics were originally lay people. Monasteries in the western world had a quite different character, particularly due to their extensive clericalization and tight organization. The patres ("fathers") are ordained priests, whilst the fratres ("brothers") are responsible for the manual and "secular" work. The person mainly responsible for organizing western monasticism was Benedict of Nursia (480–547), founder of the Benedictine Order in 529 (monastery of Monte Cassino). Through organized communities of monks, this order spread across the whole of western Europe, and with its famous rule "Ora et labora" (pray and work) produced significant achievements in agriculture, schooling and science.

The reform movements, started in the monasteries of Cluny and Gorze in the 10th and 11th centuries, became the driving force for an overall renewal within the Church. In protest against an increasing secularization of the old orders – in the Middle Ages the monasteries had become a depository for the younger children without inheritance of large families or the nobility – a number of different reformed orders were formed. Outstanding examples were the Cistercians in the 11th and 12th centuries, founded by Bernard of Clairvaux (1091–1153), which soon became just as powerful as the Benedictine Order, and the "Friars Minor" (Franciscans) at the beginning of the 13th century, founded by Francis of Assisi (1181–1226), who are committed to the

Christian ideal of poverty and caring for the sick. In addition, there were the preaching orders (Dominicans) founded by Dominic (Guzman) (1170–1221) who were soon entrusted with the church's fight against heretics and with carrying out the inquisition ("Canes Domini" = watchdogs of the Lord).

During the Middle Ages, and to some extent into the age of Enlightenment, the monasteries in Europe were rich and powerful, many of them independent land owners. A storehouse of spiritual education and scholarship, they often formed a kind of "church within the church". The Order of the Jesuits, founded by Ignatius of Loyola (1491–1556), attained outstanding significance in the age of the Counter-Reformation, with many Jesuit monks serving as missionaries to the Far East and political advisors to Catholic rulers.

The Christian Mission

The missionary activities and spread of Christianity are the clearest signs of the great vitality of this religion. No other religion was able to organize its mission so thoroughly and extensively and expand it to cover all the continents of the world. What was in many respects a new chapter in the spread of Christianity began with the move to proselytize the American continent just after its (re-)discovery in 1492. And yet earlier, both in terms of its zeal and its sense of mission, proselytization activities had been characterized by the military style reconquista (re-conquering) of the Iberian Peninsula from the remnants of Islam. The apostle Paul had undertaken his immense work of travelling and converting people in Europe and Asia under the pressure of the directly imminent return of Christ and the pressure of time connected with that. This hyperactivity meant that many missionaries never recoiled in the face of physical hardship and danger, including the risk of martyrdom.

Whilst the Orthodox Church usually adapted its missionary efforts to regional structures and languages (the variety of organizational forms particularly in the Near East bears witness to this), the western Churches took a far more centralized and strict approach.

The two leading Catholic seafaring nations, Portugal and Spain, undertook extensive missionary activity beginning in the 15th century, often with violent and Eurocentric character-

The Dream of Pope Innocent III (1198–1216)
Fresco by a Franciscan master, c. 1260, Assisi, S. Francesco

In the 13th century, a counter-movement focused on early Christian ideals of poverty and itinerant preaching arose, including the influential Franciscans order. The Church's short-lived resistance is explained by legends about the Spanish Dominicus (1179–1221) and the Italian Francis of Assisi (1182–1226), including dreams that convinced the Pope that the new orders were pillars for the shaky edifice of the church.

istics, whilst the Protestant sea nations of England and Holland carefully combined their missionary zeal with trade interests. Intense missionary activity has characterized the Catholic holy orders at all times.

This form of missionary activity is very different from the efforts at establishing an "inner mission" which can be found in all churches, but especially the Protestant ones, in the form of movements of renewal and re-awakening. In the Protestant sphere, these efforts started particularly with Pietist groups (August Hermann Francke, Count Zinzendorf) who called upon people to "change their ways." Sections of the "Young Churches" and many church youth and renewal movements (such as the YMCA or "Catholic Action") have adopted these concepts.

CHRISTIANITY UP TO THE REFORMATION

The Early Church and the Roman Empire

While some members of the early church initially wanted to confine Christianity to a law-based religion in the Jewish world and restrict its mission to converting Jews (particularly under James and initially also Peter), in other words to become a Jewish Christian sect, Paul saw more clearly than anyone the future of Christianity in converting Gentiles.

Based on the extensive message of renewal of the NT, there was a turn away from Judaism, which had fatal consequences for the relationship between the two religions, particularly for Judaism. Very soon the Jews were accused of being as stubborn as the Gentiles, and the tendency already present in the evangelists to depict the Jews as the actual "murderers of Christ" increased.

Mass in St. Peter's Square in front of the Church of St. Peter in Rome (during the 2nd Vatican Council)

The general assemblies of the Catholic Church, at which only bishops are allowed to participate, are called councils (Greek: "synod"). While all eight ecumenical councils of the ancient church were convened by the Roman emperors, and primarily served to establish or further develop doctrine, the councils convened by the Curia during the Middle Ages and in modern times usually took place within the field of tension between claims to ecclesiastical and secular power. They often served to combat any attempts at reform, and to consolidate traditional positions on the law and faith. The culmination was the First Vatican Council (1869/70), which affirmed the universal episcopate and papal infallibility. The fundamental idea underpinning the councils was the conviction that the Holy Spirit would also be at work in the assembly of bishops.

Through Paul, and even more through the early Church Fathers, the apologists ("Defenders") of young Christianity found a spiritual connection to the Greek-Hellenistic world and its claim to universality, which seeped into Christianity. As described in the prologue to John's gospel, Christ was equated with the Greek logos, and interpreted as universal reason, and church teachers, particularly in the East, developed Christianized neo-Platonic philosophies. Generally speaking, it can be said that Christianity adopted the education system of antiquity and "Christianized" it.

The relationship to the Gentile Roman state underwent a great transformation. Christianity first came into contact with a state cult in Judea, where the Christians were treated as a Jewish sect by the Roman administration. The principal offence for both the Christians and the Jews was the Roman cult of the emperor which, after the consolidation of the hereditary or adoptive dynasties, had led to a god-like veneration of the emperor. The Christians rejected this as a form of idolatry, although Jesus's words with regard to secular authority are not entirely clear. Times of suspicious tolerance alternated with grave persecution of Christians, the harshest being under Emperor Nero (54–68), Septimius Severus (193–211), Maximinus Thrax (235–238), Decius (249– 251) and Diocletian (285–305). In these times the number of martyrs grew, their fearlessness strengthening the faith and the profession of it. At the same time, Roman thought had a great influence on Christianity, which led to the faith becoming far more legalistic. Many devotional and structural features of the church today have pagan-Roman origins.

Emperor Constantine (306–337, from 324 sole ruler) was the first emperor to recognize the potential of Christianity to uphold state power, and in 311 issued the Milan Edict of Tolerance which guaranteed Christians the freedom of religious practice and state recognition. The victory of Constantine over his Co-Emperor Maxentius at Milvius Bridge in 312, allegedly fought under the sign of the cross, was later elaborated into a Christian legend, while the so-called "Donation of Constantine," on which the Pope later founded his claim to the secular rule of central Italy (Church States), subsequently turned out to be a forgery. In 392, under Emperor Theodosius (379–395), Christianity became the state religion, and the state prohibited all pagan cults. The subsequent Christian emperors of Western Rome proved to be for the most part politically weak, but intervened heavily in the affairs of the young State Church.

The Orthodox Church and Byzantium

After the division of the Roman Empire in the 4th century and definitively after the fall of Western Rome (476), the Eastern Roman Empire of Byzantium gained increasing significance and power. Byzantium (Constantinople) flourished culturally as a "second Rome," and the Patriarch of Constantinople, who was under the protection of the emperor as the spiritual leader of the Greek Orthodox Church, gained equal status with the Pope in Rome around the year 500.

Rome and the Western Church also became increasingly independent of Byzantium. With the adoption of some of the Byzantine court rituals into the Orthodox Church, the Eastern Church became more closed towards Rome, which was surrounded by Arian Germanic peoples. The Orthodox Church spread throughout the entire Slav region, as far as and including Russia. Theologically, the main difference between the Eastern Church and the Roman Church is that the former places greater emphasis on the supremacy of the person of God, and sees the Holy Spirit as proceeding only from the Father and not from the Son as well (Filioque, meaning "and from the Son").

The Byzantine Empire was at the height of its power under the Emperor Justinian (527–565), but in the 7th century it began to lose its territory in the Near East due to the rapid advance of Islam, and soon found itself under threat. This threat continued through several phases until the fall of the Eastern Roman Empire (1453). Due to the vast number of saints, and their extensive depiction in paintings, icons and relics, an often bloody battle over the use of images (iconoclasm) raged between 726 and 843 in the sphere of influence of the Eastern Church. It centred on the legality and appropriateness of these forms of veneration (accusation of idolatry). The church and the emperor were equally involved in the battle, which weakened the empire from the inside.

Hostility between the Eastern and Western Churches increased as a result of the disputes over dogma and the question of Roman primacy, and culminated in the schism which has existed since 1054, the separation of the two Churches after reciprocal ostracizing and condemnation. After the conquest of Constantinople by the Turks in 1453, the Greek Orthodox Church led a tolerated existence under the rule of the Ottomans, while the Russian Orthodox Church saw itself – with Moscow as the "Third Rome" – as the legacy and storehouse of old Orthodoxy, and played an important role in the spiritual life of Eastern Europe and Eurasia. The Russian tsars adopted important aspects of Byzantine Caesaropapalism and the system of being a state church.

The Western Church of the Middle Ages and the Papacy

The Western Church gained impetus from the suppression of the Arians and the conversion of the Western European Germanic peoples to the Roman Catholic faith in the 5th and 6th centuries. Due to the early Christianization of Ireland and parts of Scotland, monastic communities grew up there and became bases for the systematic proselytization of Western, Central and Northern Europe. The most famous monk was the Anglo-Saxon Winfried (approx. 673–754) who carried out missionary activities amongst the Franks under the name of Boniface, at the beginning of the 8th century, and suffered martyrdom at the hands of the Frisians.

To counter the growing influence of Eastern Rome and Constantinople, the Pope, as Bishop of Rome, claimed his primacy over the whole Church, referring to the fact that Jesus had called Peter the "rock" on which the church should be built (Matthew 16:18). As the Byzantine Empire became politically weaker Rome gained increasing autonomy. Pope Gelasius I (492–496) developed the doctrine of the separation of ecclesiastical and temporal power, with ecclesiastical power having precedence ("Doctrine of Two Swords"). This was developed by Pope Gregory the Great (590–604) into a doctrine on the primacy of the Roman popes.

In the 8th century Rome began to push for political separation from Byzantium and directed its attention to the empire of the Carolingian Franks that was gaining strength. With the coronation of Charlemagne as Holy Roman Emperor by the Pope in Rome at Christmas 800, the Frankish rulers, and later the German Emperors, became the protectors of the Church. After the Roman papacy in the mid-9th century – the so-called "Dark Century" – had sunk into the chaos of rival Roman aristocratic cliques, the German emperors undertook attempts at reform with their Roman campaigns in the mid-10th century, but in doing so they brought the Church into a situation of complete dependency on temporal power. Nevertheless, through this re-structuring Western Christianity was able to achieve huge successes in its conversion activities in Eastern Europe and in Scandinavia.

The reform movement within the Church, initiated by the monasteries of Cluny and Gorze, successfully opposed the dependency on secular power. Their figurehead was the monk Hildebrand who, as Pope Gregory VII (1073–1085), worked within the Church to oppose lay investiture (putting lay people into ecclesiastical office) and simony (sale of ecclesiastical positions), and in 1077 forced Henry IV into his famous penance at Canossa.

The papacy gained further influence and wealth through the Crusades movement (end of the 11th to the 13th century). The relationship between the pope and emperor became strained, particularly during the 11th century, in the so-called "investiture dispute," which centred on the right to invest bishops, and at times there was open battle. The disputes reached their climax under the Staufers (12th/13th centuries), who also gained control of Sicily and lower Italy. At the same time the Middle Ages saw a period

Mother of God
Icon, Moscow School, 16th century

The images of saints of the Greek Orthodox Church, known as "icons" (Greek: "likeness, image"), as distinct from idols, have long been used as devotional images both in churches (iconostasis, icon screen) and in private prayer. In the context of the Iconoclastic Controversy (iconoclasm, 8/9th century) they became stylized in a form that has lasted until the present day. In defence of the cult of the Virgin Mary this had a specific effect on the depiction of the Mother of God. The type known as "Miraculous Image" (Hodigitria) shows Mary as the Mother of God with the child in her arms giving the blessing of Christ.

Greek Orthodox Celebration of the Eucharist
Contemporary photograph

Henry IV in Canossa in 1077
Eduard Schwoiser, book illustration,
late 19th century

The conflicts between the Curia and
the territorial rulers, particularly the
German King and Holy Roman
Emperor, escalated in the so-called
"investiture controversy" triggered by
Pope Gregory VII's revoking the right
of lay people (emperors) to invest
clerics with ring and staff as a sign of
their office, and thus to bestow
temporalities. For political reasons,
Holy Roman Emperor Henry IV
(1056–1106) had no option but to
subject himself in 1077 to a three-
day penance imposed by the Church
before the gate of the castle at
Canossa. This event is seen as a
symbolic expression of the peak of
Papal power. Later popes, such as
Boniface VIII (1294–1303), through
abuse of power, nepotism and
obsession with power, contributed to
the eventual implementation of the
principle of separation of powers.

Pope Boniface VIII 1294–1303
Arnolfo di Cambio, Bust, ca. 1300,
Rome, Museo Petriano

in which western monasticism and scholastic learning flourished; a number of universities and monasteries were founded as spiritual centres, and church art of the Romanesque and Gothic periods produced great masterpieces.

Under Innocent III (1198–1216) and his direct successors the papacy as an institution reached the zenith of its power. The Pope was the spiritual, political and legislative head of an entire culture, and proudly called himself the "head of the entirety of Christendom" (Caput christianitatis). However, in his bull "Unam Sanctam," which declared obedience to the Pope in all matters to be necessary for salvation, Boniface VII (1294–1303) went far beyond the claims of the papacy to secular supremacy. It was the last failed attempt to assert a spiritual and cultural central institution in a diverging world.

The subsequent decline was rapid: transferred to Avignon between 1305 and 1377, the popes came under the dominion of the French king. The "Great Schism of the Western World" (1378–1415/17) then followed. During this time three Popes resided simultaneously in Rome, Avignon and Pisa, until the Council of Constance (1414–1417) put an end to this chaotic situation. During the Age of the Renaissance, the papacy regained its position of power but became caught up in a process of total secularization, political intrigue and immorality. Through unrestrained simony and nepotism the popes attempted to set up Italian principalities for their families. The pontificates of Alexander VI Borgia (1492–1503) and Leo X. Medici (1513–1521) can be regarded as the climax of this secularization. Nevertheless, these prince-bishops of the Renaissance patronized the arts to a hitherto unprecedented degree, from which virtually all the artistic geniuses of the Renaissance were able to profit.

THE REFORMATION

The Radical Spiritual Change

As the 16th century began, a radical change which formed a bond with the Age of the Renaissance, humanism, and the beginning of modern times spread across the whole of Europe, affecting all spheres of life, and made itself felt particularly strongly in the Church. Whatever their differences, the great reformers shared a concern for the salvation of the human soul and the integrity of Christian

teaching, and it was this concern that led them to take up a very critical position with regard to secularization tendencies and human inadequacies as well as luxurious living, wealth and abuse of office that were rife in the Church. Faith again became more "personalized," feelings of human sinfulness could no longer be paid off by money, and the original message of the Holy Scriptures was to be liberated from all later additions that were narrow-minded and specific to their time. In the view of the reformers, rituals, cults, practices and dogma that had been added later hid the essence of the original message.

The Protestantism (from the Latin pro-testari = publicly testify) which developed from the teachings of the great reformers appealed to the sole authority of the Bible, the freedom of conscience of the individual, the call of the preacher to inner change and a faith that comes from within, and paid no heed to external symbols such as the pompous cult of saints, mysteries and relics.

The reformers were inspired by the crude abuses in the Church, and they had a number of role models to which they could make recourse. The English reformer John Wiclif (c. 1320–1384) had protested as early as the mid-14th century, against the financial antics of the Roman Curia and argued for the Church to return to "apostolic poverty." Jan Hus, a preacher from Prague (c. 1370–1415), took a more theologically grounded approach to his judgement of the secularization and greed of the Church. He made clear the crisis of faith of pious Christians for which – despite having been assured free safe conduct – he was burned for heresy at the Council of Constance. Girolamo Savonarola (1452–1498), the Dominican monk who attacked the Borgian Pope and the financial hegemony of the Medicis in Florence, and combined his uncomfortable admonishments with an appeal for messianic policies, suffered the same fate. Nevertheless, the great reformers of the 16th century were to enjoy lasting success.

Martin Luther

Martin Luther (1483–1546) was originally an Augustinian monk in Erfurt, and from 1512 was a professor of Bible Studies in Wittenberg. In 1517 he published his 95 theses against the Roman practice of selling indulgences (which legend has it he nailed to the door of the castle in Wittenberg), and thus set in motion a movement that was to have repercussions far beyond his own sphere of influence. What Pope Leo X. initially dismissed as "a group of squabbling monks" soon developed into a broad reform movement, particularly when in the years to follow Luther defended, systematized and elaborated his theses in various (critical) articles. In 1520 he burnt the Roman bull threatening his excommunication and thus sealed his break with Rome.

He reduced the number of Church sacraments to two – baptism and the Eucharist – and was filled with a deep, inner trust in the grace of God and a strong consciousness of the sinfulness of humankind. In the course of the conflicts Luther became increasingly impatient and aggressive; in the end the Papacy seemed to him to be the rule of the Antichrist. His often quite coarse language, calling for active reform of the Church, caught the public imagination. Very soon a number of German princes began to stand by Luther and placed him under their protection, in particular the Elector of Saxony and the Landgrave of Hesse, so that in 1521 Luther was provided safe conduct and could appear at the Diet of Worms before the emperor and envoy of Rome.

Attempts to achieve unity failed; Luther stuck by his theses. In the years to follow matters came to a head: at the Diet of Augsburg in 1530, Luther's followers (he himself was not present) radicalized his theses and the split in faith in Germany began. The religious discussions that were repeatedly initiated were no more able to bring about unity than was the "Schmalkaldic War" (1546/47) between the emperor's army and the Protestant princes. In the religious Peace of Augsburg of 1555 a precarious balance between Protestants and Catholics in the empire was negotiated, the fragility of which became particularly evident in the Thirty Years War (1618–1648). Lutheranism enjoyed great success in Northern Europe. In Sweden, King Gustav I Wasa introduced the Reformation along Lutheran lines in 1527, and King Christian III followed in Denmark, Norway and Schleswig-Holstein in 1536.

Ulrich Zwingli

Ulrich Zwingli (1484–1531), from 1519 spiritual advisor at the Old Minster in Zurich,

shared much of Luther's criticism, but was more deeply rooted in humanism and spiritualism, which is why his teachings are closer to those of the Baptists. From 1523/24 Zwingli preached in the spirit of the Reformation, introduced the Lutheran Lord's Supper, and he and his followers advocated baptizing adults a second time, which the City Council and Catholic authorities of Zurich took action to prevent. The Swiss cantons split on Zwingli's Reformation. In 1529, during the religious debates on the question of the Lord's Supper, Zwingli spoke out against both the Catholic doctrine of the "transformation" of Jesus into bread and wine (doctrine of transubstantiation) and against Luther's adherence to the actual presence of the Lord in the Eucharist (real presence). For Zwingli, the Lord's Supper was a purely commemorative act. Zwingli – like Calvin after him – then tried to eliminate dissenters from his own ranks. In October 1531 he was killed in the Battle of Cappel against the Catholic confederates.

John Calvin

John Calvin (1509–1564) was the youngest and in many ways the most radical of the great reformers, and the one who also had the most far-reaching influence. From a family of clerics who lived in a tense relationship with the Church, he was educated in France, but moved from there to Basel, where he came into contact with the Reformation. In 1536, he became a pastor in Geneva, and in 1537 drew up articles regulating the organization of the Church, based on Reformation principles, which he sought to implement rigorously. Forced to flee, he returned triumphantly to Geneva in 1541 and achieved legal status for his church articles of organization. Calvin and his followers set up a strictly organized "theocracy" in Geneva, and in 1559 founded an important theological college from which his philosophy spread to the whole of Europe.

In his prophetic sense of mission, Calvin defended the right of protest in the face of the unjust and un-Christian authorities, and radicalized the teachings of previous reformers. Calvin believed in election by God through faith in him, with a good and successful Christian life a preparation for being chosen. He emphatically asserted his theory of "double predestination," that is that some people are absolutely prede-

Martin Luther preaching
Lucas Cranach the Elder, reformation altar, detail, 1548, Wittenberg, Stadtkirche

The group of paintings created two years after Luther's death by his friend Lucas Cranach shows the reformer interpreting the message of the bountiful and merciful justice of God which can only be pronounced through the word of the Bible, and experienced through faith. In contrast to the Latin mass, in which the Eucharistic sacrifice is the most sacred moment, for the Protestants the pronouncement of the Gospel ("good news") "in the appropriate vernacular" became the central focus of the liturgy. Luther's outstretched arm is pointing to the crucified Christ in the centre of the predella, as the only symbol of God's act of grace which liberates people from the fear of sin and death.

The Pope as Antichrist
Satirical leaflet, woodcut, 16th century

St. Bartholomew's Day
Francois Dubois, late 16th century,
Lausanne, Musée des Beaux-Arts

The spread of the ideas of the
Reformation provoked opposition
from the Catholic Church and,
particularly in the territories under
Catholic rule, led to the often bloody
"Counter-Reformation." One of the
first climaxes was the persecution of
the Calvinist Huguenots
(confederates) by the French royal
dynasty, under Catherine of Medici.
The first public executions took place
as early as 1559 and 1560 (blood
tribunal of Ambois), and continued
despite an edict of tolerance (blood
bath of Vassy, 1562). Although in
1570 Admiral Coligny managed by
force to convince the sovereign to
give in (Peace of St. Germain, 1570),
she took revenge two years later
when the Huguenots were in Paris
to celebrate a royal wedding (blood
wedding). In the night of the 23-24
August 1572 she had some 2,000
Huguenots killed, including Coligny
(St. Bartholomew's Night). The wave
of murders spread from Paris to the
towns and villages. Sources speak of
100,000 victims. It was not until the
Edict of Nantes in 1598 that free
practice of religion was permitted.

termined to be blessed and others to eternal
damnation. His severity and earnestness run
through the entire Calvinist doctrine, and his
ideas of a life lived according to God's will had
a decisive influence on the Protestant work
ethos of modern Europe, the adherence to an
"inner asceticism" (Max Weber). Despite bloody
persecution, the new doctrine had particular success in France, where the Calvinist
Huguenots ("Confederates") soon became a
significant force. A number of aristocrats joined
their ranks, and Admiral Coligny was an able
leader until the Massacre of St. Bartholomew's
Day in 1572. France remained Catholic, but
King Henry IV, himself a Huguenot, guaranteed
them free practice of their religion in the Edict
of Nantes (1598). However, the edict of tolerance was retracted in 1685 by Louis XIV and
the Huguenots were then driven out of France.
Calvinism also had great success in the
Netherlands where it became the spiritual
driving force behind the Dutch struggle for independence from Spanish rule. In 1571, Calvinism
became the state religion in the northern
Netherlands, and from there also advanced to
German territories around the Lower Rhine. A
number of German principalities such as the
Palatinate and Brandenburg-Prussia also
became Calvinist – at least for a short time. In
Scotland, John Knox led a Reformation along
Calvinist principles whose influence also spread
to England. The seafaring nations of Great Britain
and Holland also took Calvinist philosophy to the
colonies and the New World.

Further Currents in the Reformation

During the Reformation, King Henry VIII of
England (1509–1547) separated from Rome

in the wake of a series of quarrels originally
sparked off by the Pope's refusal to grant him
dispensation to divorce his wife. After dissolv-
ing the monasteries he founded the Anglican
State Church in 1534, directly under the King's
own authority. In many respects the Anglican
Church adopted a position somewhere between the Roman Catholic and the Protestant
Churches. In 1539 the King pronounced the
six articles of faith based on the Reformation
which, among other things, included a denial
of the Catholic doctrine of transubstantiation.
With the 42 articles of faith issued in 1553
and the "Acts of Supremacy and Uniformity"
1559, England's definitive conversion to
Protestantism was implemented under Edward
VI (1547–1553) and later, after a short-lived
attempt at re-Catholicization, finalized under
Elizabeth I.

The Reformation period also saw a number of
radical movements that were defeated both by
the Catholics and by the more moderate
Protestants. From about 1520, particularly in
southwest Germany, a number of peasant
revolts were fomenting, with which some of
the knights joined. In 1521, after a number of
"zealots" or "visionaries" had come and gone
as leaders, they finally found a leader for their
protest, in the figure of Thomas Müntzer
(1489/90–1525), who had a deeply religious
and messianic character. In 1524 he tried to
set up a chiliastic "theocracy" in Mühlhausen
and advocated the violent overthrow of the
non-Christian authorities and princes. After
some initial success the peasants' army was
defeated and annihilated in 1525 at the Battle
of Frankenhausen. Müntzer was executed and
the religiously motivated independence struggles of the peasants were bloodily repressed,
as Luther had urged the authorities to do.

Under the influence of the Anabaptist prophet Melchior Hofmann (before 1500–1543,
died in prison), who preached in Amsterdam
and Strasbourg, and Bernhard Rothmann
(c. 1495–1535), a chaplain from Münster, the
Anabaptists expelled the bishop in 1534/35
and set up a new "Kingdom of Zion" in
Münster, supported by some of the
Reformation-minded middle classes. The
Dutch Anabaptist leader Jan Matthys (died in
combat in 1534), followed by the prophet
Johann Bockelson of Leyden, became the spiritual leaders of the Anabaptist Kingdom and

using rigorous and violent means set up a "Kingdom of God" on earth. The attempt was violently put down in 1535 and its leaders tortured to death.

The Catholic Counter-Reformation

The successes of the Reformation from the mid-16th century onwards set in motion a reform movement within the Catholic Church that became famous as the Counter-Reformation. The point of departure for this movement was the Council of Trent that met with interruptions between 1543 and 1563. It abolished a number of abuses in the Church and created new foundations for the Catholic Church. The form of the sacraments, the celibacy of priests, the monastic rules, missionary activity as well as the "Roman Catechism" (1556) were re-defined, and the pastoral role of the church placed on foundations which are still valid today.

The driving force behind the Counter-Reformation was the Order of Jesuits, founded by Ignatius of Loyola in 1540, who were entrusted with overseeing the Catholic universities and educational institutions and missionary work. In the wake of the strict and severely organized Counter-Reformation, but also due to the persecution of heretics, spiritual tutelage of believers developed, along with the Inquisition and a spate of witchhunts. Their manic superstition – a sign of spiritual insecurity – reached its tragic climax in the first half of the 17th century in central Europe, and somewhat later even in the largely Protestant new world of North America. It resulted in developments that – just like the magnificent triumph of the church during the Baroque Age – led to a radical critique of religion as the Age of Enlightenment dawned.

CHRISTIANITY FROM THE ENLIGHTENMENT TO THE PRESENT DAY

Enlightenment and Criticism of Religion

Just as no other religion experienced a triumph comparable to Christianity, no other religion has been called into question on the same scale as Christianity by the Enlightenment and scepticism of the western world. On the Protestant side, Christianity was linked to the principle that the religion of the ruler was the religion of the people ("cuius regio, eius religio") and thus to a degree dependent on political power. In the Catholic Church, state absolutism and the principle of national sovereignty led to attempts to "nationalize" religion and place it under the power of the respective state, illustrated, for example, by the 18th century Gallicanist, Jansenist and Episcopalist movements in France and Germany.

The new spirit of the Enlightenment taught above all a "natural religion" or a "natural Christianity" as an inner moral principle in human beings, dictated by reason, that did not require supernatural revelation, belief in the afterlife or institutionalization through a church. Important philosophers such as John Locke in England or Leibniz, Thomasius, Wolff and Immanuel Kant in Germany, represent such ideas. Via Jean-Jacques Rousseau, they had an especially strong influence on the French Revolution.

The "Enlightened Absolutism" of Frederick the Great of Prussia or Joseph II of Austro-Hungary was largely indifferent to denomination, and intervened radically in the affairs of the church, cutting back the ceremonial aspects and subjecting religion to principles of state rationale and the welfare of the people. The power of the Catholic Church in particular was severely restricted by Austrian "Josephinism:" Emperor Joseph II (1765–1790) rigorously appointed enlightened bishops, replacing the monastic institutions with secular educational institutes.

The French Revolution (1789–1794) radically rejected all privileges of the clerics who from 1790 had to either swear an oath of allegiance to the civil constitution or emigrate. Church property was confiscated and religion confined to developing the "noble instincts in human beings." Maximilien de Robespierre, in particular, implemented the "Cult of Reason" and faith in a "Supreme Being" guided by reason (modelled on Rousseau's ideas). After the Revolution it was above all Napoleon Bonaparte who forced the Church – amongst other things by interning the Pope and his cardinals – to bow to civil jurisdiction, and brought about the separation of state and church.

At the beginning of the 19th century, the extensive secularization (in 1803 the secular power of the church was abolished in Germany by resolution of the estates of the empire) brought

Pilgrimage Church of the Castigated Saviour
Dominicus Zimmerman, Wieskirche, 1754–1757, Wies near Steingaden, Upper Bavaria

The century of religious wars (Huguenots, Dutch independence struggles, Thirty Years' War 1618–1648) led to a schism between Eastern and Western Europe which brought consequential shifts in economic and social developments in its wake. The papacy celebrated the outcome of the Counter-Reformation as the victory of the Church (ecclesia triumphans). One of the expressions of this feeling was an impressive spate of building along with an abundance of figures, colours and light in Baroque churches (horror vacui); the believer bows in awe before their transcendental splendour.

Storming of the Bastille
from a drawing by Jean Louis Prieur, late 18th century, Versailles, Musée Historique

The storming of the Bastille, symbol of absolutist power, by the people of Paris on July 14 1789 became an expression of the Enlightenment conviction of the right of human beings to self-determination. Reason was postulated as the sole source of knowledge and guidance for behavior, with the role of religion reduced to the "development of noble instincts". The privileges of the clerical class were withdrawn, and holders of office had to submit to the civil constitution and civil law. The attempt of some revolutionary leaders to replace the masses' need for religion by belief in a "Supreme Being" guided by reason and a "cult of reason" was short lived. Napoleon, who emerged as victor out of the confusion of events, implemented the separation of state and church, and ended the clerical claim to universality by annexing the Church States and imprisoning Pope Pius VII.

about a radical change in the religious and ecclesiastical situation in Europe. The church, and ultimately the Christian religion, had finally lost its spiritual and educational monopoly; the sovereignty (also in spiritual matters) of the nation states had won the day over the church's claim to universality.

Apart from this external curtailment of its political power, Christianity also underwent radical religious criticism in the wake of the Enlightenment, particularly in the 19th century. It shook not only the church, but also the principles of the Christian faith to the very core. With "spiritual secularization" and the increasing "disappearance of magic from the world" due to the tremendous surge in the natural sciences, technology and the economy, traditional Christianity was increasingly experienced as inhibiting intellectual freedom and experimental scientific progress.

It was principally the different schools of scientific materialism, wanting to free people from the traps of tradition and religion and enable them to produce great technical and scientific achievements, that protested against the very foundations of the Christian religious world view. For example, the sociologist Auguste Comte (1798–1857), the founder of scientific positivism, assumed that human thought was subject to a "three-stage law" according to which intellectual progress moved from a theo-

logical-religious to a philosophical, to a positivist (empirical) interpretation of the world that ultimately would abandon all religious concerns. The biologism and evolutionary theory of Charles Darwin (1809–1892) and his successors shook the foundations of faith, particularly belief in the biblical creation story and the fact that people had been made in the image of God.

In his strivings for a radical anthropocentrism, Ludwig Feuerbach (1804–1872) undertook a comprehensive criticism of religion in general and Christianity in particular, in which he interpreted religion as man's self-alienation (projection thesis), which hindered human attempts at self-perfection. Karl Marx (1818–1883) and Friedrich Engels (1820–1895) gave Feuerbach's criticism an economic and social underpinning. Religion, with its emphasis on the afterlife, was a hindrance to people's political struggle for improved social and material living conditions ("religion as the opium of the people") in this world.

Friedrich Nietzsche's (1844–1900) criticism of Christianity was particularly aggressive and enduring. He took up Schopenhauer's scepticism towards Christianity, reproaching it for fostering the supremacy of a resentment-ridden "morale of slavery" of weakness and mediocrity (stereotyping) instead of the free development of the strong and artistic individual (supermen). Richard Wagner's attempt to revive a strong Germanic neo-paganism in art was influenced by a similar train of thought. Sören Kierkegaard (1813–1855) actually pleaded for an inner renewal of Protestant Christianity. With his emphasis on the isolation of individuals and their decisions, and his criticism of merely external forms of what he described as comfortable church-going Christianity, he heralded the existentialist movement in philosophy which later became strongly critical of religion. The treatment of the religious function by Sigmund Freud (1856–1939) had a particularly powerful impact, though it only evolved gradually. In his attempts to enlighten people about certain inner compulsions, Freud with his psycho-analysis theory examined the religious images of the "super-ego" (conscience) as ideas of morality that in some cases caused illness and which could, for example, be traced back to over-powerful and frightening father figures.

The Churches in the 19th and 20th Centuries

The Christian Churches, which after the 1815 Congress of Vienna tried to re-establish their old structures under new conditions, were at best confused and at worst rejected and con-demned by the fundamental challenges of the 19th century – revolutionary achievements in science and technology, secular belief in progress, democratization movements, liberal-ism and later socialism. In the 19th century, the Protestant Churches led the debate about a conservative or liberal Christianity, liberal theol-ogy seeking connections with scientific ration-alism, and in some respects became more opened to liberalism after 1848. The spiritually dominant figure was Friedrich Schleiermacher (1768–1834), a significant force in the re-newal of Protestant theology. Outwardly, (con-servative) Protestantism was the pillar of a late-absolutist system of State Churches, espe-cially in Prussia and thus after unification in 1871 throughout the whole of Germany. Through state pressure, Prussia forced the Protestant Churches to form a union (Protestant Christian Church), and most other German states followed Prussia's example. In the second half of the 19th century, Protestant-ism began to look closely at social questions, as did the Catholic Church.

The situation of the Catholic Church was con-siderably more complicated. After 1815, the papal see became a hot-bed of all kinds of reac-tionary tendencies. The reactionary movement culminated in the pontificates of Leo XII (1823–1829), Gregory XVI (1831–1846) and Pius IX (1846–1878). Since the 1830s, Rome had indulged in disciplining and relegating open-minded theologians and university pro-fessors throughout Europe. Through its inflex-ibility in questions to do with the mixed marriage rules practised by the state, Rome pro-voked the "mixed marriage dispute of Cologne" (1837–1841) which caused a difficult situation for the church in Germany and all other coun-tries with a mixture of denominations.

Rome's centralism brought the national Catholic Churches into situations of grave con-flict. This centralism was strengthened and uncompromisingly imposed, culminating in the "Syllabus" of 1864 (condemnation of the 80 "errors of modernism" which included the principal ones of liberalism and democratiza-tion), the establishment of the dreaded Papal Index of Prohibited Books (list of books forbid-den for Catholics) and above all the controver-sial dogma of "Papal Infallibility" of 1870.

A hard-fought battle broke out in Belgium and France over schools and culture. Relations with France were severely marred anyway by the fact that the Catholic Church could not initially bring itself to recognize the republic following 1871. A whole series of modern currents were arbitrarily dismissed as so-called "Americanisms," which did not exactly do much to help the situ-ation of the Catholic Church in America, viewed in any case with scepticism and suspi-cion. In Italy itself the relationship between the Pope and secular power degenerated into open hostility following Garibaldi's feat of unifi-cation, which had led in 1870 to the disappear-ance of the Church State. The Pope had described himself as a "prisoner in the Vatican." Generally speaking the democratic and liberal movements in all countries that had previously been under Catholic rule (Italy, Spain, Portugal) showed distinctly anti-Church tendencies.

In the German Empire, Bismarck, who wanted to "de-politicize" the Catholic Church as much as possible, placed all schools under the authority of the state in 1871 and unleashed the so-called "kulturkampf," in the course of which several Catholic bishops were impris-

Karl Marx (1818–1883)
Coloured photograph, around 1880

With the scientific and technological achievements of the 19th century, the Enlightenment's critique of religion became both more fundamental and more radical. Atheism emancipated itself from heresy and developed its own autonomous view of the world. The most lasting effects came in the field of science from Charles Darwin (1809–1892, theory of evolution) and in social politics from Karl Marx. Marx's analysis decried Christianity, with its emphasis on the after-life, as an ideological "superstructure," whose aim was to minimize the economic profit share of the exploited classes who create the added value ("Religion as the opium of the people"). The historical materialism founded by Marx influenced 20th century renewal movements in theology, particularly in the Third World. The 19th century philosophical critique of Christianity, marked by a spirit of scepticism, was extremely diffuse in its attempt to set ethical values, and thus open to abuse by nationalist or racist ideologies (Arthur Schopenhauer, Friedrich Nietzsche).

Friedrich Nietzsche (1844–1900)
Hans Olde, 1899

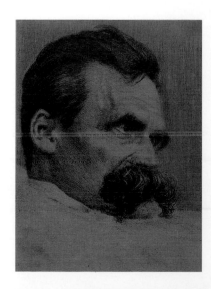

oned or forced to emigrate, many bishoprics remaining deserted for years. It was only under the pontificate of the skilful and flexible Leo XIII (1878–1903) that the situation in France, Germany and Italy started to become less tense in the 80s and 90s.

Under Leo XIII (Encyclical "Rerum Novarum" of 1891) the Catholic Church began to draw up its own social theory and cautiously open up to the working classes. However, under his successor Pius X (1903–1914), the fight against modernism took on a new dimension with the "Anti-Modernist Oath" of 1910, under which Catholic clergy were obliged to reject all modern tendencies. The spirit of this suspicious anti-modernism was (with a number of variations) dominant until the end of Pius XII's pontificate (1939–1958).

After the Bolshevist revolution of 1917, the Russian Orthodox Church experienced a phase of grave and bloody persecution. By connecting to the traditional state church philosophy, the Soviet leadership gradually managed to make the Church compliant and persuade it to cooperate with the state's aims. Nevertheless, Bolshevist or Stalinist-style socialism remained an acutely anti-religious and anti-church movement under which the Western Churches of Eastern Europe (Poland, Czechoslovakia, Hungary, Romania, Bulgaria and Yugoslavia) also suffered after 1945. Here, too, phases of persecution (particularly at the end of the 40s and beginning of the 50s) alternated with a policy that sought either to render them socially harmless or incorporate them into the aims of state socialism.

In Central Europe, both the Catholic and Protestant Churches developed a reserved and equivocal relationship with the democracies that had been formed after 1918. The Catholic Church In France was even actively involved at the head of the anti-democratic and pro-Fascist "Action francaise." In Austria, Spain and Portugal the Catholic Church also supported openly anti-democratic tendencies.

Both Churches failed in the face of Fascism or Nazism, particularly in its early days. While in the Protestant Church, under the influence of the ever-worsening methods of government after 1933, the opponents of Nazism formed the "Confessing Church" (Barmen Declaration), and split off from the German Christians (Reichskirche), who remained true to the state to the very end, the Catholic Church remained ambivalent for a long time. Impressed by the concordat with the Fascist governments (1929 with Italy, 1933 with Germany), the protests issued by Rome remained carefully considered and diplomatic until 1945. True resistance in Germany in both Churches was to be found only in individual movements or individuals. In Italy and Spain and in some Latin American dictatorships the Catholic Church identified to a great degree with these regimes well into the 60s and 70s.

After 1945, as a new order was established, people in Christian circles too began to reflect on what had happened and to work out guidelines for the future. All churches, particularly in Central Europe and North America, issued a clearer commitment to democracy and the conservative-style social state. Many Christian youth and peace movements have since become actively involved in working for international understanding and a policy of peace and disarmament motivated by Christian principles. The ecumenical movement has become more popular in all churches, which can mainly be ascribed to the World Council of Churches founded in 1948, with its headquarters in Geneva.

In the Catholic Church, the pontificate of John XXIII (1958–1963) and Paul VI (1963–1978), with their policies of "Aggiornamento" (modernization) and the Second Vatican Council (1962–1965), brought a rapid opening to the modern world. Apart from many innovations

German Protestant Church Congress, Leipzig, 1954

After 1945, the church congresses and other similar events in all Christian churches developed into a forum to discuss the problems of Christianity in the modern world. Topics of discussion included ecumenism, disarmament, the peace movement and social justice.

such as reform of the liturgy, a stronger lay movement and the rise of modern and critical theological theses, it was above all the young churches of Africa, Asia and particularly Latin America who made themselves heard at the Council, with their own concepts such as liberation theology. Despite certain signs of renewed conservatism (under John Paul II, since 1978) this trend has continued.

Both within the Catholic Church (even into the Roman Curia) and within the Protestant-dominated World Council of Churches, a distinct "internationalization" – and thus a renewed universalization of Christianity – is taking place. Due to the enormous social problems of the so-called "Third World" countries, and the increased self-confidence of Christian women (feminist theology) the churches are going to be forced to re-evaluate their attitude to the "poor countries" and to the role of women in Christianity. On the other hand, fundamentalist Christian groups are enjoying renewed popularity and – originally emanating from conservative Protestant groups in the U.S.A. – are trying, particularly in the countries that are traditionally predominantly Christian, to counter the complexity of Modernism with a rigorously literal interpretation of the Bible.

CHRISTIAN SPLINTER CHURCHES AND SECTS

The Old Churches of the East

The centralism of church organizations has made Christianity exclusive and intolerant of people with different opinions and different interpretations of the same message. Yet the history of Christianity is full of battles of faith and struggles to understand its own teachings, most of the time with various groups fighting over the same scriptures.

Since the elimination in the 4th and 5th centuries of the Arians who were mainly confined to Western Europe, the Monophysites in Syria, who believe that Jesus Christ had only one nature, namely a divine nature, formed a separate Christian church which still exists today. In Syria they are known as Jacobites after their pioneer Jacob Baradai (died 578); their head is the Patriarch of Antioch. The Monophysites also include the Coptics (whose beliefs differ somewhat), the Egyptian Christians whose head, the

"Coptic Pope," resides in Cairo (originally with the title of Patriarch of Alexandria) and the state church of the Abyssinians (Ethiopians), which has been a patriarchy since 1949. Besides the canon of the Bible, Abyssinians recognize a large number of additional NT apocryphal scriptures. The Armenians, too, under their own "Catholicos" (high priest) belong to the Monophysite faith.

In the struggle against the Monophysites, the Nestorians were formed, named after the Patriarch Nestorius of Constantinople (deposed for heresy in 431). They make a clear distinction between the divine and human natures in Christ and claim that only the human nature was born and suffered on the cross, not the divine nature. The Nestorians formed their own church in East Syria which at times enjoyed Islamic protection and early on carried out missionary activities in China and Mongolia. The Thomas Christians from Southern India are also part of the Nestorians. They are named after the apostle Thomas who is said to have brought Christianity to them. Today they are also represented in North America as the so-called "Assyrian Church." They have retained ancient Syrian as their ecclesiastical language and have a prohibition against eating pork.

In the Sphere of the Catholic Church

Since it is strict about the uniformity of its doctrine, the Catholic Church has always persecuted deviant groups particularly harshly and

Second Vatican Council

While the First Vatican Council (1869/70), with its definition of the claim to universality of the Roman episcopate and the dogma of papal infallibility, represented a final culmination of anti-liberal Catholic conservatism, the Curia was somewhat at a loss in the face of the fast and furious developments of the 20th century (world wars, nationalist dictatorships, October Revolution, East-West confrontation, end of colonialism). Not until Pope John XXIII (1958–1963) and Pope Paul VI (1963–1978) did the Church begin to adapt to the conditions of a changing world (aggiornamento). The modernization efforts of the entire Church were expressed in Vatican 2 (1962–1965), which initiated numerous reforms (including reform of the liturgy and participatory rights for the laity) as well as a lively debate on the theological and social concepts of the "young Churches" in Africa, Asia and, above all, in Latin America which confronted the primacy of Church doctrine with the needs of "Christianity as it is practised."

Martin Luther King (1929-1968)

Martin Luther King, Methodist minister and victim of a racist assassination, became the worldwide symbol of the civil rights movement and liberation movements that were based on Christian ethos. The principle of non-violent resistance to racial apartheid that he unerringly put into practice and the success he ultimately achieved through it provided an example of the possibility of combining Christian and political action which has had lasting influence. In 1964 Martin Luther King received the Nobel Peace Prize.

barred them from the Church. The highest goal, however, is the unity of all Churches and thus the Catholic Church succeeded in splitting off sections of virtually all Eastern Churches and uniting them again with Rome as the "Uniat Churches." They allowed these churches to retain authority over their own ritual and language so that representatives even within the Catholic Church can be clearly recognized as members of Eastern Churches by their dress and rites.

Of the United Churches the (United) Coptics of Alexandria (under the patriarch of Cairo), the Syrians of Antioch, the Greek Melchites (based in Damascus), the Maronites in Lebanon (based in Bkerke near Beirut), the Chaldeans of Babylonia (based in Baghdad) and the Armenians of Cilicia (based in Beirut) all have their own own patriarchate, the (united) Ukrainians of Lvov (Lemberg) and the Syro-Malabars of Ernakulam (India) created their own sees within the Roman Catholic Church. In protest at the promulgation of the dogma of papal infallibility at the 1st Vatican Council of 1870, the "Old Catholics" in Germany separated from Rome. They have their own bishop, do not recognise papal infallibility and various other dogmas, and have once more allowed priests to marry. In many respects, such as women's rights or voting rights within the church for the laity, they are a liberal variation of the Catholic Church.

In the Sphere of the Orthodox Church

The most important splits took place not in the Greek Orthodox but in the Russian Orthodox Church. Due to the great emphasis on the cult of mysteries and the rich store of different kinds of liturgical acts and gestures, a number of off-shoots with very bizarre features developed in Russia.

In the 17th century the "old believers," also known as Raskolniki ("schismatics"), split off in protest of the reform of the Orthodox rite introduced by the government. A section of them, the "Bezpopovtsy," do not have their own priests.

A number of visionary movements grew up, usually harshly persecuted by the state, such as the Khlysty ("flagellators") who operate clandestinely, and whose leader saw himself as God the Father incarnate and who elected their own "Son of God" and their own Apostles. An extreme form of the Khlysty were the Skoptsy ("castrated"), whose men and women (after procreation) systematically mutilated their genitals in order to deaden the desires of the flesh. Sects with a pronounced spiritual and inward character were the Molokane ("milk-drinkers"), who appeared in the 18th century. They lived largely in communities, sharing their property, and refusing to perform state or military service. Another sect were the Dukhobory ("wrestlers with the spirit"), the majority of whom emigrated to North America to escape persecution.

In the Sphere of the Protestant Church

There are many religious communities which are basically "protestant" in origin. In the U.S.A., for example, there are over 200 registered churches that are fundamentally Protestant. However, in many cases only vestiges of the original reform movements now remain, or they have merged with other groupings. These include the remains of the Waldenses, who were persecuted towards the end of the Middle Ages. Their centre is Piedmont, and they have formed tightly organized communities.

Similarly the "Bohemian-Moravian Brethren" are leftovers from the reformation movement started by Jan Hus in the early 15th century, whose followers split into two groups. Expelled from Bohemia, they settled mainly in Saxony and merged with the "Herrnhut Brethren" (named after the town Herrnhut in Saxony), founded in 1722 by Count Nikolaus of Zinzendorf (1700-1760). They were joined by Lutheran and Reformed followers.

The survivors of the Baptist Kingdom of Münster of 1535, formed Mennonite groups after 1537 under the priest Menno Simons (1496-1561) in Friesland. They were tolerated in Holland and in parts of Germany, and later spread to Russia and North America. At the end of the 17th century a number of them split off and still live today as farmers in North America. Known as the Amish People, they live a very conservative, isolated life and reject all modern forms of living, and most technological achievements. Even more visionary in character are the remains of the Schwenckfeldians, named after the German spiritualist and mystic Kaspar of Schwenckfeld (1489-1561), whose centre today is in Pennsylvania, and the "Remonstrant Brethren" in the Netherlands, both of whom developed out of pantheistic and visionary Christian movements in the 16th and 17th centuries.

From the 16th century, the different Protestant churches and movements became caught up in incessant quarrels with one another, particularly in the German states. While the Calvinists remained separate, in most countries, the Lutheran and Reform Churches united under pressure from the state, as in 1817 in Prussia.

In England's Anglican Church there have also been a number of splits throughout the various phases in which the Anglican faith was formulated. For example, there are two movements within the "Church of England" – the "High Church," which is modelled on the Medieval Church, and the more Puritanical "Low Church." Influenced by Calvinism, the severe "Independents" or "Congregationalists" split off from the main Church in 1581. Like the "Puritans" (or "Presbyterians"), they gained significant influence, mainly in North America and Australia.

Different Baptist communities became independent, the most significant of which is the Methodist Community, founded by John Wesley (1703–1791), who developed enthusiastic missionary activity in many countries. An offshoot of the Methodists is the Salvation Army, founded in 1865 by the preacher William Booth (1829–1912), which combines a purely practical Christianity with a military form of organization.

The community of the Quakers, the popular name for the Society of Friends, also originated from within the Anglican tradition. They lead an intense inner religious life, based on love of one's fellow human beings, and have few ecclesiastical forms of organization. They settled mainly in the U.S.A., notably in Pennsylvania. Other radical Free Church forms of organization, such as the "Shakers" and the Darbists ("Community of Brethren"), also set up communities there. They should be distinguished from a number of chiliastic and apostolic communities, who all make great reference to the apocalyptic texts in the Bible and put forward speculations about the end of the world. These include a number of Adventist communities as well as the Jehovah's Witnesses, the sect founded in 1874, for whom the Thousand Year Kingdom began in 1914. The "New Apostolic Church," founded in Germany in 1860, is also one of these groups.

Even more remote from any kind of orthodoxy are groups who base their belief on additional pronouncements and revelations. These include the "Inspiration Communities" in Europe and the U.S.A. and the "New Salem Society" of the "prophet" Jacob Lorber (1800–1864). The "Community of Christians," based on the philosophy of Rudolf Steiner, and the Christian Science movement founded by Mary Baker Eddy (1821–1910), also belong to this category.

One of the most curious and independent institutions is the Mormon Church, which calls itself the "Church of Jesus Christ of Latter-Day Saints." Its founder, Joseph Smith (1805–1844, murdered) wrote down the "reformed gospel," the Book of Mormon, which the archangel Moroni started to dictate to him in 1827, and founded the Mormon Church in 1830. After Smith was murdered by a lynch mob his successor, Brigham Young, migrated to the Great Salt Lake with his followers, imitating the exodus of Moses from Egypt. From their centre in Salt Lake City the Mormons farmed in the state of Utah, which became a federal state of the U.S.A. in 1896.

There are also countless chiliastic groups and sects inspired by Christianity in Africa, Latin America, Japan and the South Sea Islands.

Village Mass in North Cameroon

In contrast to other world religions such as Hinduism and Buddhism, the relationship to the community, the "for many" (Matthew 26:28, Mark 14:24) and "for you" aspects (Luke 22:20), as well as the command to love one's fellow human beings are distinctive features of Christianity. Historical developments have thus always challenged theological doctrinal opinions and ecclesiastical structures, leading to a plethora of interpretations and forms of organization, all claiming to be based on the New Testament. Due to Marxism and the formation of new nation states in the Third World, with their demand for an autonomous form of their own, 20th century Christian Churches are experiencing perhaps the greatest dynamic force for change since the Reformation.

ISLAM

The word Islam means "submission to God." In uncompromising monotheism, the youngest of the world religions emphasizes the uniqueness of Allah, and the workings of God in the daily life of humankind. For Muslims the Koran is the eternal and direct revelation of God, brought by the Archangel Gabriel to the prophet Mohammed who epitomizes a life lived according to God's will. The "Five Pillars of Islam" regulate the religious life of the believers. In everyday life, Islam sets particular store by its practically-oriented legal system (shari'a) and makes a strong link between its religious and social components. Early on, the very charismatic Shi'ites broke away from the more legalistic Muslim majority (Sunnis). Throughout the history of Islam, which had its first cultural heyday in the Middle Ages, runs the thread of a strong link between religion and politics, and the search for the right relationship between these two elements also characterizes modern conflicts in Islamic countries.

The Archangel Gabriel brings the message to Mohammed
Turkish miniature

Mohammed, a successful and well-regarded caravan manager, was 40 when the angel Gabriel appeared to him in a dream in a cave near Mecca. He gave Mohammed a book, commanded him to read and to proclaim God's message. Mohammed put up strong resistance to this apparition, initially thinking it was the work of the devil. But when the vision came again he accepted his calling to prophecy after long inner struggles and began to make public appearances in his home town of Mecca, preaching and admonishing the people. As a result, the rich Meccans forced him to emigrate to Medina (hijra).

MOHAMMED AND THE PROPHETS

The Life and Significance of Mohammed

Mohammed (Arabic: Muhammad) is the founder of Islam, prophet (an-nabi) and messenger sent by God (rasul allah). He did not, however, see himself as the founder of a new religion, but as someone who brought to completion the only true monotheistic primal religion pronounced since the beginning of time.

Mohammed was born in 570 in Mecca. His parents died when he was young and he went to live in the house of his uncle Abu Talib (the father of the 4th caliph Ali, the Prophet's cousin). As a young man he tended herds of animals in the desert, and at the age of 25 became a caravan manager for the rich widow Khadija, a woman considerably older than he was, whom he later married. As a caravan manager, he went on journeys to Syria, and it was in this melting pot of cultures and religions that he first came into closer contact with the Jewish and Christian faiths and with the so-called "hanifs," the ancient Arab God-seekers who wanted to overcome polytheism and who taught the belief in one God.

Mohammed experienced his first calling when he was about 40. Sura 96, the oldest Sura in the Koran, relates how the angel Gabriel appeared to him in a dream, held out a book and commanded him to read. Again and again Mohammed resisted in his sleep although put under strong pressure by the angel. However, when he awoke "the scripture had been written on his heart." Gabriel announced to him that he – Mohammed – was the prophet of

God. Mohammed's reaction was despondency and helplessness. In a deep depression he first sought solitude, and even thought of suicide, but after considerable soul-searching he eventually accepted his mission.

In about 610, Mohammed began to make his first public appearances in Mecca, admonishing the people and preaching against the decline in morals, religious laxity and social indifference. In the style of a social reformer, he exhorted people to live according to God's will, and preached a decisive monotheism: God (Allah) alone, he said, was the Lord of the Ka'aba, the ancient Arab polytheistic shrine in Mecca.

He became more and more uncompromising, and Mohammed was seen by the rich citizens of Mecca as a troublemaker and increasingly felt to be a threat to their accustomed lifestyle. He was the victim of numerous campaigns to malign and ridicule him, led both by the Arabs of Mecca and the Jews and Christians, until finally he and his followers were banished from Mecca. His conflict with the Meccans became more and more acute, culminating in open hostility, but at the same time he gained a number of new followers.

In 622, Mohammed and his followers moved to Medina (at the time the city was still called Yathrib; only later did it become known as Medina = the city of the prophet). This exodus (hijra) marks the beginning of the Islamic calendar. Mohammed was given a warm welcome in Medina. He made skilful use of the rivalry between Medina and the richer Mecca, gained great status there, and several times was appointed to mediate in disputes. He skilfully smoothed out the tensions between his old followers and the new believers from Medina, and changed more and more from a radical prophet to a careful and considered statesman. In 623 Mohammed worked out the first community constitution for his followers and tried, but failed, to gain the support of the Medina Jews. In particular vis-a-vis the Jews, he formulated the closeness yet separateness of Islam. He emphasized the importance of Abraham and his son Ishmael, and declared that the Ka'aba in Mecca was a shrine built by Abraham in honour of monotheism.

In the subsequent years, Mohammed concentrated very much on the imminent conflict with the people of Mecca. In 625 there was an out-and-out battle against them, in which the Muslims lost and Mohammed himself was wounded. In 627 the Meccans besieged Medina. Mohammed proved to be a brilliant defender in the so-called "Battle of the Trench" and forced an end to the siege. In 628 there was an amnesty with Mecca, but just two years later Mohammed took up arms against his home town and made the Ka'aba into a purely Muslim, monotheistic shrine. After Mecca had surrendered, the Prophet exercised leniency, declined to hold any major court trial to enforce punishment, but removed all the polytheistic images of gods from the city.

Mohammed continued to live in Medina, formulated the Islamic faith, and sent messengers to various rulers asking them to accept Islam. In March 632, he and his followers made the first Islamic pilgrimage to the Ka'aba in Mecca, upon which contemporary pilgrimages (hajj) are modelled. In the midst of preparations for the campaigns against Persia and Byzantium the Prophet fell ill, and died in Medina on June 8, 632.

Mohammed was a pious man who was sincerely convinced of the truth of the revelations he experienced. He was a psychologically gifted leader, imbued with a sense of mission, who was characterized more by feeling and strong will than by a sober analytical intellect. He pronounced a doctrine that was secular in focus, which was in harmony with the requirements of day-to-day politics, warfare and a sophisticated social order, yet which did not completely lose itself in worldly concerns. He was able to openly admit to his short-comings, but nevertheless throughout his life remained extremely sensitive to the ridicule of his opponents. He seems to have originally believed that he would easily be able to persuade Jews and Christians to accept his message, but opposition and ridicule on their part increasingly provoked Mohammed's anger.

Two distinct periods in Mohammed's activity can be distinguished: the prophet from Mecca, who was concerned with more general questions about God and faith and people's focus on the after-life, became in Medina a far-sighted statesman who establishes very detailed legal and social regulations on how the believers were to live together. Throughout his entire life he relied on his personal authority, the

steadfastness of his faith, and his political success. His life can serve as a model for the pious Muslim in every respect. One of his earliest direct successes was in establishing the universality of Islam, overcoming the ancient Arabic tribal loyalty and replacing it by a community of believers. It was only later that popular Islamic devotion made the practical, down-to-earth prophet into an infallible saint who had known no sin.

The Significance of Prophets in Islam

The greatest proximity of Islam to Judaism and Christianity is seen not only in their concept of God, but also in the significance they attach to the prophets. The Koran says that God has always sent prophets to all peoples, and that those prophets are always from within the population. The Koran distinguishes between simple prophets (nabi) who admonished and warned people, and the Messengers of God (rasul) who are specially chosen.

Mohammed is believed to be the last link in a long chain of prophets, and in Sura 33:40 is called the "Seal of the Prophets." For Islam the most important prophets before Mohammed were also those significant for Judaism and Christianity: Abraham (Arabic: Ibrahim), Moses (Arabic: Musa) and Jesus (Arabic: Issa). Islam believes in the original revelation and covenant between God and Adam as the first human being, but rejects the idea of original sin. It emphasizes the special correlation between divine revelation and natural human reason: people can directly recognize and rationally understand God's actions even though they cannot fathom the mystery of God. Abandoning one's faith is thus for Islam always tantamount

Mohammed Prays before the Kaaba
Turkish miniature

Mohammed's original intention was to make the Ka'aba into a shrine for all monotheistic religions. However, after his emigration to Medina he distanced himself from the Jews and Christians. He proclaimed the autonomy of Islam and declared the Ka'aba, which he said had been built by Abraham, to be a Muslim shrine. Since then believers no longer turn to face Jerusalem when praying, but to Mecca.

Mohammed Preaches to his Disciples
Turkish miniature

Mohammed appeared in Mecca as the leader of the early Islamic community, warning compatriots to turn away from idolatry and that God's judgement was nigh. In Mecca his principal work was teaching the faith, and he soon gathered followers around him. The essential content of his revelations focused on the goodness and omnipotence of God and God's concern for people as well as his call for people to return to the one God, Allah. He exhorted people to revere God and give him thanks and to be generous to their neighbours.

to abandoning reason. For Islam, all prophets announce what is ultimately one and the same message. Abraham is regarded by believers as the epitome of piety and obedience to God. The Koran mentions him specially as "example" and "friend of God" and he is seen as the archetypal seeker of God (hanif). Moses is referred to in the Koran as the "Chosen One," and is particularly significant for Islam as the pronouncer of the law, about which the Koran has a good deal to say. The Koran regards Jesus in many respects as directly prefiguring Mohammed. It mentions the Virgin Mary as being chosen by God to give birth to Jesus. The statements about Mary in the Koran resemble those in the Christian apocryphal scriptures in many respects. Islam sees Jesus as an important prophet who was ridiculed by the Jews (as Mohammed was by his people), but it makes no mention of his role as redeemer of mankind, and decisively disputes that he was the Son of God. God is One (Allah), He has no son and does not "associate" himself with any other person. The Koran commentators believe, however, that Jesus will come again at the end of time: he will come again as a perfected Muslim and rule as the righteous king over a unified world.

The Koran deals in great detail with Mohammed's call to prophecy, and defends him against the criticism of his contemporary opponents that he was either a liar or was possessed by demons. Mohammed knew that as God's Chosen One he would be guided by God and that he should ask Allah to forgive people's weakness. The series of prophets ends with Mohammed as the "Seal of the Prophets." Islam is thus the religious and temporal completion of the religion that God intended from the beginning. Mohammed is both an ordinary person and a chosen prophet at one and the same time.

THE KORAN: ALLAH'S MESSAGE

Structure and Significance of the Koran

For religious Muslims the Koran is the sacred book, in which God's direct revelation is written down as it was announced to the people by Mohammed. The Koran is for them the ultimate reference for how to behave in the world, a book of guidance, teaching and edification for all believers.

The word Koran is spelt "Qur'an" in Arabic and comes from "qara'a" = to read, read aloud. The Koran is thus the book that is to be read or recited. Appropriately, the first word of God's revelation to Mohammed, recorded in the oldest Koranic Sura, Sura 96, is: "Recite!" (iqra!). The Koran comprises 114 Suras (chapters) of different lengths, each named after a characteristic word in the text. They are not in chronological order, and are a mixture from the different periods of Mohammed's pronouncements, which occasionally leads to some rather contradictory statements. However, the rule of thumb is that the statement of a later Sura in the Koran takes precedence over an earlier one. All Suras (with the exception of Sura 9) begin by invoking the name of God (basmala).

The Arabic of the Koran is regarded by believers to be inspired by God, which is why Muslims were disinclined and for a long time opposed to translating the Koran into other languages. That opposition to some extent still exists.

The Koran is believed to be of divine origin, eternal, not created, but existing with God before the creation in the form of a "heavenly archetypal book" (umm al-kitab; literally the "mother of the book") and the "word of God." Its message was given directly and without change to Mohammed.

On the basis of differences in style and content, four periods of revelation recorded by Mohammed in the Koran can be distinguished. Three periods are before the hijra (emigration) of 622, and these are known as the Meccan periods; his utterances in Medina constitute the fourth period. All the Meccan revelations aim at converting non-believers, and describe in graphic terms the joy experienced in paradise by the believers and the tortures suffered in hell by the non-believers. The Suras of the first Meccan period are short, rhythmic and full of poetic charm. The second Meccan period is calmer and more considered in style. It tells exemplary stories from the ancient Arab world and draws upon themes similar to those in the Bible. The third Meccan period is very prosaic, and full of repetition. The Medina period is concerned with fighting for the autonomy of Islam, particularly to distinguish it from the Jewish faith. After Mohammed's death in 632, the divine revelation was regarded as completed. The sayings of the Prophet were collected under the first three caliphs, evaluated and systematized. Under the third caliph, Uthman (644–656), the Koran was presented to believers in the version that is still used today.

The Koran and Hadith

Apart from the sayings of Mohammed, the exemplary life of the Prophet also presented believers with a problem of interpretation, more precisely the reliability of the transmission (hadith) of his actions and beliefs in different concrete situations. This caused the sunna (Arabic "sunna" = usual way of behaving,

custom) – the exemplary life of the Prophet – to be accorded much higher value.

In the 9th century, the six orthodox compendia of the traditions (sahih: literally, authentic) were compiled. They are known as the hadith collections. They are not only commentaries on the Koran, but more importantly collections of references for the concrete legal problems of daily life, traced back to the example of the Prophet and his environment. Especially important is the proof of a "chain of transmitters" (isnad) that has as few gaps as possible, and the compatibility with other recognized transmissions. The hadith collections are, after the Koran, the second main source for the statements of Islamic theology and law.

DOCTRINE AND RELIGIOUS LIFE

The Only One – Allah:
Creator – Guide of the World – Judge

Belief in Allah, the one and only God, is at the heart of Islam. Muslims express their uncompromisingly theocentric view of the world in their unqualified surrender to and worship of God and by unconditionally subjugating themselves to his will and wisdom.

The fight against any kind of polytheism and the exclusive emphasis on the oneness of Allah are central points in the religious warnings that Mohammed repeatedly issued. In the Koran, God is the free creator of everything, the act of creation being depicted as the division of heaven and earth out of one coherent mass.

God created mankind in a way similar to that described in the Old Testament, out of earth or clay. On occasions the Koran emphasizes that

Fragment of the Koran on Parchment
Iraq or Syria, 8th–9th century

Solon and Disciples
from: The Selected Sayings of
Wisdom and Finest Speeches
(Mukthar al-hikam wa-mahasin al-
kalim by al-Mubashshir), Syria, 1st
half of 13th century

This miniature painting arose out of
the need to illustrate the Arabic
translations of scientific Greek works.
The Solon miniature gives an
impression of the beauty and high
degree of realism that characterizes
miniatures of the first half of the 13th
century. The picture shows the Greek
sage Solon teaching a group of
pupils. His red beard, showing that
he is a foreigner, contrasts with the
black beards of his audience, who
are dressed in Arab-style clothes. The
attentive expressions on their faces,
alert postures and lively gestures
show how fascinated they are by the
power of his words. The scene
symbolizes how the legacy of the
Ancient World was transmitted to the
Arab world, the chain of tradition
that links the Classical Age to the
Islamic Age.

the creation came about simply through God pronouncing the creative words "Let there be" (and there was). The Koran stresses the rational orderliness of the entire creation, and how all things are interconnected. All the laws of the world, including causality, come directly from the will of God and divine wisdom. The creation is seen as a permanent and continual process (Latin: creatio continua); the world does not possess an autonomous coherence, but is created each moment anew by God. This also applies to humankind.

Everything that happens to people is predetermined by God (predestination). In the examination of the relationship between God and man the strong emphasis on predestination has made the problem of human free will a particularly controversial point in Islamic doctrine. The question arises as to why God leads some people to the correct faith and thus to salvation and lets others perish through their lack of faith. Thus, in early Islam, those who denied human freedom (Jabarites, from the Arabic jabr = compulsion) argued against the emphatic defenders of the freedom of human beings to decide and act (Mu'tazilites; the official state religion in the 9th century). It was the school of Ash'arites, who asserted themselves in the 10th century, who emphasized the unrestricted predetermination of everything by God, but also the responsibility of the human being. The Ash'arites believe that all actions have two levels: each action is created by God in human beings but the individual consents to this and takes it upon himself in an act of "acquisition"

(kasb or itkisab), which gives him the feeling of freedom. But the capacity to take this upon himself, this act of acquisition, is in turn something that God has created in man. The starting point for this idea are the commandments of God pronounced in the Koran. Ethical rules can only be appropriately established if people have the ability to differentiate between good and evil (and also the freedom to choose between these two possibilities).

The main enemy of the Islamic concept of God is polytheism in any form. Again and again the oneness of Allah is stressed in different formulae, such as the passage in the short Sura 112: "Say: God is One, the Eternal God. He begat none, nor was He begotten. None is His equal." (Sura 112:1–4).

The worst sin that even God does not forgive is "associating" (shirk) other gods or persons of God with God (Sura 4:48). This is aimed principally at the ancient Arabic polytheism that Mohammed was confronted with. Many passages of the Koran protest vehemently against the idea of a God who fathers children or has children: "Never has God begotten a son, nor is there any other god besides Him" (Sura 23:91). The idea of another God or a further person of God is for Islam tantamount to giving up the belief in the indivisible omnipotence and supremacy of God, and a weakening of God's sole supremacy. It is thus not only erroneous and based on a falsehood, but is also a form of blasphemy.

Gradually this reproach was directed towards Christianity and its emphasis on Jesus Christ being the Son of God. Despite the fact that the Koran holds Jesus in high esteem, Islam denies the claim of the historical figure of Jesus to be divine, or even that he said he was the Son of God. It considers statements of that nature to be a subsequent exaggeration in the Christian scriptures. Similarly, the Christian dogma of the trinity is for Islam a kind of "disguised polytheism," undermining the oneness and uniqueness of God.

The Koran situates the angels as the "servants of God" between the absolute transcendence of God and the world of humanity. It ascribes clearly defined tasks to them and regards the jinn as spirits created out of fire being somewhere between the angels and humanity. The Koran also pronounces the existence of the devil (Iblis) and his demons, who lead people astray.

Islamic Ideas of the Afterlife

The belief in the Day of Judgement and Allah's severe judgement of the life the believer led on this earth is a central element of Islam. For Muslims, death is the separation of body and soul, the moment when special angels of death (especially Izra'il) lead the person's soul to heaven. The Final Judgement, described as the "supreme disaster" (Sura 79:34), is depicted in a martial and graphic manner, similar to John's Apocalypse in Christianity. The deeds of each individual, which are recorded in books, are recited and shown to the person. God then pronounces judgement and separates the saved from the damned. Both the tortures of hell and the joys of paradise are depicted in extreme and sensory terms. When calculating the good deeds, it is not simply faith that counts, but the practical expression of that faith, in other words the link between faith and good deeds is considered crucial. In several places, the Koran mentions the superabundance of food and pleasures of the senses in paradise, as well as the joy of sexual intercourse with the virgins of paradise (huri). It will, however, be possible for only a few chosen believers to look upon God, and then only for a few moments.

The "Five Pillars of Islam"

In devotional practice Islam rests on what are known as the five pillars (arkan). The first pillar is the public and visible profession of faith (shahada). It has to be said in Arabic and means "I testify (confess) that there is no God but the one God (or: that there is no god besides God); and I testify (confess) that Mohammed is the Messenger of God." The profession of faith is something to be said both by the individual and the community. It affirms the oneness of God (tawhid) and the unity of all created things and humankind in direct connection with the Creator. These words accompany a Muslim for life, gather the believers for the communal act of worship, and form the core of all prayers and all affirmations about God. The shahada is the only one of the five pillars that is the object of theological dogma and is not a law of the Shari'a. With the conscious and serious pronouncement of this formula in front of witnesses, a person becomes a Muslim. Once having been accepted into the community, the state of being a Muslim is irrevocable, and turning away from

God is punishable by death. Scholars of Islamic law thus stress the grave consequences of this step and advise careful examination of inner readiness. The acceptance of the faith can only be an act of free will, without any coercion.

A particular form of profession of faith and ritualized act of worship is the salat, the liturgical praying that is obligatory at certain times of day. This is the second pillar of Islam, and is a communal prayer. Before performing the salat, the believer must be in a state of purity. He or she therefore carries out a series of ritual ablutions. Ritual purity (tahara) is the prerequisite for all religious and devotional acts. The five fixed times of prayer – morning, noon, afternoon, sunset and evening – are intended to remind Muslims day and night of their position as worshippers of Allah. A muezzin (caller to prayer) summons the faithful, by chanting from the tower of the mosque.

The salat has to be performed by believers wherever they happen to be, but it must be performed in the mosque by at least some believers. The link between Muslims throughout the world is emphasized by the fact that everyone prays facing the Ka'aba in Mecca. At a sign from the imam (prayer leader), men and women gather in separate rows or separate rooms in the mosque, but move close together as a sign of their connectedness.

Uniformity is also guaranteed by the imam, who takes up his position in the prayer niche (mihrab) of the mosque that marks the direction of Mecca. Their gaze fixed on him, the believers pray as if one person. The posture for

The Dome of the Rock (Omar Mosque, Kubbat al Sakhra) in Jerusalem
Built 688–91 under the caliph Abdelmalik on the spot occupied by the Ark of the Covenant in Solomon's Temple.

The brilliant gold dome of the Dome of the Rock built on the Temple Mount towers majestically over Jerusalem's Old City. Persian tiles decorate the outer facades of the octagonal mosque that, alongside the Ka'aba and the Tomb Mosque of Mohammed in Medina, is one of the most important Islamic shrines. Legend has it that people's souls are weighed on the arcades that edge the mountain plateau in order to determine their place in the afterlife. Inside the dome is the Sacred Rock on which Abraham was meant to sacrifice his son Isaac. Faithful Muslims claim to see the hoof-marks of Buraq, Mohammed's mount that carried him on his journey to heaven.

Friday Mosque in Isfahan
Inner courtyard with great iwan on the southern side

As far as we know, building of the Friday Mosque began in the mid-12th century during the Seljuk era. It is the oldest mosque with a four iwan structure. Of the four iwans, or open vaulted halls, that are grouped around a central courtyard, the southern iwan is the most striking due to the beauty of its magnificent colored tiles. The arch which leads into the domed hall in front of the mihrab is decorated by 14 medallions, divided up by rosettes from the Safavid era bearing prayers in honour of Mohammed, his daughter Fatima and the 12 imams. Characteristic for Persian architecture are the tapering minarets that tower above the building, each crowned with a pavilion-like ambulatory.

prayer is also fixed, and consists of a series of motions performed in a specified sequence. Each of the five daily acts of prayer is terminated by repeating the praise "Allahu akbar" ("God is the Greatest") and a recitation of the 1st Sura of the Koran, which is itself a prayer. Each of the people praying then says the "Salamu alaikum" (Peace be with you) to their neighbours to the right and the left.

The Friday worship service in the mosque at midday is of great significance. In contrast to the Jews and Christians, Mohammed chose Friday as the day for communal worship. It is not, however, a civil day of rest, in other words not a holiday in the Christian sense. The core of this act of worship is a sermon, which the preacher delivers in a standing position.

Almsgiving, zakat, is the third pillar of Islam. Generally speaking, it is the duty of a believer to share his wealth with other members of the faith who are less well off or are in need. This is the foundation of the social actions of all Muslims. Unlike in Christianity, zakat is not based on free will, but is a religious obligation. Generally speaking zakat can be described as a tax. The Koran says little about how often or how much must be given, but concentrates on the inner value of giving and the ethical attitude of the giver. It is similar to the sayings of Jesus in the New Testament in that it values quiet giving more highly than a public show of generosity which is always subject to the suspicion of self-righteousness.

The Islamic legal system grew up after Mohammed's death, particularly in connection with questions as to how the giving of alms should be organized. The Shari'a sets out precise regulations about the levies, depending on the different types of property and the goods to be offered. The Muslim pays his zakat on agricultural crops, cattle, gold and silver in different amounts and – to put it simply – 2.5 % of his annual cash earnings from merchandise used in trade. The recipients of the alms are divided into eight groups. At the top are the poor and needy, but orphans, the sick, and travellers in distress have to be taken into account as well as public works to the glory of Allah.

Zakat serves to strengthen Muslims' sense of moral and social responsibility for one another, their care for those in socially weaker positions, and as a corrective against exaggerated egoism, vulgar striving for profit or social indifference. The believer also gives special alms and gifts to the needy at various annual Islamic festivals, particularly at the end of Ramadan, the month of fasting. In the zakat system the combination of a religious, devotional duty and a sophisticated taxation law with secular overtones is striking. Politically-minded Muslims see in zakat, as the institutionalization of reciprocal social responsibility, an anticipation of modern state welfare systems.

During the period of holy fasting, Ramadan, the 9th month in the Islamic calendar, the pious Muslim abstains throughout the entire month from eating and drinking, smoking and sexual intercourse between the hours of sunrise and sunset. Ritual fasting (sawm) is the fourth pillar of Islam. Fasting, too, stresses the community aspect of Islam. Physical self-discipline is meant to lead to inner purification: the individual reflects upon his duties to and actions for the community and seeks reconciliation with his partners in faith. In this aspect of inner reflection, the fasting month of Ramadan is comparable to Lent in the Christian calendar. In fasting, thanks is given for the gifts of everyday life by reminding oneself of them through abstention. Ramadan is the month of patience and the reward for patience is paradise. According to one of the sayings of Mohammed, fasting is God's preferred form of prayer because no one sees it but him. Nevertheless the Shari'a does have limitations on the commandment to fast and also recognizes mitigating circumstances. For example, only healthy adult Muslims are obliged to keep sawm; old people, the sick, pregnant women and nursing mothers, people doing heavy manual work and travellers are exempt. They can either fast at a different time or perform a specified act of penitence. This is especially important for believers who live and work in non-Islamic countries. Generally speaking, the flexible principle applies that fasting should only be done if the health of the person fasting is not jeopardised. The mosques are particularly full toward the end of the month, when on 27 Ramadan in the "Night of Power" or "Night of Decree" (laylat al-qadr) the descent of the Koran from heaven and the beginning of Mohammed's life as a prophet are commemorated.

The fifth pillar of Islam is hajj, the pilgrimage to Mecca and its surrounding area. Every Muslim should – if health, financial means and the safety of the routes allow – undertake this pilgrimage at least once in his life. Hajj is a pilgrimage to the holy places where Mohammed lived and worked. The central focus is the black, cube-shaped Ka'aba with the sacred stone built into its walls in the mosque at Mecca, which according to the Koran was built by Abraham with the help of his son Ishmael as a sign of the veneration of Allah.

Visiting Mecca is at any time an important religious practice for Muslims, but particularly so in the 12th month of the Islamic calendar, the month of pilgrimages Dhu al-Hijja, when the "great pilgrimage" begins and believers from all parts of the Muslim world stream into Mecca by the thousands. When they get close to Mecca the pilgrims enter a certain state of ritual purity and sanctity (ihram) and formulate for themselves the meaning of their pilgrimage, put on a simple white pilgrim's robe as a sign of preparatory purity, and subject themselves to particular rules.

In the great mosque of Mecca they walk seven times around the Ka'aba (tawaf) and then walk seven times back and forth between the hills of al-Safa and al-Marwa. This is a reminder of the distress of Hagar (one of Abraham's wives) and her son Ishmael in the desert, when God saved them by causing the spring of Zamzam to well up out of the sand of the desert. The believers then drink from this well, its water being thought to have miraculous powers, before they continue a few kilometres further to Mount Arafat.

Here the high point of the pilgrimage takes place, with the pilgrims standing in meditation and prayer from noon to sunset. After sunset, they walk to nearby Mina, breaking their journey in Muzdalifa where they spend the night and collect pebbles which, on the next morning in Mina, are thrown onto three heaps of stones. This custom is a reminder of the steadfast faith of Abraham and the wondrous rescue of his son, Ishmael (Isaac). To commemorate this, the believers sacrifice sheep and camels as a sign of their humility, and have their hair cut. The Feast of Sacrifice (id al-adha) lasts for four days and is celebrated throughout the Islamic world. The meat of the sacrificial animals is given to the poor. Mohammed saw this festival as the fulfilment of the Muslim community.

The pilgrimage means that Mecca is held in high esteem as the centre for Muslims throughout the world. The gigantic gatherings of believers in Mecca and the surrounding area during the "great pilgrimage" often result in outbreaks of mass panic, and clashes between different groups of pilgrims. The culmination of conflicts of this kind was the violent occupation of the mosque at Mecca by radical Muslims in 1979, and the suppression of the revolt by Saudi Arabian troops. Since the conquering of the holy sites in 1924, the members of the ruling family as-Saud regard themselves as protectors or guardians (sharifs) of the holy sites and all matters concerning pilgrimages. Indeed, the Saudi King Fahd even renounced his official title as king in 1986 and has since called himself "Protector of the Two Holy Sites" (Mecca and Medina).

ISLAMIC LAW

The Islamic Legal System: Shari'a

Islam is a "lay religion," that is to say it rejects the need for a separate class of priests to lead people to God and salvation. It is also a religion of laws. The religious obligations and the "Five Pillars of Islam" apply equally to all believers.

There is a genuinely Islamic theology, but due to the many and varied social obligations of the individual towards the community, the legal problems of daily communal life have moved more and more into the foreground for the mass of believers. Thus the pious Muslim goes not to the priest but to a legal expert (faqih,

Muslim at Prayer

The salat, the strictly ritualistic prayer, is one of the fundamental religious obligations of every Muslim. It is said at fixed times, wherever the believer happens to be. As a sign of total surrender to God the person praying kneels down and lays his or her forehead on the ground. The person at prayer faces the sacred Ka'aba in Mecca, symbolizing the community of all Muslims throughout the world.

For example, Sura 64:16 says "Fear God, in so far as you are able, listen and be obedient.

In the Koran, the law is depicted as the light that gives people insight and understanding and enables them to make a (fair) judgement. The Koran emphasizes the parallel between the significance of its law for Muslims and the Torah for Jews, or the Gospels for Christians. The law is meant to create and preserve unity among Muslims.

Islamic Teaching on Obligations: Classification of Actions

In early Islam there were vehement arguments about how human deeds came to be classified as "good" or "evil." The Mu'tazilites assumed an inner quality of every action that can be recognized by human powers of reasoning and does not directly depend on God's decision. Orthodoxy (the Ash'arites), by contrast, assumes to this day the absolute sovereignty of divine will that, by its decree alone, determines what is good and what is evil. Mankind merely has to establish what God's commandments are, interpret them and follow them.

Human deeds are thus divided into five categories with regard to the divine law:

a) Actions which are obligatory. Their performance is rewarded, their omission punished.

b) Actions that are recommended, that are advantageous for the religion and the community. Their performance is rewarded by God, but their omission will not be punished.

c) Actions that are allowed, that are morally neutral. Their performance will not be rewarded by God, their omission will not be punished.

d) Actions that are disapproved of, that limit religious obedience. Their omission will be rewarded by God, but their performance will not be punished.

e) forbidden actions. Believers are commanded to refrain from them and will be rewarded for doing so; their performance will be punished.

Human sins are divided into major and minor sins. The gravest sins are those against God and the faith, followed by those against fellow humans and their right not to suffer harm, and thirdly are those against the means of daily life, i.e. offences against property, character defamation and false witness. According to the Koran, God forgives all sins if he so wishes, with the exception of not believing. The Koran commands respect for human life, and has

Mihrab, Prayer Niche at the Mosque in Cordoba

The mihrab wing of the mosque, which only the caliph and his retinue were allowed to enter, symbolizes the secular power of the ruler, and is the focal point of the building. Magnificent gold mosaics with vine scroll decoration on different colored backgrounds decorate the facade of the mihrab (designed by a Byzantine master), and give the space an air of mysticism. The golden inscriptions on a blue ground surrounding the tympanum are quotations from the Koran and praise the name of al-Hakam II (961–976). In a horseshoe-shaped arch flanked by four marble columns the facade opens onto the mihrab, the prayer niche. A perfect octagonal space, its chapel-like design represented a new departure in Islamic sacred architecture, and was the model for virtually all later mihrabs in Spain and North Africa.

plural: fuqaha) for advice and help. The Islamic legal system (Shari'a) is a fundamental element of Islam, which has the capacity to underpin the community of Muslims and unite it. Islamic scholars (collective term: ulama) are thus always knowledgeable in both religious and legal matters. Even Mohammed commented on ancient Arabic common law, and announced his ethical and moral principles in forms that were based on legal thinking. This is particularly true of the precepts.

The Koran stresses both the positive and negative characteristics of human beings. God gave mankind responsibility for the earth, but with clear instructions and laws. But, according to the Koran, mankind tends toward non-belief or even evil, and depends upon the grace of God. Without divine guidance, people are by nature too weak to be able to tread the path of goodness. Nevertheless, it is thought that God does not want to make it difficult for people; he makes it easy. Consequently, virtually all the commandments of Islam have easier forms or exceptions.

severely restricted the ancient Arabic laws of blood revenge, although killing out of retribution is not necessarily considered to be unjustified. Human sexuality is affirmed without reservation as having been given by God, but it is subject to clear rules. Promiscuity and lack of chastity incur drastic punishment under the Koran. Repeatedly, justice is cited as the outstanding virtue of Muslims and the meaning of the divine order in the world.

The Four Sunni Law Schools

The legal language of Islam is to be found in virtually all areas of Islamic life and also characterizes the testifying character of the profession of faith (shahada).

After the death of the Prophet, the caliphs and scholars of Islam very quickly wanted to establish a comprehensive legal system to regulate life in Muslim communities. In the majority Sunni Islam (from the Arabic sunna = custom, habit), four orthodox law schools (madhab, plural: madhahib) were formed and still exist today:

a) The Hanafi school, named after its founder Abu Hanifa (699-767), was the first to be formed and is still the most widespread of all the law schools. It is also the most liberal, and allows more room for rationality and individual opinion (ra'y), something for which it is reproached by its opponents. It has a great love of legal niceties and introduced into the Islamic legal system a number of procedures and ways of thinking with general validity. It is dominant in Central Asia, India, Pakistan, Turkey, Afghanistan and in parts of Egypt and Tunisia.

b) By comparison, the Maliki School, named after Malik ibn Anas (715-795), is conservative and makes great reference to the common law valid in Medina at the time of the Prophet. Its legal interpretations are sometimes very rigorous. It is dominant in the Maghreb, North and West Africa, Mauritania, the Sudan and Kuwait.

c) The Shafi'i School, named after al-Shafi'i (767-820), a pupil of the two previous schools, is the most systematic of the law schools and occupies a position in the centre, between the more liberal Hanafis and more conservative Malikis. It has gained a reputation mainly for its subtle differentiation of legal principles. It is widespread in the entire Near East, and predominant in Indonesia, Malaysia, Jordan, Palestine, Syria, Lebanon, and parts of Egypt.

d) The Hanbali School, named after Ahmad ibn Hanbal (780-855), represents severe and uncompromising traditionalism of great piety, which due to its rigidity did not gain great popularity. Since the early 19th century it has found increasing respect in the Arab world through the Wahhabi reform movement. The Hanbali School is predominant in Saudi Arabia and some small states on the Arabian peninsula, and also has some supporters in Syria, Iraq and Algeria.

Whilst in the early days the law schools feuded with each other, sometimes vehemently, over the course of time a process of mainly practically-oriented adaptation to one another has taken place. The four law schools share a common adherence to the four "roots" (usul) of jurisprudence, namely to the two legal sources, the Koran and hadith, and two legal procedures. The first is drawing an analogy between one legal case and a similar one (qiyas) – a procedure that has its origins in the early days of Islam and is based on individual judgement (ra'y), and the second is consensus (ijma), or rather the "agreement of the scholars" on a technical question. The latter goes back to Mohammed's belief that an individual might err, whereas God's guidance could never unite the entire community of believers in erroneous thought.

By stressing the consensus of scholars, Sunni Islam has (since approximately the 11th century) "closed the doors" on independent research (ijtihad, literally: exertion) by the individual believer into the Koran and hadith. The believer, as well as entire groups or governments, thus turn in case of doubt to a

On Mohammed's Birthday in Akbar Nagar, Bihar

The mawlid, the Feast of Mohammed's Birthday, is the climax of the "Mohammed Cycle," the festivals that celebrate the life of the Prophet. As a sign of their veneration, the faithful wear a white pilgrim's robe for their processions and carry green flags and banners, the colours of Mohammed, who as a child is said to have worn a white woolen dress and lain on a green silk blanket.

Islamic Feast of Sacrifice
in a village, K'maras province, Turkey

To mark the pilgrimage to Mecca (hajj), believers celebrate the Feast of Sacrifice, the most important feast in the Muslim calendar. Sheep are ritually slaughtered to commemorate Abraham's willingness to sacrifice his son. The meat is not for personal consumption but, as a sign of the community of faithful Muslims, is given to friends and distributed amongst the poor and needy.

legal expert and ask him to draw up a concrete legal opinion (fatwa), which incidentally eliminates the responsibility largely from the individual who has faith in the knowledge of the legal expert.

The Law in the Daily Lives of Muslims

In Islamic law there is a strange dualism in ethical-religious and legal interpretations, although for pious Muslims the two aspects neither simply concur nor can be clearly separated. The Shari'a distinguishes between the rights of God and the rights of human beings, and between the obligations to God and obligations to fellow humans.

Islamic law is not consistently uniform, and can often be interpreted in different ways – which is where the skills of the legal expert are all-important. A number of transgressions, particularly in matters to do with God's rights, are not punished by the judge (qadi): in this the maxim generally applies that it is not the individual failure to fulfil the law, nor the individual transgression, that makes a person a non-believer, but the denial of the binding nature of the requirements of the law. In virtually all Islamic countries the relationship between Shari'a and political or state power is not as simple as it should be according to the Islamic ideal. Virtually nowhere do state law and religious law reflect each other perfectly. Although Turkey has a deliberately and explicitly secular law (due to the reforms of Kemal Atatürk after

World War I), in other Islamic countries there are clearly secular tendencies, or at least an increasing secularization of state legislation. For complete legal capacity according to Islam it is necessary to be in full possession of one's mental faculties and be of age, yet restriction of legal responsibility begins at birth. For that reason, legal regulation of tutelage and other relationships of dependency plays an important role. Family and marriage legislation with emphasis on conjugal obligations and modern forms of divorce are also given a good deal of attention. Inheritance law with an exact regulation of quotas (which relative is entitled to which share), property law with its emphatic prohibition of charging interest and usury, and criminal law with its restriction of the ancient Arabic idea of blood revenge and an exact graduation of punishments – from corporal punishment to blood money, to the death penalty – these were all central issues in the Koranic idea of law as long ago as Mohammed's time in Medina, and were developed and systematized after his death.

FURTHER DEVELOPMENTS OF ISLAM AND ISLAMIC CULTURE

Islamic Thought in the Middle Ages

Islam produced great cultural achievements in virtually all fields. The capitals of Islamic kingdoms, such as Baghdad, Damascus, Cairo and Cordoba, were also important centres of culture, and developments there had great impact on all Islamic countries. The heyday of Islamic art, culture and science was between the 8th and 13th centuries, and left a particularly deep imprint on the 9th to 11th centuries, extending far beyond Islam's sphere of religious influence.

Islamic philosophy grew principally out of commentated translations of Greek philosophy, particularly the works of Plato and Aristotle, and it was via Islam that these works arrived in the West. The main areas of Islamic philosophy were metaphysics (which was very close to theology), logic, epistemology, ethics and political philosophy. The theology-related questions were concerned principally with the nature of God and (possible) attributes of God, knowledge of God, the beginning of time and creation, and when the world would end.

Astronomy was also closely linked to philosophy, looking at the hierarchies and cycles of the cosmos and furthering knowledge of the Ancient Orient to great effect. Arabic mathematics assimilated the knowledge of the Ancient Greeks and soon exceeded it. The word "algebra," for example, is of Arabic origin (from al-gabr). Arab-Persian medicine, which was exemplary for the entire world at the time, combined empirical observations with speculations about the nature of human beings, incorporating some of the legacy of Greece and India and establishing its own schools. The writings of Hippocrates and Galen were known in translation. The important Islamic thinkers were, like their Greek role models, universally educated. Almost all of them also worked as physicians, astronomers and mathematicians, and often held high positions in court or state.

Al-Kindi (died 870) combined Aristotelian philosophy in an original way with neo-Platonic elements. He put forward his own philosophical theory of prophecy and divine revelation, and is said to have left behind 300 articles, of which some 70 are extant. Al-Farabi (870-950) is the most important Islamic commentator on Greek philosophy. With his "Model State," he had a decisive influence on the political thought of Muslims, and his legal philosophy had as strong an influence on Judaism as on Islam. Ibn Sina (latin: Avicenna) (930–1037) is regarded as having perfected Islamic philosophy. As a systematician he developed a synthesis of philosophy and theology. He mastered all the sciences known at the time and was widely famed. Ibn Rushd (latin: Averroes) (1126–1198) purged philosophy, particularly that of Aristoteles, of later theological and mystical interpretations. He was more active in the West than the Arab world, being particularly popular in France, and had a direct influence on Thomas Aquinas, the most important Western thinker in the Middle Ages. A very original Islamic thinker was the Tunisian Ibn Chaldun (1332–1406), who developed his own philosophy of history and a very modern sociology and theory of culture which was not really appreciated until centuries later, when it influenced the thinking of Karl Marx and Emile Durkheim, for example.

All the arts and sciences were greatly promoted by the ruling Islamic dynasties, particularly by the Abbasid caliphs of the 9th and 10th centuries and the Moorish rulers of Spain, who developed their residence cities into centres of contemporary art and science.

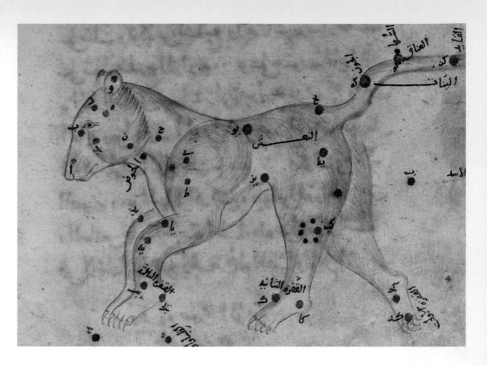

Islamic Mysticism: Sufis and Dervishes

Islamic mysticism, a rich and complex tradition, was always in a relationship of tension with the official Islam propagated by the rulers, warriors and legal experts. It has many links to non-Islamic influences and has always maintained itself in a strange balance between turning away from the world and calling for an inner renewal of Islam.

The spiritual origins of Islamic mysticism lie in the praise of penitent asceticism, which the Koran clearly endorses, but also in the encounter of Islam, as it spread to other countries, with the forms of piety found in those cultures that had been incorporated into the Islamic world. For example, the influence of the Christian monastic system is unmistakable, as is the incorporation of the ideas of Indian and Buddhist itinerant monks and the Persian-influenced neo-Platonists and Gnostics.

The initially pious asceticism soon developed into deliberate seeking after God, which centred on ideas of fear of and trust in God, coupled with renunciation of the world, and the search for inner peace. The central focus was complete reliance on God (tawakkul) which included concepts of "submission" (taslim), namely of oneself to God, and "trusting" (tafwid).

Meditation (fikr) and constantly remembering God (dhikr) became important. The intuitive recognition of God, which for the mystic is the inner measure of the truth of the individual's faith, has greater importance for the mystic than scholarly knowledge and mere external

Depiction of the Great Bear from: Star catalogue of al-Sufi (1009/10)

Islam has produced outstanding cultural achievements in all fields, both in the arts and sciences, with astronomy and astrology held in particularly high esteem. Even in pre-Islamic times, the nomads used the stars to guide them and calculated their movements in order to determine where they were and tell time. The stars were also seen as higher powers, holding the promise of good fortune or misfortune. The legacy of knowledge inherited from the Greeks also played an important role in Islamic astrology. The influence of the constellations on the planets was recognized, knowledge which was used particularly in medicine. The individual constellations were assigned to certain parts of the body and used to diagnose illnesses. The "Great Bear" constellation comes from Al-Sufi's star catalogue, which was published in Europe in Latin translation and contributed to the Arab names for the stars becoming widely known in Europe. The Arabic handwriting on the picture appears as it does on the Ptolemaic celestial globe.

Abu Said (967–1049) – a Persian Mystic and Strict Adherent to Sufism
from a Maqamat manuscript (Book of Collections), probably Syrian, around 1300

This miniature shows the Persian mystic Abu Said preaching in the mosque at Samarkand. The sermons of the mystic, based on his practical and intuitive experiences, were often more successful than the speeches of the scholars, which intensified the conflict with orthodoxy.

Dervish Dancing in a Trance
Dotted engraving, around 1810

Dervishes, members of Islamic mendicant orders that were formed by disciples of the mystics (Sufis), dance themselves into an ecstatic state of euphoria in order to achieve direct union with God. Their magnificent costumes, consisting of a full skirt and hat or turban, varies according to the order and distinguishes the different ranks within the community.

adherence to the law. Conflict between Islamic mysticism and the official theology and political orthodoxy was thus inevitable. The metaphorical language of mysticism, which came mainly from Ancient Persian metaphysics, was suspicious to official Islam, as was the appearance of many mystics as preachers issuing admonishments and advocating reform, and venerated by the masses as saints.

Repeatedly, the feelings of suspicion escalated to actual waves of persecution, culminating in the execution of the important mystic al-Halladsch in 922. The great mystic and theologian al-Ghazzali (1058–1111) attempted to reconcile mysticism with official theology. The Andalusian mystic Ibn al-Arabi (1165–1250) claimed that by increasing his inner faith he had penetrated to the nature of God and had experienced unity with God. A particular high point of Islamic mysticism was the work of Jalal al-Din Rumi (1208–1273), whose passionate poetry displays great musicality and rich imagery.

In the 12th century, religious orders grew up as specific organizations of mystics (tariqa), some of which were organized in actual monasteries and brotherhoods, others in associations. The mystics became known as "Sufis" (from the Arabic suf = wool) – those wearing a woollen robe. The religious orders were very similar to the organized and formal Buddhist and Christian monastic orders, and had a strictly hierarchical structure. The sheikh, to whom the brothers had to show absolute obedience, acted as head of the order. One rule for example was: "You should be in the hand of your sheikh like a corpse in the hand of the person washing it."

The brotherhoods assumed a charitable and pastoral function. In the early days they formed a number of fortified monasteries to defend the borders of the Islamic areas (ribat) and thus prefigured the Christian Orders of Knights of the Middle Ages. The members of the Islamic brotherhood were known in Persian as "Dervishes" (etymology not entirely clear). The type of order and structure of the communities and monasteries varied greatly and was not centrally coordinated. Some brotherhoods, such as the 19th century Sanusiya movement in Libya, also became politically significant, and led the combative Islamic reform movement.

THE POLITICS AND HISTORY OF ISLAM

The Caliphs – Successors to the Prophet, and God's Representatives on Earth

It was clear that early Islam, after Mohammed's death, saw itself as a union of politics and religion, extending the example set by the Prophet. The successors to the Prophet – known as caliphs (from the arabic chalifa = representative, successor) – assumed not only the religious leadership of the community, but also the organization of an area of state responsibility that became steadily larger. Their dual role is expressed in their title "Ruler of the Believers."

Since the Prophet left no clear instructions about succession, the first caliph elected by the tribes after his sudden death was his father-in-law Abu-Bakr (632-634), who was the father of Mohammed's favourite wife Aisha. He had been one of Mohammed's earliest followers, and through the respect he enjoyed was able to hold together the community that was already beginning to diverge in different directions. The second caliph, Umar (634–644), was also a father-in-law of Mohammed, and had been part of the Prophet's closest circle of followers. Within a few years he completed Islam's conquest of Mesopotamia, Syria, Palestine, Egypt and Persia, which had begun under Abu-Bakr. These rapid military and political successes were seen, and in fact still are seen, by Muslims as "proof" of the fact that Islam is right and cannot be resisted.

During the military conquests that followed, Islam adopted a skilful attitude of political tolerance, placing the "People of the Scriptures" (also known as "People of the Book") – Jews, Christians and in Persia the Zoroastrians (followers of Zarathustra) – as "officially protected people" (dhimmi) under the protection of Islam. They paid a special poll tax to the Islamic ruler, in return for which they were allowed to practice their faith within the realm of Islam. The dhimmi principle is still practised today, although in some states it seems to be in jeopardy from local nationalist movements.

The third caliph, Uthman (644–656), came from Mecca but had joined Mohammed early on. More interested in religion than politics, he completed the compilation of the Koran that has remained valid ever since, as well as the early hadith collections. Following his murder, Mohammed's cousin and son-in-law Ali (656–661) became the next caliph. He is still regarded by the Shi'ites as the only legitimate successor to the Prophet. It was under Ali, a personally religious and righteous man who had difficulties dealing with his political opponents, that the unity of the Muslim community definitively disintegrated. For example, it was during his reign as caliph that the first major split in the Muslim community took place in 657, with the Kharijites (from the Arabic kharaja = to move out, split off) forming a separate community, and calling for a return to an original Islam based strictly on the Koran. In the course of a number of unsuccessful military campaigns to restore unity, Ali was murdered in 661.

Sunni Muslims call these first caliphs the "Four Rightly Guided Caliphs." They regard their lives and actions as exemplary in every respect and it is they who, together with the example of the Prophet, constitute the sunna (literally: custom) in political terms. In all Sunni discussions about political fairness and guidance, the age of the "rightly guided" caliphs plays an important part. After Ali's murder, the Muslim governor of Syria, Mu'awiya, who had formerly been Ali's fiercest opponent, assumed the title of caliph and founded the hereditary caliph Umayyad dynasty (661–750) with its established residence in Damascus. The Umayyads extended and consolidated the empire and equipped it with appropriate administrative structures. In 749/50 the Umayyads were violently overthrown by the Abbasid Dynasty (750–1258).

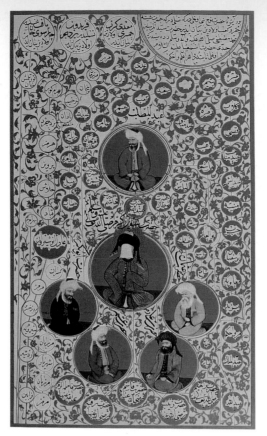

After the second Abbasid caliph had established Baghdad as the new residence, the Abbasids centralised the administration and commerce and developed the caliph court into an important centre for science and the arts. They were strongly influenced by Persia in their political way of thinking and also in ceremonial aspects, and had great admiration for the culture of the ancient world. The dynasty reached its cultural apogee under caliph Harun al-Rashid (786–809), famous from the "Arabian Nights" stories. He strove to establish a cultural exchange with other international centres, and his highly educated son al-Ma'mun (813-833) made Baghdad into a world centre of philosophy and science.

The decline of the caliphate began as early as the 10th century, as it started to become dependent on various military dynasties to "protect" it. The caliphs of Baghdad met a bloody end in the storm of the Mongols under Hulagu Chan in 1258. The empire disintegrated and the rise or expansion of various local ruling dynasties began. The most prominent of these was the military dynasty of the Mamelukes who ruled in Egypt, Syria and Palestine. In the 13th century, under the energetic and very capable Sultan Baibar (1260–1277), they managed to stop the advance of the Mongols into the Orient and eliminate the last of the Christian crusader states.

The Encounter between the Orient and Occident: Merchants and Crusaders

The flourishing caliphate empire established regular trade relations with both Asia and Europe, with the Italian seaboard republics of Venice and Genoa in particular amassing great wealth through their trade with the Orient. The trade cities of the Eastern Roman Empire and Moorish Spain were also centres for the exchange of goods between the Occident and Orient.

Of lasting significance for the relationship between Christianity and Islam was the crusader mentality that had been developing since the 11th century in Europe, and with which all classes of society – from the nobility to farmers and the poor – had joined in a strange mixture of piety, expectation of salvation, striving for material gain, spirit of adventure and fanaticism. It was the first focused expansion of Christian Europe, and its principal declared aim was to re-conquer Jerusalem for Christianity.

Although several crusades ended in total disaster, the Latin Kingdom of Jerusalem that was established in 1099 was able to claim a number of other Christian crusader states for a time in Syria and Palestine. The image of the "barbaric infidel" which the crusaders projected without differentiation onto Muslims and Jews alike, and sometimes even onto oriental Christians, was the cause of a series of massacres during the conquests for which the Muslims in turn exacted retribution.

Only gradually did the two sides gain respect for one another. The outstanding figure in this respect on the Muslim side was the Kurd Sultan Saladin (1138-1193) who, through a mixture of bravery and astuteness, tough negotiating and courageous chivalry, brought Egypt and Syria under his control, and in 1187 in the Battle of Hattin annihilated the Latin Kingdom of Jerusalem. The attention paid to this figure has endured, and also led to an engagement with Islam, of which Gotthold Ephraim Lessing's play "Nathan der Weise" is an example.

The last crusader states lasted until well into the 13th century, finally coming to an end in 1291 with the capture of Akkos by the Mamelukes.

Islam in Europe: Moors and Turks

After 711, Arabs arrived in Spain and Portugal via Gibraltar and settled there (and in a few provinces in the north). They advanced into France, where they were defeated in 732 in the Battle of Tours and Poitiers. The political and spiritual centre of Islam in Spain was the emirate of Cordoba that had been established in 756 by a branch of the Umayyad dynasty. In the following years, Moorish Spain became a stronghold of intellectual, commercial and artistic life and had a lasting influence on the sciences in Europe, particularly due to the juxtaposition of Islam, Judaism and Christianity in its various forms.

Islam experienced its first heyday in Spain under the mighty Emir Abderrahman III (912–961), who built the palace city of Medina az-Zahara and took the title of caliph in 929 (third caliphate alongside Baghdad and Cairo), and his scholarly son al-Hakam II (961–976), who collected together over 400,000 books in Cordoba, one of the most extensive libraries in history.

Separate forms of culture and art also developed due to the Christians living in Spain under Arab supremacy (Mozarabs), and the Muslims living under Christian supremacy (Mudejars). As early as the 11th century, the caliphate of Cordoba disintegrated into numerous small Arab kingdoms (reyes de taifas), some of which produced remarkable achievements in science and the arts, yet due to incessant feuds with one another fell victim to the advance of the Christian kingdoms in Spain (reconquista).

The Berber dynasties of the Almoravides and Almohades, who ruled in both Morocco and Islamic Spain between the 11th and 13th centuries, were not able to do more than delay this development. The kingdom that held out the longest was the Moorish kingdom of Granada

The Conquest of Jerusalem
from: Wilhelm von Tyrus, La très noble et excellente histoire des saintes croniques d'outremer. France, 14th century.

The Medieval crusades long marred relations between the Orient and Occident. European Christianity set out to liberate Jerusalem from the "infidels", i.e. the Muslims, and win it back for Christianity. After an almost four-year march, the army of crusaders reached Jerusalem and on July 15, 1099 began to storm the city. The massacre of Jews, Muslims and even some oriental Christians that followed the conquest of Jerusalem determined Islam's view of Christianity for a long time to come.

in the south, under the rule of the Nasride dynasty. It was eliminated in 1492 by the Catholic kings after enjoying a final cultural heyday (Alhambra in Granada).

In the wake of the storm of the Mongols, Islamic tribes advanced from Central Asia towards Europe in the 13th century. The most successful and significant were the Turks, who had been under the rule of the Ottoman dynasty since 1281. Since the 14th century they had been advancing from Anatolia into the Balkan region and surrounding the Eastern Roman Empire of Byzantium that had been weakened since the crusades. They finally defeated it in 1453, when under Mehmed the Conqueror they took Constantinople and made it into the capital of the Ottoman Empire (Istanbul). In the early 16th century they occupied Egypt, Tunisia, Azerbaijan and Hungary in rapid succession and ruled many of the Mediterranean islands. In 1529 and 1683 the Turks were outside the gates of Vienna and through a mixture of alliance and war became one of the most important factors in European politics.

Despite attempts at reform in the 19th century, the Ottoman Empire increasingly disintegrated. After World War I Mustafa Kemal Atatürk abolished the sultanate and made Turkey into a republic, and undertook massive modernization measures in an attempt to create a secular state, particularly through reforms in the education system. Mustafa Kemal Atatürk thus gave Islamic Turkey the opportunity of closer links with modern Europe. This, however, resulted in a deep rift between the modern state and tradition, and also between different regions, as is the case today in many modernized Islamic countries.

Islam in Asia

While Islam arrived in India both via conquests and trade (as early as 712, regions in what is now Pakistan belonged to the Islamic realm), Southeast Asia, particularly Indonesia and Malaysia, had since the 13th century fallen increasingly under the influence of Islam through the entirely peaceful route of trade relations.

Consequently, Islam there has a number of distinctive features. For example, it is much less of an exclusive religion, and in some regions exhibits astonishing mixtures with the indigenous religions of those areas. In the anti-colonial freedom fights of the 20th century, this flexible Islam took on a significant role. For example, in Indonesia – the Islamic country with the largest population – Islam is the state religion, but is mixed with the specific political principles of that country which ensure the coexistence of different forms of religion.

In Northern India, Babur, the descendant of the Timurides, founded the Islamic Moghul kingdom (Persian from "Mongol") in 1526. He and his successors declared the local Hindus to be "officially protected" (dhimmi) and strove to integrate the two forms of religion in an empire ruled by Islam. The consolidation of the state proceeded under Babur's significant and tolerant grandson Akbar (1556–1605), who attracted scholars of all religions to his court, and in 1582 founded a "Community of Divine Faith" which strove to bring together all religions and to give them equality in a kind of "state religion" in the Moghul empire. After the death of the last great Moghul, Aurangzeb, in 1707, the empire disintegrated and fell under British colonial rule in the 19th century.

The Lion Fountain in the Courtyard of the Alhambra
Spain, Granada

The Court of the Lions was originally designed as a courtyard under Mohammed V (1354–1359 and 1362–1391). It is regarded as the most impressive building produced by Islamic art in Europe. As the residence of the Sultan, the courtyard and palace buildings surrounding it were reserved for private use only. Water runs along small channels from the fountain pavilions at either end of the courtyard to the central lion fountain that gives the courtyard its name. Twelve archaic-looking lions spewing water carry the marble dish of the fountain. Squat and heavily stylized, they contrast effectively with the filigree of the surrounding columned gallery. On the edge of the dish an Arabic banderole praises the play of water, stone and light that creates such atmosphere.

Since the 19th century, the increasing tension between Hindus and Muslims in India has exploded in a series of bloody conflicts, and following India's independence in 1947 led to the founding of Pakistan as a separate Muslim state. Relations between the two states are still delicate and full of tension, increased by the conflicts of the Indian central government with the Muslim minorities in its own country.

THE SHI'ITES: LIFE IN EXPECTANCY OF THE IMAM

The Great Split in the Islamic Faith

The Shi'ites or Shi'a are the Muslim minority who split off from the majority Sunnis or Sunna. They currently make up some 10 to 15 per cent of all Muslims. They are, however, very strong in certain regions and have had a lasting influence on Islamic spiritual life. The division goes back to the early days of Islam, immediately after Mohammed's death, and was sparked off by the question of who was then the legitimate leader of the Muslim community.

The Shi'ites stressed the special role of Ali, the cousin and son-in-law of Mohammed, who had married Mohammed's daughter Fatima (the Prophet's only surviving child). They see him as the only legitimate successor to the Prophet, and take their name from him: Shi'at Ali, meaning the party of Ali.

The canon that forms the foundation of their faith consists of some words Mohammed spoke about Ali in the Koran. While for the Sunnis Ali is

the last of the "Four Rightly Guided Caliphs," the first three caliphs are for the Shi'ites mere usurpers. The Shi'ites similarly do not recognize the dynasties who ruled after Ali's murder in 661 – the Umayyad and Abbasid caliphates – but see the line of Imams (leaders of the community) as continuing through the direct descendants of Ali and Fatima, who historically have been largely excluded from political power. The Shi'ites have always seen these Imams from the house of Ali as the true leaders of the Muslim community and generally speaking contrast the charismatic figure of the Imam, who is directly inspired by God, with the legalistic and ultimately monarchistic figure of the caliph.

This very soon led to faith in the Imam taking on strong overtones of salvation, and it began to mingle with belief in the "Expected One" (mahdi; al-mahdi, literally: the rightly guided). In this way a belief in a saviour grew up that was strongly linked with chiliastic expectations and with corresponding social and political utopias. For this reason, religious and political impatience, combined with an active yearning for salvation, is a thread running through the history of the Shi'ites, who to this day tend to want to revolutionize society.

In many respects, particularly in practical devotional aspects, Shi'ism is not a completely different form of Islam. The "Five Pillars of Islam" are equally valid, as is the great importance attached to the legal system. It is, however, characterized by a number of additions and distinctive features. For example, to the general profession of faith (shahada), the Shi'ites add "and Ali is God's friend." To the obligatory almsgiving (zakat), the Shi'ites add another levy that was mentioned in the Koran, the "Fifth" (al-khoms). In addition to the pilgrimage to Mecca (hajj), pilgrimages to the tombs of the Imams are also considered meritorious. Through their active hope for a kingdom of justice on earth and equality among the Imams, who will return, Shi'a has over time become a melting pot for people who are discontent with society and have revolutionary aspirations. Its sophisticated cosmology and integration of very different intellectual schools of thought has also meant that it has always exercised a great attraction for Islamic intellectuals. In some points – messianism and chiliastic expectation of salvation, the cult of martyrs, incorporation of neo-Platonism and

Gnosticism, infallibility of the Imams – the ideas of Shi'a bear more resemblance to (early) Christianity and Judaism than to Sunnite Islam.

Doctrine and History of Early Shi'a

After the murder of Ali, whom they regard as the first Imam, the Shi'ites recognized as Imams the sons from his marriage to Fatima, the daughter of the Prophet. The first of these was the eldest son Hassan (2nd Imam), who showed no leadership ambitions, then the younger son Hussain (3rd Imam). After a badly planned attempted revolt, Hussain and his entire clan were deserted by their allies from Kufa, encircled in the desert near Karbala (Iraq) by troops acting on the orders of the Umayyad caliph Yazid, starved, and on 10 Muharram (October) 680, annihilated.

The martyrdom of Hussain is a trauma for the Shi'ites, which even more than the life of Ali became the actual hour of birth of the religious Shi'a. For the Shi'ites the failure of the Kufans to help Hussain represents a kind of "historical original sin." The episodes from the martyrdom of the family, over the centuries embellished with additional legends of piety, are re-enacted in plays staged each year, particularly by Shi'ites in Iran and Iraq, on the relevant days of Muharram ("Ashura Days"), accompanied by processions of mourning with people flagellating themselves with chains. After the tragedy at Karbala, the line of Imams continued through one of Hussain's surviving sons and his descendants. There are, however, differences in the person with which the different Shi'ite groups see the line of Imams ending. Thus a basic distinction is made between the "Fiver Shi'ites," "Sevener Shi'ites" and "Twelver Shi'ites," named according to the number of Imams they recognize.

The family tree of the Shi'ite Imams explains the early divisions of the Shi'a. The early Shi'a in particular was characterized by religious impatience and revolutionary expectation of salvation, which is true for the different branches of the Isma'ilites (Sevener Shi'ites). Alongside many splinter groups that are barely still in existence, the following three branches of the early Shi'a can be distinguished:

a) The Zaidites or Fiver Shi'ites: for them the line of Imams ends with Zaid, a son of the 4th Imam, who fell in the year 470 during the revolt against the Umayyads. They are moder-

ate and tolerant, particularly towards the Sunnis (for example they do not revile the first three caliphs). Their faith does not include waiting for the mahdi nor the idea of the concealed Imam. One distinctive feature is that they stress the successful fight of the appropriate person for the imamate and thus reject the principle of heredity, which the other Shi'ites adhere to. Zaidite dynasties ruled in Yemen for over 1000 years, from 901 to 1962.

b) The Isma'ilites or Sevener Shi'ites: they are the most heterogeneous and mysterious of all the Shi'ite movements, yet characterized by exceptional vitality. For them the line of Imams ends with Isma'il, a son of the 6th Imam, who was designated by his father as his successor but died before him in 760. Sections of the Isma'ilites accord Ali special status and see the line of 7 Imams as ending with Isma'il's son Mohammed. They profess a chiliastic expectation of the mahdi and share with the Twelver Shi'ites the idea of the Hidden Imam. Their ideas are philosophically very speculative and contain numerous Ancient Persian and neo-Platonic elements. To some extent they claim that the initiated have secret knowledge, and differentiate between an inner (secret) and external (visible) divine revelation.

The Isma'ilites, particularly in their early days, had great missionary zeal, and chalked up a number of political successes by setting up the

Akbar Crosses the Ganges
Miniature from the Akbar-nama

This picture is part of the "Akbar-nama," the illustrated epic that recounts the heroic deeds of Akbar, Indian Moghul emperor from 1556-1605. Here he is crossing the Ganges with his elephants and troops. As a successful general he managed to extend his empire beyond the borders of north-west India. He tried to bring together the Hindus and Muslims in this large territory by founding a non-denominational religion. He was also tolerant of Parsees and Christians. Akbar, highly cultivated but illiterate, showed great interest in all religions and anything connected with mysticism and had representatives of the different religions explain their faith to him. As a statesman he skilfully and ambitiously put down many rebellions in his empire. He pursued a clever policy of marriage and led the Moghul empire to great prosperity. Akbar was an impassioned architect. His imposing mausoleum is in Sikandra near Agra.

Mohammed and Ali Remove the Idols from the Ka'aba
Illustration from the "Raudat as-Safa" by Mir Havand, Iran (Shiraz), between 1585 and 1595

This scene illustrates the Islamic prohibition on images. In many of his sayings and speeches Mohammed expresses the rejection of pictorial depictions. After the conquest of Mecca he had the depictions of people that decorated the interior of the Ka'aba removed. This Persian miniature stresses the special role of Ali in helping Mohammed carry out this important action.

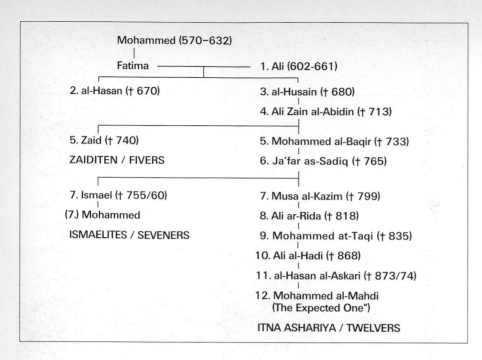

Mohammed (570–632)

Fatima ——————— 1. Ali (602-661)

2. al-Hasan († 670)   3. al-Husain († 680)

4. Ali Zain al-Abidin († 713)

5. Zaid († 740)   5. Mohammed al-Baqir († 733)
ZAIDITEN / FIVERS
6. Ja'far as-Sadiq († 765)

7. Ismael († 755/60)   7. Musa al-Kazim († 799)
(7.) Mohammed   8. Ali ar-Rida († 818)
ISMAELITES / SEVENERS   9. Mohammed at-Taqi († 835)

10. Ali al-Hadi († 868)

11. al-Hasan al-Askari († 873/74)

12. Mohammed al-Mahdi
(The Expected One")

ITNA ASHARIYA / TWELVERS

Family Tree of the Shi'ite Imams

The Shi'ites recognize as Imams only the direct descendants of the Prophet Mohammed and his daughter Fatima, who married Ali, Mohammed's cousin. The 4th Imam Ali Zain al-Abidin was the only survivor of the tragedy at Karbala (680). His (elder) son Zaid ibn Ali, the 5th Imam of the Zaidites, fell at Kufa in combat against government troops, which is why the Zaidites believe in the fight for the most suited person to be the Imam. The 6th Imam, Ja'far as-Sadiq, is seen as the great legal teacher of the Shi'ite (Ja'faritie Law School). According to the belief of the Seveners, his son Ismael, who was designated by his father to succeed him, died before his father. All Ismaelite groups nevertheless acknowledge him as the rightful Imam, while the Twelvers see the line of descent as continuing through his brother Musa al-Kazim. The Imams of the Twelvers all lived supervized or guarded by the Abasid caliphs, and according to the belief of the Twelvers all met a violent death (martyrs). On the death of his father in December 873 or January 874, the 12th Imam, Mohammed al-Mahdi, still a child, went "into hiding."

Isma'ilite Counter-Caliphate of the Fatimids in Cairo (909–1171), whose followers split into two different political and theological movements in 1094 (Musta'lis and Nizaris). Today, major Isma'ilite groups (Nizaris) live in Syria, Yemen, Afghanistan, Turkestan and in different African countries, as well as India where they are known as "hodschas." Their leader is the Aga Khan. Musta'li communities live in Yemen and India where they are called "Bohras."

The Isma'ilites include – mainly as a result of divisions during the Fatimid period – a number of extreme political and religious groups, some well-known, such as the Druzes who live in Syria and Lebanon (named after their founder, the Fatimid missionary al-Darazi). They venerate the Fatimid caliph al-Hakim (996–1021) who disappeared in 1021 as an incarnation of the Supreme Being.

The most famous were the dreaded Nizari assassins (from the Arabic hashishiyun = hashish eaters) operating out of fortresses in Northern Persia and Syria, to whom leading Sunnis and also crusaders fell victim in spectacular suicide attacks between the end of the 11th century and 13th century. The assumption that the attackers carried out their actions under the influence of drugs is still under dispute. Their leader in Syria was the mysterious "Old Man of the Mountain" about whom Marco Polo wrote in his travelogues. They were annihilated in the 13th century by the Mongols in Iran and the Mamelukes in Syria. The word assassin has remained in many European languages.

c) The "exaggerators." Part of early Shi'a were a number of extreme systems of religious thought who were described by all other sections of Islam, including the other Shi'ites, as "exaggerators" (ghulat or ghaliya). Today they are regarded as an Islamic sect. Common to almost all of them is the belief that God was immanent in Ali, or that Ali and the other Imams had divine attributes, in other words that the Imams are earthly incarnations of God. Vestiges of their community still exist in Syria (Nusayris), Iraq and Iran.

The Twelver Shi'ites

The Twelver Shi'ites, also known as Imamites, call themselves Itna Ashariya (= Twelvers) and constitute the largest Shi'ite grouping. They believe in a series of 12 Imams, the last of whom, like the Prophet, was named Mohammed. On the death of his father (the 11th Imam) in December 873 or January 874 he, still a child, went into hiding, whence he will return at the end of time as the "Expected One" (al-Mahdi).

For the Twelvers, the idea of martyrdom plays an important role, as expressed in the plays re-enacting the tragedy at Karbala already mentioned. For them all the Imams (with the exception of the 12th, concealed Imam) were martyrs who fell victim to the power of the Sunni caliphs. The Twelvers talk of the group of "14 Infallibles" who are free from any error or sin; that is, the 12 Imams, plus Mohammed and his daughter Fatima. The Twelver Shi'ites have their own subtle legal system, the fundamentals of which are ascribed to the 6th Imam Ja'far al-Sadiq (died 765) and which is therefore called the Ja'fari School. The collection of sayings ascribed to the Imams also has canonic value.

The legal system of the Twelver Shi'ites has some distinctive features which explains the outstanding role of the Iranian legal experts, the mullahs (Persian, from the Arabic mawla = lord, master). The Shi'ites do not understand theological and legal knowledge to be a "closed book," a process which the Sunnis consider complete since the 11th century, but stress the importance of rational reflection, following the principle of the ijtihad (literally exerting oneself), in other words the individual's own attempts to solve problems. For example, the Iranian mullahs and ayatollahs describe themselves as "mujtahid" or exerting themselves. Every fatwa and every piece of advice must be considered rationally, and is therefore fallible – and another person, particularly a legal expert living at a later date, does not necessarily have to follow that same decision. For this reason – contrary to popular opinion – the Shi'ite system is the least fundamentalist of Islam's legal systems. Ijtihad is, however, the sole perrogative of the mullah; the humble believer is obliged to "imitate" (taqlid). It was through this power that, since the 16th century, a hierarchically structured separate class has emerged in the mullahs, who could be described as the "Shi'ite clergy." After may years of study and issuing opinions (fatwas), the mujtahid or mullah can acquire certain titles of honor. The first stage is known as "authority (proof) of Islam" (hujja al-islam); the next is "Sign of God" (ayatollah, or more precisely ayatu'llah) and the few generally recognized major ayatollahs bear the title "Source of Imitation" (marja at-taqlid).

The Shi'ites in Iran

Iran is the only country in which Twelver Shi'a is the state religion. Immediately after the Safavids seized power in Persia in 1501, Shah Isma'il declared the Twelvers and the Ja'fari School of Law the official state religion. The rise of the mullahs began, although they were initially under strict state control. The energetic Safavids made Persia, and especially the capital Isfahan, into an important centre of culture and the arts. The political zenith was the reign of Shah 'Abbas the Great (1587–1629), who overthrew Azerbaijan and Georgia, and set up a great number of Shi'ite religious foundations (waqf). In 1779 and 1796, the Qajar dynasty came to power (until 1925) and made Tehran the capital of Persia. Itna Ashariya remained the state religion.

In the 19th century, conflicts intensified between the Iranian rulers and the Shi'ite spiritual leaders, who accused the state power of becoming westernized and joining Europe. This intensified in the second half of the 19th century after the Shah had sold various trade privileges and monopolies to British companies. Following the referendum on the new constitution in 1906, riots and persistent conflicts were the order of the day.

However, the mullahs did not begin to show open opposition to this assimilation trend until after Colonel Reza Shah took power (1925–

1941) and founded the Pahlavi dynasty. He was an admirer of the reforms of Kemal Atatürk, and aimed to achieve extensive secularization of the country. He withdrew the judiciary and the education system from the mullahs' control, and used authoritarian means to limit their influence to religious matters. Under his son Reza Pahlavi (1941–1978) there was a temporary calm, which in the sixties turned into harsh conflicts about the Shah's western-style reform attempts ("White Revolution").

The propaganda of the politically oriented mullahs enjoyed great support from all classes of Iranian society, and was particularly encouraged by the unrestrained corruption of the Shah's regime and the obviously dictatorial government measures. Nevertheless, the majority of ayatollahs, particularly the higher-

Isfahan: Sheik Lotfallah Mosque

Under the dynasty of the Safavids, the Persian empire enjoyed a new cultural heyday. Shah Abbas the Great (1587-1629) made Isfahan the capital of his empire and designed the new Isfahan to the south of the old city centre on an imperial scale. The small Lotfallah Mosque, integrated into the King's Square, which Abbas had built at the beginning of the 17th century in honour of his father-in-law, is one of the most beautiful and important works of architecture of the Safavid era. The single-skinned dome is unique in structure and form. Its sand-coloured ground of tiles is covered with white vine weaving, edged in black with blue flowers and buds. The exterior facades are more restrained, while the interiors of the mosque are dominated by the exquisite turquoise and sapphire tones of the Safavid empire.

Shi'ite Procession in Iran, Flagellators

Muharram or October 10, the anniversary of the Battle of Karbala in 680, in which the 3rd Imam Hussain was killed in battle against the army of the Umayyad caliph Yazid, is commemorated by the Shi'ites particularly in Iraq and Iran as one of the highest holy days. As a sign of mourning, all public institutions are closed and black flags and cloths are hung from the bazaars and mosques. The climax of the commemoration is the procession of people flagellating themselves, beating their fists against their breasts and performing acts of bloody self-castigation with iron chains.

ranking ones – even after 1978/79 – showed little inclination to get directly involved in day-to-day politics.

The overthrow of the Shah was followed by the return of the Ayatollah Ruhollah Khomeini (1902-1989), who had been in exile for 60 years. He had always been a political leader of the Shi'ites but was never the sole leader nor the undisputed religious leader. With his return, the religious and political means to mobilize the masses came to fruition, strengthened by the revolutionary ideology and politicized expectation of salvation of Shi'a, with its strong emphasis on theocracy and on the concept of martyrdom.

Through the inherent dynamics of the revolution and its followers Khomeini felt increasingly under pressure to step into the foreground and assert his principle of "rule exercised by the legal scholar" (Persian: velayat-e faqih), with Shi'ite legal experts having supreme power. His own role as revolutionary leader remained undefined, vacillating between making general guidelines and issuing concrete political instructions. He codified the position that the Iranian government see itself as the earthly representative of the concealed Imam in Article 5 of the Constitution, with an additional clause asking that Allah should hasten the return of the mahdi.

His authoritarian regime with strong theocratic tendencies also acted as a signal to other Shi'ite communities, particularly in Lebanon. Since Khomeini's death, the political and religious leadership of Iran have once more separated. Apart from in Iran, the Twelver Shi'ites also make up the majority of the population in the south of Iraq, and large communities also live in Lebanon.

MODERN ISLAM

Colonialism and the Islamic Reform Movements

Since the beginning of the 19th century, Islamic countries have experienced a spate of modernization due to their renewed encounter with the West. These contacts had manoeuvred these countries into relationships of ongoing political and economic dependency. In the age of colonialism, virtually all these countries (with the exception of the Ottoman Empire) became direct colonies or "protectorates" under the tutelage of the major European powers. The end of colonialism in the 20th century brought about a revaluation of Islam in these Islamic countries, in both religious and political terms, since Islam was actively involved everywhere with anti-colonialist independence movements.

Napoleon's landing in Egypt in 1798 is regarded as the first event in this renewed, initially entirely one-sided encounter with the Islamic world. The Orient then swam into the consciousness of Europeans, albeit in a very transformed and romanticized form. The colonial powers won over the ruling elites of the Muslims and deepened the rift between the thin elite layer of society, which was strongly European, and the ordinary people who were mostly illiterate and deeply rooted in tradition. Islam on the whole was on the side of the simple people, who formed the majority of the population.

The Islamic world's experience of colonialism included the forced recognition of the military and technological superiority of the West (which resonated with Islam's own superiority in the early days of the religion), the experience of being refused political autonomy, and a feeling of discrepancy between the superiority of the Islamic religion and the concessions it had to make in the face of actual political and military helplessness.

Islam increasingly became more self-confident, identifying with the independence struggles of colonialized countries and peoples. The reformers of Islam were aware that they were walking a fine line: they had to confront the modern age and the achievements of the West, taking care neither to adopt them without criticism nor to condemn them out of hand. Their position was thus defined as decisively anti-colonial, but not necessarily anti-modern. It was more important for them to work out how many modern political and economic achievements actually already existed within Islam.

The Islamic modernist movement began in earnest in the second half of the 20th century, and contained many elements now ascribed to "fundamentalism:" These included attempts to recover the authenticity and original nature of Islam, a yearning for original Islam and an Islamic unification movement instead of the large number of existing systems, the defence of Islamic culture against oppressive external influences, the emphasis of the equality of all believers before God, and demands for the social and charitable commitment of the individual. However, at the same time, the reformers also wanted Islam to be at the forefront of their own modernization movement, not merely to be a "backward-looking utopia." They called for harmony between faith and modern human freedom, stronger political commitment of believers which would include self-determination, a radical reform of the educational system in Islamic countries, and a narrowing of the gap between rulers and the ruled. They made reference to the conditions in the original Islamic community, and attempted to fulfil the requirements of modern economic policies and achieve improvements in social welfare.

A significant fundamentalist movement that also had reforming tendencies was, and still is, the puritanical Wahhabi movement, named after the Hanbali reformer Muhammad ibn Abd al-Wahhab (1703–1792) who had called for radical monotheism, the destruction of the oriental belief in saints, and adherence to a rigorously strict moral code. Of political significance was the connection between al-Wahhab and the Arabian ruling family as-Sa'ud, who had conquered a large part of the Arabian peninsula in the 19th century (including the Holy Sites of Islam).

The most successful representative of the as-Sa'uds in the Arab world was Abd al-Aziz, known as Ibn Sa'ud (1880–1953). Together with his militant "ikhwan" (=brother)-warriors he conquered the whole of what is now Saudi Arabia in the early decades of the 20th century, and in 1932 established a kingdom with hereditary descent. With its oil wealth, Saudi Arabia became an important major power, and is still the major financial backer of projects to support and spread Islam throughout the world.

Other centres of Islamic reform movements grew up at the end of the 18th century in India, Yemen and Libya, where the combative order of mystics, the Sanusiya (Sanusi Movement) became the forerunner of a self-confident Islamic renewal in the 19th century, which spread to the entire Maghreb and which still influences Libya today.

Significant reformers were the Indian Ahmad Khan (1817–1898), who travelled throughout England, tried to establish relations between modern Islam and Christianity, and called for a radical education reform for young Muslims. The Afghan Jamal al-Din al-Afghani (1838–1897) formulated Islam's anti-colonial struggle and influenced a great number of Islamic rulers. The Egyptian Muhammad 'Abduh (1849–1905) worked toward a revival in Islamic literature and political journalism, and also strove to reform Islam's criminal law.

Where the 19th century created the foundations for a reform of the Islamic world, the 20th century wanted to see these ideas translated into action. World War I and its effects were – seen quite rightly – in Islamic countries as a sign of the bankruptcy of the European colonial system. The changes that followed in Europe were watched in the Islamic world critically, but with interest.

Politically-minded Muslims criticized the individualism and egotism of European societies, and in some instances developed their discomfort into a criticism of capitalism. They found the polarization in western societies as a result of the feuding between democratic parties highly suspect. Islam, they argued, occupied a position in the centre, between democracy and dictatorship, taking from the former the idea of the freedom of the individual and from the latter social stability. The forms of "guided democracy" and similar constructs that were later implemented in Muslim countries testified to this idea. The economic system of Islam, the reformers and political thinkers continued, was neither capitalist nor socialist; it took from capitalism the freedom of the individual to act, and from socialism the principle of solidarity in society. Later, Islamic countries also tried to find a way out of the polarization of the two power blocks headed by the U.S.A. and U.S.S.R., and confidently proclaimed that Islam was the superior "third way." Thus a famous Islamic battle cry was "Neither West nor East – Islam!"

Ayatollah Ruhollah Khomeini (1902–1989)

The Ayatollah Khomeini distinguished himself from many other Shi'ite scholars by his strong involvement in politics. He agitated against the "un-Islamic" modernism and westernization of the Shah's regime which tried to severely limit the influence of the mullahs. He advanced the cause of the Iranian revolution from Paris, where he lived in exile, and returned home in 1979 after the overthrow of the Shah. In the "Islamic Republic" which succeeded the Shah's regime and which gave the Islamic spiritual leaders a leading role, Khomeini occupied the position of the "Guiding Legal Expert" and thus had the power to decide all political and religious matters.

Arab Nationalism and "Islamic Socialism"

The idea of the "eternal mission of the Arabs" was propagated from the early 20th century, in particular by educated and progressive forces in Arab countries. However, Arab nationalism was also fostered by religious minorities, notably by oriental Christians, who through the "dhimmi" system felt themselves to be second-class citizens, more closely allied through shared nationality than through their religion. (This is the basis of the Ba'ath Party in Syria and Iraq, founded by the Syrian Michel Aflaq). Nationalism in Islamic countries went hand in hand with education. However, programmes aimed to standardize caused the ethnic minorities – such as the Kurds in Turkey and Iraq, and Jewish communities in Iraq – problems in asserting their autonomy, leading to increasing intolerance on the part of the nationalist central governments. These problems were often erroneously ascribed to Islam as a religion, but are actually more the result of nationalist politics aimed at standardization.

Socialism has had a strong influence on Islam since the end of 19th century. Due to high reciprocal social obligations, the almsgiving system (zakat) and a highly developed social ethos, the word "socialism" does not have a negative connotation in Islam. At the same time, Islam decisively rejects Marxism and Bolshevism on the grounds that they propagate materialist atheism. Islam sees itself as a major pillar of socialism, and the spiritual spearhead in the fight against what is considered to be pan-European materialism.

"Islamic socialism" crystallised after World War II, particularly in Syria (Ba'ath party), in the fight for social justice. The Egyptian president Gamal Abdel Nasser (ruled 1954-1970) became the leading figure of a self-confident "Arab socialism" with modernist elements, and his ideas and projects still have a strong influence on the pan-Arabic movement. Today "Arab socialism" continues to play a major role in countries such as Syria, Iraq and Algeria, and in Libya since 1969 under Colonel Muammar al-Qaddafi (Ghaddafi) it has been incorporated into a fundamental re-Islamization of the foundations of society (Way of the "Green Book").

The ideas of Pan-Arabism or Pan-Islamism, which became stronger after World War II, aim – at least ideologically – for greater unity amongst the Arab countries and Islamic countries in general. The countries committed themselves to the politically self-confident concepts of Arab nationalism and Islamic socialism. The Arab League, founded in 1945, was joined in 1974 by the "Organization of the Islamic Conference," in a major international efforts toward political autonomy for the whole of Islam. Despite some efforts, the differences between the various Islamic countries have since become more marked, and later efforts at Islamic unity – such as those of Ghaddafi in Lybia, the early Iranian Revolution (1979–1982) or by Iraqi President Saddam Hussein in the 1991 Gulf War – have been relatively unsuccessful and isolated.

Fundamentalism and Islam's "Holy War"

The self-confidence and vitality of the Islamic movement, combined with the problems of migrants living in European countries, have

Summit of Arab Statesmen, 1970 in Cairo

The photograph shows (left to right): King Faisal of Saudi Arabia, General Muammar al-Qaddhaffi (Libya), President Abdul Rahman Iryani (Yemen) and President Gamal Abd el-Nasser (Egypt). After World War II, Arab statesmen strove actively for the political autonomy of Islamic countries. With his nationalization of the Suez Canal in 1956, President Nasser secured himself a leading position in the Arab world. The conference was convened in September 1970, in order to establish consensus on the Palestine question and avoid a fraticidal war and the division of Yemen. A few days after this meeting Nasser died of a heart attack. As early as January 1964 the first summit had been held in Cairo at his instigation.

meant that the militant aspect of Islam has become the focus of attention of Western consciousness in recent years and has to some extent been stereotyped as a threat to Europe or even the whole of Western culture. It cannot be denied that militant and radical Islamic groups exist, some of whom have declared war on pluralist modernism. But they have often been subsumed under the over-simplified term "fundamentalist" (although this term actually comes from U.S. Protestantism), and identified with violence and intolerance. To some extent they have been carrying the can for a dubious negative overall view of Islam.

The association of "Muslim Brotherhood" (al-Ikhwan al- Muslimun), founded in 1928 in Egypt by the teacher Hasan al-Banna (1906–1949, murdered), can be regarded as pointing the way towards a radical and often militant Islam in our century. They initially took part in the national independence struggle, but then very quickly took a radical turn, and by shortly after World War II their membership had grown to 500,000. Following a number of assassinations and acts of violence, the Muslim Brotherhood has been under pressure from the government since 1948, but has spread its influence into Jordan, Iraq, Lebanon and particularly Syria. In Syria and Egypt (since Nasser's time) it has been closely watched. It now forms an oppositional force to all secularization tendencies and has to be taken seriously.

A similarly strong movement is the "Islamic Community" (Jamaat-i-Islami) founded in Pakistan in 1941 by Abu-l-A'la al Mawdudi (1903–1979) which, since the founding of the state in 1948, has been successfully working for a complete Islamization of society. Radical splinter groups in various countries, whose structure is often quite difficult to comprehend, use some violent methods to fight to set up an Islamic order as they understand it.

The question of Islamic militancy flares up again and again when it comes to the meaning of the "Holy War" (jihad). As a universalist religion of salvation, Islam – like Christianity – clings to its claim to absoluteness. The Islamic legal system, for example, divides the world into two areas: the "Abode of Islam" (Dar al-Islam), envisaged as a realm of peace, and the "Abode of Warfare" (Dar al-Harb) in which non-believers and non-Muslims live. In times of peace this can, however, become an "Abode of

Treaty" or even an "Abode of Peace." And that is the situation de facto, since for a long time now no Islamic country has gone to war for purely religious reasons.

Mohammed was concerned with questions of war, and in particular with wars of defence. He condemned all wars that were not motivated by religious issues. He called upon believers to fight for God and the religion, but he also warned them to keep the peace with the non-believers as long as they for their part also kept the peace (see, for example, Suras 8:61, 4:90 or 4:94). The Koran repeatedly stresses peace as the goal that should take precedence in human life.

The term jihad means "striving for the cause of Islam" and has a much broader meaning than is reflected in the translation "Holy War." As the fight for the faith and supremacy of Islam, this striving is the obligation of every Muslim. Yet many Islamic legal experts stress that war is only the "small jihad," subordinate to the "great jihad" – the spiritual, moral and missionary efforts to further the spread of Islam. Nevertheless, radical Islamists again and again use the term "Holy War" to legitimize violence. Apart from stressing the jihad, Islam also has a great tradition of peace, with which most Muslims identify.

Demonstration of Islamic Women
Nabatiye, Lebanon

Since the second half of the 19th century a process of increasing politicization of Islam has been seen in the Arab countries. The political consciousness of Muslims is sparked off particularly by areas of permanent crisis, such as Palestine. In Lebanon, the Shi'ite Hezbollah, which represents a radical and militant form of Islam, gained huge impetus through the Iranian revolution. Like most fundamentalist movements, it works by mobilizing the masses. Women also take part in political protest demonstrations.

ILLUSTRATIONS

The publisher thanks the institutions, archives and photographers for permission to reproduce their illustrations, and for their kind help during the preparation of this book. Despite much effort, however, we were unable to contact all of the copyright holders. Any inquiries concerning copyright should be addressed to the publisher.

Archive for Art and Architecture, Berlin 61bottom, 62, 63, 65 top, 67, 68, 69 top, 69 bottom, 72, 78 bottom, 79, 81, 84 bottom, 85 bottom, 86, 88, 89 top, 89 bottom, 92, 115; (Hilbich) 88; (Erich Lessing) 57, 58 top, 59, 60, 61 top, 73, 74, 75 top, 75, 80, 82, 99

ARCHEFOTO 113

Bednorz, Achim 102

Berger, Friedemann Cover, 22, 24, 25, 27, 28, 30, 31, 32 top, 32

bottom, 33, 34 35, 36 top, 37, 41 top, 41 bottom, 42 top, 42 bottom, 43 top, 44 bottom, 46 top, 46 bottom, 47, 101

Beyer, Klaus G. 18 bottom, 77, 83 top, 83 bottom, 85 top

Bibliothèque Nationale de France, Paris 108

Bildarchiv Preußischer Kulturbesitz, Berlin 21, 56, 58 bottom (Alfredo Dagli Orti), 65 bottom, 70, 78 top, 96, 97, 100, 106 bottom, 110, 111 bottom (AP)

Bodleian Library, Oxford 105

British Museum, London 109

Christoph, Henning/DAS FOTARCHIV 93

Deutsches Historisches Museum, Berlin 84 top

dpa/Central Press 38, 91

farabolafoto 80 bottom

Hansmann, Claus 12 top, 106 top

Imber, Walter Cover, 9 top, 11 top, 13 top, 13 bottom, 19, 20 103

IPPA (Israel Press & Photo Agency 64 bottom, 71 top

JAPAN aktuell 36 bottom, 48, 51, 53, 54 top, 54 bottom

JAPAN-Photo-Archiv/Hartmut Pohling 52 bottom

Jüdisches Museum in der Stiftung Stadtmuseum Berlin, Foto: Hans-Joachim Bartsch 64 top, 71 bottom

Keilhauer, Peter 16 bottom

Lachmann, Hans 90

laenderpress 6 bottom

Michael O'Mara Books 49, 50, 52 top, 55

Moore, Charles/DAS FOTOARCHIV 29

Newman, Marvin 66

Österreichische Nationalbibliothek, Vienna 107

Poncar, Jaroslav/transparent 39,

R. Maro/version 104

Riedmüller, Andreas/DAS FOTO-ARCHIV Cover, 76

Staatliche Museen zu Berlin, Preußischer Kulturbesitz, Museum für Indische Kunst 7 top, 7 bottom, 8 top, 10, 14 top, 14 bottom, 15 top, 16 top, 17 bottom, 18 top

Süddeutscher Verlag 114

Topkapi Saray Museum, Istanbul 94, 95 top, 95 bottom, 98

Ullstein Bilderdienst 117

Victoria & Albert Museum 111 top

Weinreb, Robert/DAS FOTOARCHIV 2,6